Contents

Inn-Sights	vii
How This Guide Is Arranged	ix
New England	1
Mid-Atlantic and Chesapeake Region	41
The South	81
The Midwest	121
Arizona, New Mexico, and Texas	161
Rocky Mountain Region	201
West Coast	241

Indexes

Alphabetical Index to Inns	281
Inns on or near a Lake	284
Inns at or near the Seashore	284
Riverside Inns	285
Island Inns	285
Inns with Cabins	286
Inn or Locations of Historical Interest	287
Inns offering Educational Experiences	288
Inns near Cross-Country Skiing	289
Inns near Downhill Skiing	290
Guest Ranches or Inns with Horseback Riding	290
Guest Farms or Inns with Farm Animals	291
Inns that Accept or Consider Pets	292

Recommended
FAMILY INNS
of America

Recommended
FAMILY INNS
of America

New England *by* Elizabeth Squier
Mid-Atlantic and Chesapeake Region *by* Brenda Boelts Chapin
The South *by* Sara Pitzer
The Midwest *by* Bob Puhala
Arizona, New Mexico, and Texas *by* Eleanor S. Morris
Rocky Mountain Region *by* Doris Kennedy
West Coast *by* Julianne Belote

edited by
Cary Schuler Hull

A Voyager Book
The Globe Pequot Press
Chester, Connecticut

The prices and rates listed in this guidebook were confirmed at press time. We recommend, however, that you call establishments before traveling to obtain current information.

Illustrations for chapters on New England, the West Coast, and the Mid-Atlantic and Chesapeake Region by Olive Metcalf.

Illustrations for chapters on The Midwest and Arizona, New Mexico, and Texas by Bill Taylor, Jr.

Illustrations for chapters on The South and the Rocky Mountain Region by Duane Perreault.

Excerpt from "The Sound of Music," p. 219, copyright © 1959 by Richard Rodgers and Oscar Hammerstein II. Copyright renewed. Williamson Music Co., owner of publication and allied rights. Used by permission. ALL RIGHTS RESERVED.

Copyright ©1989 by The Globe Pequot Press

All rights reserved. No part of this book may be reproduced or transmitted in any form by any means, electronic or mechanical, including photocopying and recording, or by any information storage and retrieval system, except as may be expressly permitted by the 1976 Copyright Act or by the publisher. Requests for permission should be made in writing to The Globe Pequot Press, 138 West Main Street, Chester, Connecticut 06412.

Library of Congress Cataloging-in-Publication Data

Recommended family inns of America / by Elizabeth Squier . . . [et al.]
 ; edited by Cary Schuler Hull.—1st ed.
        p. cm.
    "A Voyager Book."
    ISBN 0-87106-646-7
      1. Hotels, taverns. etc.—United States—Guide-books. 2. United States—Description and travel—1981—Guide-books. I. Squier. Elizabeth. II. Hull, Cary Schuler.
TX907.2.R43 1989
647.947301—dc20   89-23304
                                                                  CIP

Manufactured in the United States of America
First Edition/First Printing

Inn-Sights

Describing a family inn can be tricky. The mind conjures up an image of a big white colonial building with children playing croquet on the grassy lawn—if you happen to live in New England, that is. A Midwesterner, on the other hand, might imagine a Victorian hotel in a rivertown, where the family can take a riverboat cruise down the Mississippi. And in the Southwest, one might picture a white-stucco building with original Southwestern art on the walls and a fascinating town to wander. The fact is, there is no one precise image of a family inn. That's because people's images of an inn differ depending on where they live. How, then, define a family inn? Let's start with the basics. Webster's defines an inn as "an establishment for the lodging and entertaining of travelers." Globe Pequot Press takes this basic definition one step further. Since 1973, with the publication of the first edition of Elizabeth Squier's *Recommended Country Inns—New England*, the Press has defined an inn as a place with a certain unique ambience that cannot be found in any other type of lodging. To Globe Pequot, an inn has something very special to offer—atmosphere, charm, history, personality, and delightful location. Where else but at an inn would you be given the opportunity to rent a pussycat to lull you to sleep with its purring, a treasured family quilt to snuggle under for the night, a cookie jar in the kitchen that you can dip into whenever you wish, a 1920s bowling alley to play on, a piano you're invited to play any time, a garden of vegetables you're encouraged to pick? . . . All these and more are the personal touches that make an inn memorable.

Also essential to the Press's definition of an inn are the welcoming innkeepers who treat their guests as friends, or even members, of the family: people like Mary McEntire at The Pines in North Carolina, who will rush out with an umbrella to greet a guest in the rain, or Michael and Holly Durfor at Dexters in New Hampshire, who will share their children's toys with visiting children, or Lew Jones at Old Pioneer Garden in Nevada, who will show guests how to milk a goat and feed the animals. Innkeepers are in this business because they love people and enjoy getting to know them around the breakfast table, on the veranda, on a trail ride, or at an evening enrichment lecture.

Inn-Sights

Now let's add *family* to this picture of the basic inn. You still have the unique ambience and the attentive innkeepers. But now you also have a relaxed, comfortable atmosphere in which children feel at home and parents need not worry about antiques being broken. Is it an inn that could be considered a romantic getaway? Probably not. Are the meals gourmet? Not necessarily. Is there an abundance of things to do at the inn or in the area? You bet. After all, it is a family inn.

A family inn can be a ranch with horses and trail rides, a farm with animals to care for, a resort hotel on a lake, or a large house on an ocean beach. It might be located in the middle of a wonderful city to explore or on an island. It can be a place that gives children the chance to experience history or one that provides outdoor activities. And a family inn certainly is a place that gives the children (and parents, too!) some unique and memorable experiences: taking private fly-fishing lessons, sleeping in a restored caboose, staying on a college campus and using college facilities, calling a lighthouse home, living on an Indian reservation, going on trail rides to a haunted house, sleeping in an old jail cell, staying in a Shaker village, and more. Whatever and wherever it is, a family inn promises fun for the whole family.

This guidebook of 126 recommended family inns provides a wealth of information for the family who wants to take a vacation together in the United States. It is packed full of potential adventures and learning experiences for children of all ages. Once you have treated your family to a stay at a family inn, you will want to do it again and again.

How This Guide Is Arranged

This inn guide contains descriptions of 126 family inns in seven regions of the United States. These inns were selected by the authors of The Globe Pequot Press's seven regional *Recommended Country Inns* guides as the best inns in their regions for families. *All the inns were personally visited by the authors. There is no charge of any kind for an inn to be included in this or any other Globe Pequot Press inn guide.*

The guide is arranged geographically by region, beginning along the Atlantic Ocean. These regions, in order, are: New England; Mid-Atlantic and Chesapeake Region; the South; the Midwest; Arizona, New Mexico, and Texas; Rocky Mountain Region; and the West Coast. Within each region, the states are listed alphabetically; within each state, the towns are arranged alphabetically.

Preceding each region's listings is a regional map and a numbered legend of the eighteen family inns found in that region. The map is marked with corresponding numbers to show where the inns are located.

Indexes: At the back of the book are various special-category indexes to help you find inns located on a mountain or at the seashore, inns with horseback riding and inns with skiing, inns with cabins and inns accepting pets, and many more. There is also an alphabetical index of all the inns in the book.

Rates: The guidebook quotes current low and high rates to give you an indication of the price ranges you can expect. They are more than likely to change slightly with time. Be sure to call ahead and inquire about the rates as well as the taxes and service charges. The following abbreviations are used consistently throughout the book to let you know exactly what, if any, meals are included in the room price.

EP: European Plan. Room without meals.

EPB: Room with full breakfast. (No abbreviation is used when continental breakfast is included.)

MAP: Modified American Plan. Room with breakfast and dinner.

AP: American Plan. Room with breakfast, lunch, and dinner.

How This Guide Is Arranged

Children's rates: The rates given for children in this guidebook are generally for children who stay in the same room or suite as their parents. These rates are likely to change with time.

Cots and cribs: Many inns have cots and cribs—some even have futons—but if these are important to you, do check. Some inns charge extra (usually around $5 to $10) for the crib, while others charge for the child using the crib.

Credit cards: MasterCard and Visa are accepted unless the description says "No credit cards." Many inns also accept additional credit cards.

Reservations and deposits: These are so often required that they are not mentioned in any description. Assume that you'll generally have to pay a deposit to reserve a room, using a personal check or a credit card. Be sure to inquire about refund policies.

Pets: No pets are allowed unless otherwise stated in the description or the special index about pets in the back of the book. Always let innkeepers know in advance if you are planning to bring a pet.

Wheelchair access: Some descriptions mention wheelchair access, but other inns may be feasible for the handicapped. Therefore, if you're interested in an inn, call to check if there is a room suitable for a handicapped person.

Air conditioning: The description will indicate if an inn has rooms with air conditioning. Keep in mind, however, that there are areas of the country where air conditioning is totally unnecessary. For example, in the Rocky Mountain region, where the inn is at a high elevation (stated in the description), you will be comfortable without air conditioning.

Television: If your preschoolers can't live without Sesame Street and your teenagers need a daily dose of soap operas, you may feel a television in the room is essential. The description will mention if the rooms are so equipped. Sometimes there's a television in a common room. *Note:* Most innkeepers say there is

How This Guide Is Arranged

so much to do at the inn or in the area that guests generally don't find the time to watch.

Telephone: Assuming that when you take a family vacation you want to get away from it all, the descriptions do not state if you will find a telephone in your room.

Smoking: Unless otherwise specified, smoking is permitted.

BYOB: It is often acceptable to bring your own bottle, especially if an inn has no bar service. If you see no mention of BYOB or a bar in the description, you may want to check in advance.

Menus: The authors often indicate some favorite foods they enjoyed at an inn, but you should not expect the menu to remain the same forever. Menus usually change seasonally or monthly. The description of the inn's food should give you a general idea of the meals served and help you determine whether your children will find foods they will like.

☛ : When you see the ☛ , it is the authors' indication of something particularly interesting, pleasing, or unusual about an inn. It is *not* intended as a rating.

E: The comment preceded by a big initial (standing for the author's name) occasionally found at the end of the inn description is one more personal statement from the author about an inn.

One final word of advice: As Sydna Zeliff, innkeeper of Christmas Farm Inn in New Hampshire, says, "When you go to a country inn, it's like going to a favorite relatives' house. Treat the inn kindly. Don't let your children jump on the beds or couches, and remind them to say please and thank you, just as you would in a relative's house."

NEW ENGLAND

by
Elizabeth Squier

Elizabeth Squier first wrote *Recommended Country Inns—New England* in 1973, a time when country inns were relatively scarce. Since then, the number of New England country inns has grown immeasurably. Now in its eleventh edition, Elizabeth's guidebook includes 223 full-service inns (where both breakfast and dinner are served) in all six New England states.

Since writing the first edition of her popular guidebook, Elizabeth has earned the well-deserved nickname "inn creeper." She tours more than 200 inns every year from top to bottom, inside and out, before recommending the best ones in her book. A recognized author on fine food and lodging, Elizabeth is a gourmet cook and has written travel and food columns for many periodicals.

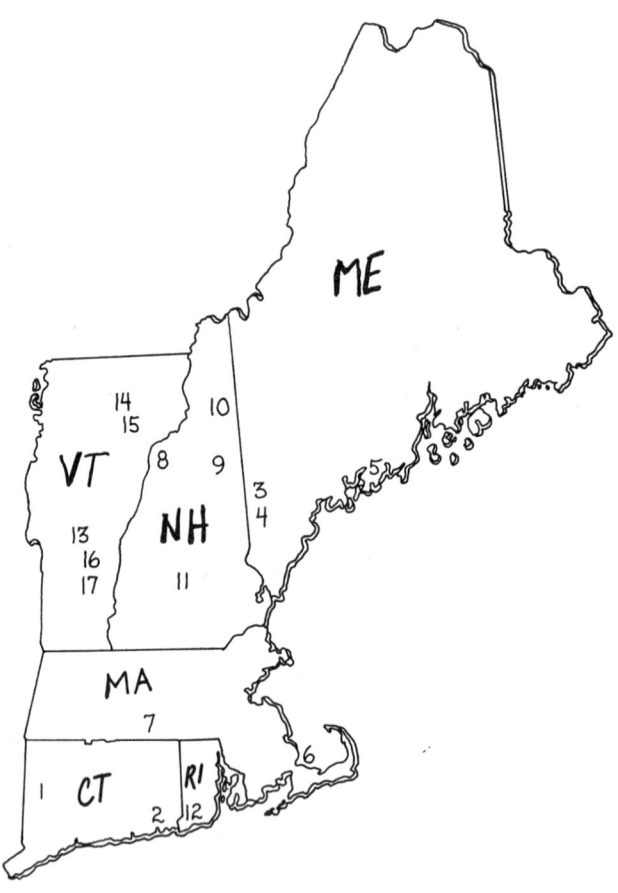

New England

Numbers on map refer to towns numbered below.

CONNECTICUT
1. New Preston, The Inn on Lake Waramaug 4
2. North Stonington, Randall's Ordinary 6

MAINE
3. Bethel, The Bethel Inn 8
4. Center Lovell, Westways Country Inn 10
5. West Boothbay Harbor, The Lawnmeer Inn 12

MASSACHUSETTS
6. Sandwich, The Dan'l Webster Inn 14
7. Sturbridge, Publick House & Country Motor Lodge 16

NEW HAMPSHIRE
8. Franconia, Franconia Inn 18
9. Jackson,
   Christmas Farm Inn 20
   Whitney's Village Inn 22
10. Shelburne, Philbrook Farm Inn 24
11. Sunapee, Dexters 26

RHODE ISLAND
12. Westerly, Shelter Harbor Inn 28

VERMONT
13. Chittenden, Mountain Top Inn 30
14. Craftsbury Common, The Inn on the Common 32
15. Greensboro, Highland Lodge 34
16. Killington, The Vermont Inn 36
17. Landgrove, The Village Inn 38

The Inn on Lake Waramaug
New Preston, Connecticut
06777

Innkeepers: Kevin and Barbara Kirshner
Address/Telephone: 107 North Shore Road; (203) 868–0563 or (800)-LAKE-INN from greater Northeast
Rooms: 23; all with private bath, air conditioning, television.
Rates: $85 to $105, per person, double occupancy, MAP. Children up to 12, $45; 12 and over, $69. Package plans available.
Open: All year.
Facilities and activities: Sunday brunch, bar. Calendar of family events. Indoor pool, sauna, exercise room, game room, meeting house, cross-country skiing, ice skating, boating, lake swimming. Nearby tennis, golf, horseback riding, and downhill skiing.

How often do your children get the opportunity to participate in an ☛ old-fashioned frog-jump jamboree? Come with your frog to The Inn at Lake Waramaug for that special summer event, and see how far the frog can jump. Maybe you'd prefer a wintertime trip to the inn to show your children how ice blocks used to be cut from lakes and hauled to the icehouse in days of old, or a March visit during the inn's maple-sugaring festival to show them how

New Preston, Connecticut

maple syrup is made. Summertime brings a traditional New England clambake and the Huckleberry Finn raft race, and October is the time for the jack-o'-lantern carving contest. This inn is well known for its year-round calendar of events. Be sure to write ahead for the calendar and plan your family vacation accordingly.

Even if you miss the special events, you will find there is much to do here, both inside and outside the inn. Winter is a fairyland. The innkeepers keep an area on the lake cleared for skating. Cross-country skiing starts just outside the door. Downhill skiing is but twenty minutes away. Summer brings boating and swimming or just enjoying the shaded lawns and sandy beach. The inn has a showboat that takes you around the lake. Bicycles are also available. Nearby are golf, tennis, and horseback riding.

Inside the inn is year-round fun. Try the heated swimming pool with a whirlpool lagoon and a sauna. Memorabilia from long ago decorate the walls of the game room that has pool, Ping-Pong, electronic and other games, and even a jukebox. The newest addition to the inn is the exercise room.

The inn has a variety of accommodations. One room has a queen-size canopy bed and a daybed. Other rooms have a double bed and a twin. Cots can be added if necessary, but there are no cribs available.

Good food is served year round in the large and well-appointed dining rooms. The breakfast buffet includes granola and fresh fruit, and hot dishes like omelets and French toast can be made to order. For dinner, children order from the same menu as their parents. The chef creates a different pasta dish every night, New York strip steak is "simply served," and duck, seafood, chicken, and lamb chops are available. The menu changes seasonally.

How to get there: From New York take I–84 to Route 7 in Danbury and follow it north to New Milford. Take a right onto Route 202 to New Preston. Take Route 45 west and follow signs to the inn. From Boston take the Massachusetts Turnpike to I–84. Exit from I–84 onto Route 4 in Farmington. Continue on Route 4 to Route 118, and in Litchfield, pick up Route 202 and follow it to Route 45 west.

E: *Christmas is a fabulous festival, with lighted Christmas trees, and a* showboat *handbell choir concert to usher in the hundreds of little lights. It's enjoyed by all, including Chester, a forty-eight-year-old Shetland pony, and Toto, the inn dog.*

5

Randall's Ordinary
North Stonington, Connecticut
06359

Innkeepers: Bill and Cindy Clark
Address/Telephone: P.O. Box 243; (203) 599–4540
Rooms: 12; all with private bath, some with air conditioning.
Rates: $80 to $135, per room, double occupancy, continental breakfast. Children, $10. Midweek package plans and winter weekend plans available.
Open: All year except Christmas Eve, Christmas Day, and New Year's Day.
Facilities and activities: Lunch, dinner, bar. Hiking and cross-country skiing on 27 acres of property. Nearby: ocean beaches, Mystic Seaport, Mystic Marinelife Aquarium.

What a perfect opportunity to introduce your children to colonial living. This inn dates back to 1685 and had additions in 1720 and 1790. The Underground Railroad hid slaves here in 1830; there's a trapdoor to prove it. Indian shutters are here, too.

The Randall family built it all and cooked their meals over an open hearth. Today the Clarks still do it the Randall way. They are ☛ self-taught in the art of hearth cooking, and they wear the colonial dress of that era.

When you walk into the rustic dining rooms, the aroma of wood is most appealing. And the food is glorious. The wood gives

North Stonington, Connecticut

the food a special taste. You can watch your lunch being prepared on one of the three open hearths. Quite a sight. I had ☞ lamb chops that were the best I've ever had. My friend had scallops done the Clarks' way that were delicious. Rhubarb chutney was served with both. It was exquisite. Roast goose with wild-rice stuffing was another lunch special.

There is one seating for dinner at seven o'clock. Reservations are a must. All three fireplaces are used in the evening. Popcorn and cheddar and crackers are offered first. Soup such as corn chowder and breads (the spider corn bread is superb) come next, and then an unhurried dinner. The Clarks try to do one poultry, one roast, and one seafood main dish. One vegetable is mashed potatoes and turnips. The desserts are colonial, such as Indian pudding.

The barn, circa 1819 and hand hewn, came from New York. It has been re-erected on this property and now houses wonderful rooms. Some of them are perfect for a family of four. Several have a queen-size canopy bed with a double-size trundle bed. Three rooms have lofts, reached by a spiral staircase. Kids love these! There are skylights and whirlpool baths and air conditioning and a tremendous and fun cattle scale, so it's the best of both worlds. The inn itself has three guest rooms with working fireplaces.

There are twenty-seven acres for wandering, cross-country skiing, or hiking. An African gray parrot named Ashes lives on the second floor. What a ham. I really think you should check this one out.

How to get there: Take exit 92 from I–95 onto Route 2 north. The inn is in ⅓ mile.

E: *One fireplace has an old round oven with a clock on top. Put the bird or roast in, hang it up, and wind the clock. The oven turns and browns the food perfectly. Children will be as fascinated by this as I was.*

The Bethel Inn
Bethel, Maine
04217

Innkeepers: Dick Rasor; manager, Ray Moran
Address/Telephone: P.O. Box 49; (207) 824–2175
Rooms: 150, in resort inn complex of 5 buildings and townhouse condominiums six minutes walking distance; all with private bath, many with fireplace, some with kitchen and television.
Rates: $53 to $125, per person, double occupancy, MAP. Infants, free; children under 12, $24; 12 and over, $40. Condominium rates available for 2 or 4 people.
Open: All year.
Facilities and activities: Lunch, bar, lounge. Gift shop. Golf, tennis, swimming pool, lake house with sailfish and canoes, cross-country skiing, saunas, hot tub, exercise room, indoor games, supervised activities for children. Own walking tour guide. Nearby: downhill skiing at Sunday River and Mt. Abram.

The Bethel Inn faces the village common of Bethel, Maine, which is a National Historic District complete with beautifully restored churches, public buildings, and private homes. The rear of the inn overlooks its own 200 acres and eighteen-hole championship golf course on 6,600 yards of rolling terrain.

Guest rooms have private baths and direct-dial telephones.

They are well done and very comfortable. A number of rooms have been recently redecorated with country-print wallpaper, thick carpeting, and fresh paint. The Fairway Townhouse Condominiums are available with one or two bedrooms. The one-bedroom townhouse includes a kitchen, dining and living room, a bedroom with two queen-size beds, a queen-size sleep sofa, and a working fireplace. The two-bedroom townhouse can accommodate up to eight people. All the townhouses have a washer/dryer—a big help for a vacationing family.

The huge living room, music room, and library are beautifully furnished for the utter comfort of the guests. The piano, by the way, is a Steinway.

Dining is a pleasure, either in the charming main dining room or on ☛ the year-round dining veranda overlooking the golf course and White Mountains. You'll find such entrees as prime ribs, roast duck, and lobster and crabmeat casserole on their extensive menu. There is something to please every taste.

The bar and lounge offers a light supper menu, which is nice for the late hiker or skier. In the winter you can have hot cider, hot buttered rum, and *glögg*. Lunch is nice in the screened-in terrace lounge.

The lake house, 3 miles away on Lake Songo, features clambakes and barbecues and all water sports. And if you like to swim, the new recreation center offers an ☛ outdoor heated pool with a built-in hot tub/Jacuzzi, available for year-round use. How fantastic to swim outdoors in the middle of winter! The center also has a fitness room, two saunas, a poolside lounge, and a game room with Ping-Pong, pool, and video games.

Skiing is super up here, with Sunday River (it now has fifty-six trails on five peaks) and Mount Abram just ten minutes away. The inn has special ski packages. Do check them. And as a special special, they have 42 kilometers of groomed cross-country trails for your pleasure.

You'll never be at a loss for something to do at The Bethel Inn.

How to get there: Bethel is located at the intersection of U.S. Route 2 and Maine Routes 5 and 26. From the south take exit 11 off the Maine Turnpike at Gray and follow Route 26 to Bethel. The inn is on the green.

Westways Country Inn
Center Lovell, Maine
04016

Innkeeper: Nancy Tripp
Address/Telephone: Route 5, Box 175; (207) 928-2663
Rooms: 7, 3 with private bath; 6 houses.
Rates: $130 to $175, double occupancy, MAP. Children under 12, $30; 12 and over, $50. Houses in season: $750 to $1,500, per week, EP. Ask about EP room rates and off-season, two-night rates for houses.
Open: All year except April and November.
Facilities and activities: Full license. Recreation building with bowling, Ping-Pong, pool, card room, lending library. Private beach and marina on Kezar Lake, swimming, boating, sailing, tennis. Nearby: canoeing on Saco River, cross-country skiing, downhill skiing, golf, antiquing, White Mountain National Forest.

Westways was built in the 1920s as the executive retreat of the Diamond Match Company. It is a look into the past that is a pure delight.

The living room overlooking Kezar Lake is large, with a huge stone fireplace and comfortable couches and chairs. On cool nights in winter, your dinner is served in here on glorious ☛ Spode china. The soup may be stracciatella. Your salad is served with homemade dressings, and the entrees consist of two nightly

10

Center Lovell, Maine

choices. One day I was there one of the choices was lobster. But your choice may be veal Cordon Bleu, or fresh red snapper, prime ribs, or steak. Great, creative desserts and coffees come next. This is indeed the way to live. Children's portions are available.

All of the rooms are gracious, most overlook the lake, and all have 🖝 libraries. The president of Diamond Match was quite a reader, and his collection is here for you to enjoy. By the way, all of the rooms are different; some have wicker headboards and some have four-poster beds. All are comfortable.

The houses are scattered over 120 acres of property. Some have a view of the lake. During the summer they are rented on a weekly basis, but in off-season they can be rented for a minimum of two nights. The smallest house has three bedrooms, one-and-a-half baths, living room, kitchen, and two screened porches. The largest has seven bedrooms and three baths; it can sleep fourteen. It also has three screened porches, laundry facilities, living room, dining room, and kitchen. Families like to come here for reunions. I can see why.

In the summertime, there's no lovelier spot than the boathouse on Kezar Lake, with its fantastic view of the White Mountains. It's a comfortable spot for reading or just idle meditation. Year round, the recreation building with its two-lane bowling alley is a great place to spend some time after a day of shopping in Conway, New Hampshire (just 22 miles away); hiking in the White Mountain National Forest; downhill skiing at Shawnee Peak at Pleasant Mountain or Sunday River (25 miles away); canoeing on the Saco River—there's a lot to do up here for everyone in the family.

How to get there: Coming either way on Route 302 turn north at Fryeburg, Maine, onto Route 5. Fourteen miles north the lake will appear on your left, and the inn's entrance (marked with a sign) is on your left about 6 miles up the lake.

❂

E: *There is a body shower in the bath on the first floor that is unbelievable. It is certainly one of a kind.*

olve Metcalf

The Lawnmeer Inn
West Boothbay Harbor, Maine
04575

Innkeepers: Sylvia and Frank Kelly; Jim and Lee Metzger
Address/Telephone: P.O. Box 505; (207) 633–2544
Rooms: 32; all with private bath, some with television.
Rates: $55 to $98, single or double occupancy, EP. Children, $8.
Open: Mid-May to mid-October.
Facilities and activities: Full breakfast, dinner, Sunday brunch, bar and lounge. Games, television, children's videos, baby-sitting available, children's parties and field trips by special arrangement. Croquet, badminton, lawn games, boat dock. Nearby: Boothbay Harbor activities, boat tours, Marine Resources Aquarium, Boothbay Playhouse, Audubon Workshop at Hog Island, YMCA.

The inn is nicely located on the island of Southport in the Boothbay Harbor region. As you sit on its porch, you are looking at a beautiful saltwater cove on Townsend Gut and watching the masts of the moored sailboats sway with the winds and tides.

The accommodations range from modern rooms in a new wing to comfortable inn suites and rooms. Some of the rooms have two double beds, TV, and 🐾 a sun deck overlooking the water. The views are really lovely and tranquil.

There are delightful sitting areas. One has a fireplace to ward off early spring or fall chills. Actually, the inn has four common rooms in all. One has a TV and a variety of games. This is a neat place for the kids—they'll find puzzles, books, Walkmans, children's videos, and more. If you'd like to sit back and let someone else entertain your children, you can arrange for baby-sitters or for field trips for them. You can even make arrangements for a children's party up here!

The two dining rooms are attractive with their nice napery and tall ladder-back chairs. One has a fireplace. A breakfast of hot oatmeal is nice, and the inn offers a full breakfast, too. The chef here is very inventive; he creates a different special every night. Would you believe lobster prepared ☞ five different ways? Even fried! There are baked, broiled, and fried seafood selections and plenty of them. The ☞ native sea scallops are grand. Of course there are meat and chicken dishes for the landlubbers. Lawnmeer's Chicken Cordon Bleu with a sharp cheese sauce is a winner. So is the sautéed veal in wine and mushroom sauce. If the children prefer, they can order from a children's menu that includes chicken fingers, hamburgers, and fried shrimp.

The inn has been operating since 1898. It is the oldest continually operated inn in the Boothbay area. Come see the puffins, craggy cliffs, coon cats, and lighthouses. It's all yours to enjoy.

How to get there: Take exit 22 from I-95 onto Route 1. Just north of Wiscassett, turn on Route 27 south. Go through Boothbay Harbor onto the island of Southport. The inn is on Route 27, 3/10 mile from the Southport Bridge.

E: *The windjammers arrive every July, and I was lucky enough to be here then. What a treat.*

The Dan'l Webster Inn
Sandwich, Massachusetts
02563

Innkeeper: Steven Catania
Address/Telephone: 149 Main Street; (508) 888–3622
Rooms: 42 rooms and suites; all with private bath and television.
Rates: $64 to $121, per person, MAP. $65 to $165, double occupancy, EP. Children under 12, free; 12 and over, $10.
Open: All year except Christmas Day.
Facilities and activities: Breakfast, lunch, dinner, Sunday brunch, bar, lounge. Swimming pool, gift shop. Privileges at local health club. Nearby: ocean beaches, golf, tennis, Sandwich Glass Museum, Heritage Plantation, Thornton Burgess Museum, Doll Museum, Cape Cod Railroad.

Bring your family to Sandwich, the oldest town on Cape Cod (incorporated in 1639), and stay at the Dan'l Webster Inn, which dates back to 1692. You can walk to many area attractions from the inn, including a ☞ really special one for little girls—Yesteryear's Doll Museum. It has early dollhouses furnished in period style, demonstrating how our ancestors lived, and a wonderful collection of antique dolls.

Hop in your car to visit the Heritage Plantation, a beautiful seventy-six-acre landscaped estate with antique cars, collections of antique firearms and military miniatures, and a working carousel. Fans of Old Mother Westwind and Peter Rabbit of the Old Briar Patch will want to spend some time at the Thornton W. Burgess Museum, where the author of these popular children's stories lived. And of course you won't want to miss lovely Sandy Neck beach, a nice ocean beach with many trails through sand dunes and picnic areas.

After a day of sightseeing, you will really enjoy coming back to the inn. All of the guest rooms are very comfortable. You'll find rooms with two double beds or a king and a variety of suites. I stayed in the Captain Ezra Nye suite in the lovely Fessenden House next door to the inn. Like the other three suites in the house, it has a whirlpool tub and a marble fireplace.

A 250-year-old linden tree, complete with bird feeders, stands outside the Conservatory, one of the inn's three lovely dining rooms. This is a glassed-in room, overlooking a beautifully landscaped courtyard and swimming pool. The Webster Room has china cabinets to display ☞ old Sandwich glass on loan from the museum. There's a portrait of Daniel Webster's second wife in here. The Heritage Room has a huge open fireplace and a grand piano on the stage for your entertainment. A ☞ dance band is here on weekends, and they sure sounded good to me.

Breakfasts are hearty, with eggs, seven different omelettes, sausage, fruit, a basket of freshly baked breads and much more. The lunch menu lists salads, sandwiches, and quite a few hot choices. Dinner is an adventure. There are numerous veal offerings, chicken, seafood specials, and, of course, beef. I had chateaubriand—very nice because it was served for one. It was very good. Desserts are sinful, and there are special coffees. You can share a plate with your small child at no charge or order from a children's menu. If you like, you can come to dinner between 4:45 and 5:45 P.M. for a less expensive meal.

Cape Cod is a delightful and very popular spot for a family vacation. Give the family a treat and stay in historic Sandwich at this lovely inn. You will like it here.

How to get there: Go over the Bourne Bridge to a rotary; go ¾ of the way around it, taking the Route 6A exit that parallels the canal. Stay on this road until you come to the third set of lights. This is Jarves Street. Go right, then right again onto Main Street. The inn is on the right, close to the corner.

Publick House & Country Motor Lodge
Sturbridge, Massachusetts 01566

Innkeeper: Buddy Adler
Address/Telephone: P.O. Box 187; (508) 347-3313
Rooms: 17 in Publick House, 4 suites in Chamberlain House, 8 rooms and 1 suite in Colonel Ebenezer Crafts Inn (1½ miles away), and 100 rooms and suites in Country Motor Lodge; all with private bath and air conditioning, some with television.
Rates: January 2 through June 29, $78 to $120; June 30 through December 28, $88 to $135; double occupancy, EP (continental breakfast at Colonel Ebenezer Crafts Inn). Motor lodge rates less. Children under 17, free (maximum of two in room with parents). Inquire about MAP rates.
Open: All year.
Facilities and activities: Breakfast, lunch, dinner, bar. Swimming pool, tennis courts, jogging trail, shuffleboard, children's play area, petting farm, bicycle rentals. Nearby: Old Sturbridge Village, golf, fishing, cross-country skiing.

Take your family back in time with a visit to Old Sturbridge Village, the largest outdoor living-history museum in the Northeast. At this re-created early nineteenth-century New England community, you and your children will meet period-costumed working men and women—a potter, shoemaker, cooper, blacksmith, farmer, and more. You will see the farmer plow his field with his oxen, using an ox yoke and plow made by woodworkers and blacksmiths of the Village. Stroll through a store, bank, houses, schoolhouse, and meetinghouse.

The Village is just 1 mile away from the Publick House, which is located on the Sturbridge Common. Popular events are the Yankee Winter Weekends, during which you have lodging at the inn, admission to the Village, entertainment, five meals, and two receptions. Also popular are the Village's summer workshops for children ages seven to fourteen. For one week, from 9 A.M. to 3 P.M. daily, children participate in Village activities, dressed in costume, while their parents relax at the inn.

Do request the Publick House calendar and plan to visit here for one of the many special events. A special favorite of mine is Christmas. The inn keeps all twelve days of it, from December 21 to January 1, with special foods and minstrels who stroll through the inn.

You have a wide variety of accommodations to choose from here. If you want to stay in the Publick House itself, which is listed on the National Register of Historic Places, your family of three might stay in the Lafayette, which has a queen-size bed and an adjoining room with a single bed. The Chamberlain House suites are larger, with a living room with a sofa bed, a bedroom with a queen-size bed, and a bathroom connecting the two rooms. The motor lodge rooms have two double beds, and the townhouse suites have a bedroom with two double beds, a living room on a lower level with a queen-size sofa bed, two baths, and a patio.

The barn, connected to the main house with a ramp, has been transformed into a restaurant. Double doors, topped by a glorious sunburst window, lead into a restaurant that serves hearty Yankee cooking such as delicious lobster pie, duckling, prime ribs, or lamb chops. At Crabapples, a second restaurant, you can order big burgers for the children, among other foods.

How to get there: Take the Massachusetts Turnpike to exit 9. The Publick House is located on the Common in Sturbridge, on Route 131. From Hartford, take I–84 to exit 3, which brings you right into Sturbridge.

Franconia Inn
Franconia, New Hampshire 03580

Innkeepers: Richard and Alec Morris
Address/Telephone: Route 116; (603) 823-5542
Rooms: 34, including 3 family suites; all with private bath; 1 with Jacuzzi.
Rates: $60 to $75, per person, MAP. Children under 3, free; 3 to 11, $18.75. EP rates available.
Open: All year except April 1 to May 25, and mid-October to December 15.
Facilities and activities: Bar and lounge; game room with large-screen television, videotapes, pinball machines; hot tub. Swimming pool and river, soaring center on property, 4 clay tennis courts, croquet, bicycles, horseback riding, ice skating, sleigh rides, cross-country skiing and trails. Nearby: downhill skiing, golf, Fantasy Farm, Whale's Tail Water Park, Franconia Notch.

This is an inn in the fine tradition of old New England hostelries. The inn is the fourth for the Morris family. It is run by third-generation innkeepers who make certain there is never a dull moment any season of the year.

Truly unique entertainment for the whole family is the inn's ☛ soaring center, which offers glider rides and biplane rides. Power plane instruction is given. Horseback riding is fun on the

Franconia, New Hampshire

inn's property, and there are trail rides through Ham Branch stream and around the hay fields. There are 65 miles of maintained cross-country trails right at hand, and instruction and rentals (even skis for the smallest kids) are available. Downhill skiing is but 10 miles away.

Inside the inn, the children's game room is well equipped with arcade pinball machines, electronic games, and a large-screen TV. Videotapes of movies can be checked out at the front desk. While the kids are kept occupied, you can relax in the lounge and listen to selected classical and popular music by the glow of the fireplace. Or try out the library, card room, or screened porch overlooking the swimming pool and the mountains. And oh, the hot tub is a great way to unwind in the evening!

Family suites sleep up to six people in two rooms. One has a double bed and a twin bed in each room, with a connecting bath. Another has a living area complete with a wet bar, small refrigerator, and small stove. These are nice, comfortable accommodations.

A lovely candlelit dining room, with pink and white napery, serves glorious food. The chef has treated escargots in an innovative way. They are marinated, baked in butter, garlic, and Ouzo, and sealed in a puff pastry shell. Superb! Bouillabaisse à la provençale is really a winner, and so is spicy ginger and soy sauce sauté. A vegetarian pastry is delightful for vegetarians. For children, the chef provides a special menu. If that doesn't fill the bill for a really fussy eater, parents can order something special in advance.

☛ Breakfast in bed? It's here, if you wish, complete with a pitcher of mimosas. I could stay forever.

How to get there: Take I–91 north to the Wells River-Woodsville exit. Go right on Route 302 to Lisbon, New Hampshire. A few miles past Lisbon, go right on Route 117 to Franconia. Crossing the bridge into town, go right to the Exxon station. There, take another right to Route 116, and you're 2 miles from the inn. Or, if you have a single-engine plane, the inn has its own F.A.A.-listed airfield with a 3,000-foot-long runway.

E: ☛ *Horse-drawn sleigh rides in this beautiful winter wonderland are my idea of heaven.*

Christmas Farm Inn
Jackson, New Hampshire
03846

Innkeepers: Bill and Sydna Zeliff
Address/Telephone: P. O. Box 176; (603) 383–4313
Rooms: 37, including suites and cabins; all with private bath.
Rates: $68 to $85, per person, double occupancy, MAP. Children 12 and under, $25; over 12, $45. Special package rates.
Open: All year.
Facilities and activities: Trail lunches available, pub. Movies nightly, game room, large-screen television and VCR, Ping-Pong, bumper pool, sauna. Baby-sitters may be available with advance notice. Large children's playground, swimming pool, putting green, tennis, shuffleboard, volleyball, 80 kilometers of cross-country trails, horse-drawn sleigh rides. Nearby: downhill skiing, Attitash alpine slide, Mt. Cranmore skimobile, Wildcat Mountain gondola, canoeing on Saco River.

Yes, Virginia, there is a Christmas Farm Inn, and they have the Mistletoe Pub and the Sugar Plum Dining Room to prove it. The food is fit for any Santa and his helpers, from the hearty, full country breakfast, which includes ☛ homemade doughnuts, muffins, and sticky buns, to gracious dinners.

There are choices of seafood, poultry, and meat entrees. The grilled lamb kebab was a real hit with me; lamb is marinated in garlic, fresh thyme, and olive oil, and cooked with mushrooms, peppers, tomatoes, and shallots. For those who want a lighter dinner, the vegetarian platter of lightly steamed fresh vegetables and wild mushrooms is served on a bed of wild rice. Dishes from the seas are real treats. Children age twelve and under have their own special menu, offering them a choice of appetizers and main courses. The desserts do indeed make visions of sugarplums dance in your head, and all are made right here. How about apple pie, carrot cake, or the Christmas Farm special sundae?

Separate from the main inn is the barn, which is the place to find a wonderful game room. On a rainy day, children will find this a great spot to be, and children's movies on videotape will be shown on the large-screen TV. There are four suites in here that are ideal for large families, each with a living room and double bed and two twin beds.

Outdoors, there is no end to the family fun you can have. Skiing—both cross-country and downhill—is good here all winter long. The children's playground is set in a wide-open field, so the children can run and play to their heart's content. There are swings, seesaws, a climbing house, sandbox, and various pieces of equipment for imaginative rides. Older kids—and their Moms and Dads—will have hours of fun playing golf on the putting green, tennis, shuffleboard, and volleyball. And if you want to go exploring, there is much to do in this town in the heart of the White Mountains.

Come on the second Wednesday in July for the annual Christmas-in-July party. The inn goes all the way with a Christmas tree, a visit from Santa Claus, and singing of Christmas songs. And where else should you be at Christmas than the Christmas Farm Inn? This is a very special holiday here, and many families come every year. Sometimes extended families meet here for a reunion. Santa must live nearby, because he never fails to arrive in a most unusual manner. And when he comes, he's eagerly greeted by the inn dog, Daffodil.

How to get there: Go north on Route 16 from North Conway. A few miles after Route 302 branches off to your left, you will see a covered bridge on your right. Take the bridge through the village and up the hill ¼ mile, and there is the inn.

Whitney's Village Inn
Jackson, New Hampshire
03846

Innkeepers: Terry and Judy Tannehill
Address/Telephone: P.O. Box W; (603) 383–6886 or (800) 252–5622 within New England
Rooms: 35 rooms and suites, 30 with private bath; 2 cottages with fireplace.
Rates: $60 to $80, per person, MAP. Children age 12 and under, $30. Packages available for 3- , 5- , and 7-night stays.
Open: All year.
Facilities and activites: Lunch in season or box lunch, bar, lounge. Television and VCR with movies. Downhill skiing, ice skating, tobogganing, tennis, swimming, boating, lawn games, and summertime hayrides. Nearby: many hiking trails, Story Land, Heritage–New Hampshire, Conway Scenic Railroad, alpine slide.

This is an authentic mountain hideaway nestled in among New Hampshire's White Mountains. It's pretty nice to be able to crawl out of bed, dress, have a sumptuous breakfast, and ☛ walk across to the lifts, trails, ski shop or ski school, all just a snowball's throw away. It is a real treat not to have to drive the car anywhere after you get here. Black Mountain, with its own snowmaking equipment, is right here. The lifts can handle about 3,000 skiers

Jackson, New Hampshire

per hour, so there is hardly any waiting. There are many trails that serve the mountain, and all are kept in the best condition possible. A lighted skating rink is right beside the inn. Bring your own skates or borrow some here. The inn also has tobogganing and sleigh rides.

Summer fun is the inn's own swimming pond, which is in such a pretty setting on the lovely grounds. It is deep enough at one end for diving. The inn owns a small paddleboat to use on the pond. There are also all sorts of lawn games—croquet, badminton, volleyball, shuffleboard, and horseshoes—and a tennis court. Inside, the game room is well equipped with all sorts of games, Ping-Pong, TV and VCR, and a selection of movies. One of the parlors has puzzles in the making, nice comfortable furniture, a Steinway piano, and lovely old oriental carpets. There are Hunter fans all over the inn. Then there is the Shovel Handle Lounge for après-ski fun and entertainment. Lunch in season is served out here.

Dining is superb in a casually elegant dining room. Mauve and tan are the napery colors. One of the soups is Yesterday's (Mom always said it was better the next day). Their Jackson-style duckling is excellent, and how nice to find a delicious stew. Roast goose is also seldom seen on a menu. There is a lobster cookout by the brook once a week in the warm weather. A really nice touch for families is a special children's table (optional). Dinner at six o'clock is followed by a movie. Parents and children both can enjoy themselves.

The guest rooms are carpeted and have comfortable beds. Some of the rooms have nice wingback chairs. The eight family suites in the chalet are nice and roomy, with a living room and bedroom. There are two twin beds and a double or a queen. The small refrigerator is nice for a family, for keeping lunchtime snacks cold. The cottages have two bedrooms, a living room, refrigerator, and a working fireplace. Try it here. You will like it.

How to get there: Go north from Conway 22 miles on Route 16. Take a right on Route 16A through a covered bridge into Jackson Village. Take Route 16B to the top of the hill to the inn.

Philbrook Farm Inn
Shelburne, New Hampshire
03581

Innkeepers: Connie Leger and Nancy Philbrook
Address/Telephone: Star Route 41, Gorham, NH 03581; (603) 466–3831
Rooms: 19, 10 with private bath; 5 cottages, some with housekeeping arrangements. Pets allowed in cottages.
Rates: $80 to $100, per person, double occupancy, MAP. Children up to age 2, free; 2 to 6, $20; 7 to 11, $25. Cottages, $350 weekly, EP.
Open: May 1 to October 31 and December 26 to March 31.
Facilities and activities: Lunch, BYOB lounge. Library, play room, Ping-Pong, pool table. Swimming pool and swimming holes in mountain streams, hiking trails, horseback riding with lessons and trail rides, cross-country skiing, snowshoeing. Nearby: downhill skiing, Santa's Village, Story Land, Fantasy Farm, Attitash, Six Gun City.

When you're traveling along Route 2, take a look across the fields, and there you'll see this lovely inn that is listed on the National Register of Historic Places. And rightly so. In 1861 Philbrook Farm started as an inn. Today it is still an inn and still has ☛ Philbrooks living here, running it in fine New England tradition.

Everything you eat here is prepared from scratch in their kitchens. The baked goods are made daily. A huge garden provides

Shelburne, New Hampshire

good vegetables. One entree is served each night. Roasts of everything you can want—pork, beef, turkey—and on and on. The New England boiled dinner is also a favorite. This is good food that will appeal to children and parents alike.

The downstairs playroom has Ping-Pong, a pool table, shuffleboard, puzzles, and fun. A lot of reading material can be found all over the inn. Fireplaces are also all over the inn. ☛ A player piano, an old pump organ—where else can you find such unique things except in an inn?

Rooms are furnished with a lot of old ☛ family treasures. There are some nice four-posters and a wonderful collection of old bowl and pitcher sets. All the cottages are different. They sure are nice if you want to linger here awhile. Some have dining rooms, some have fireplaces, and some have porches. For example, the Lodge has five bedrooms, one-and-a-half baths, a living room with fireplace, dining room, and kitchen. Birch Cliff is nestled under a cliff. There are a living room, kitchen, bedroom, and bath on the first floor, and three bedrooms and a bath upstairs. You can sit out on your veranda to enjoy the view. What a nice place for a weeklong family vacation!

With more than 1,000 acres, the inn has plenty of room for you to roam any season of the year. Look across their fields to the Carter-Moriah and Presidential mountain ranges. Behind the inn rises the Mahoosuc Range. This is the Androscoggin Valley. Horseback riding lessons and trail riding are available at the Philbrook Farm stables. What a heavenly place for a horseback ride. I saw a foal about two weeks old when I was here. A real little beauty. The inn cats are Cobweb and Fuzzy, and the inn dog, Leibschen, is a German shorthair pointer.

How to get there: The inn is 1½ miles off Route 2. Going west, look for a direction sign on your right, and turn right. Cross the railroad tracks and then a bridge. Turn right at the crossroads and go ½ mile to the inn, which is on North Road.

Dexters
Sunapee, New Hampshire 03782

Innkeepers: Holly and Michael Durfor
Address/Telephone: 25 Stagecoach Road; (603) 763–5571 or (800) 232–5571
Rooms: 17, all with private bath; 1 cottage with kitchen and laundry facilities. Pets permitted in annex rooms at $10 per day.
Rates: $120 to $160, double occupancy, MAP. Cottage, $350 for 4 people, MAP; weekly EP rate available. Children under 12, $35; over 12, $45. Package plans available.
Open: May through October.
Facilities and activities: Lunch in July and August, bar. Recreation barn with television, Ping-Pong, bumper pool. Three all-weather Plexi-cushion tennis courts, swimming pool, croquet, horseshoe pit, shuffleboard. Baby-sitters available with advance notice. Nearby: canoe rentals on Connecticut River, golf club privileges, fishing, Mt. Sunapee, New London Barn Playhouse summertime Magical Mondays.

Dexters is a nice family inn, run by four innkeepers—Holly and Michael, four-year-old Hartwell (who enjoys ringing the dinner bell), and one-year-old Hayley Marie. Hartwell enjoys playing with young guests, and the Durfors' supply of baby equipment may be borrowed if necessary.

Sunapee, New Hampshire

These are rooms you'll want to linger in. They are a bit above average, with marvelous wallpapers and heavenly ☛ pillows made of feathers. Some of the rooms are favorites with families. One has a loft; others have king- or queen-size bed and twin beds, a double shower and a double sink; and another has a connecting room. The cottage is ideal for a family, as it has two bedrooms, each with a king and twin bed; a full kitchen; living room with fireplace; screened-in porch; and a washer and dryer. Come for a week!

The inn serves good, homemade, healthy food and takes pleasure in keeping a family happy. A family can be served dinner at 5:00 P.M., if necessary, or the inn will arrange to find a baby-sitter so that parents can eat by themselves later. For dinner, children can order small portions of honey-sesame chicken, New York strip steaks, and spaghetti or sandwiches from the luncheon menu. Children (parents too) think the inn's famous grilled peanut butter and bacon sandwich is a real treat.

Outdoor sports? You name it. Tennis is taken seriously here. Three all-weather ☛ Plexicushion tennis courts with a pro and shop are provided for your enjoyment. After a game there is a lovely outdoor swimming pool to cool off in. Croquet, a horseshoe pit, and shuffleboard are also available. For a good summer or fall activity, there are some of the loveliest walking and hiking trails right on the inn's property. And the inn's annual Afternoon in 1908 Summertime event, when kites are flown and period costumes are worn, has become a real hit.

There is a special recreation room in the barn for all ages, but it is keyed to those under seventeen who need a place of their own when the five o'clock cocktail hour begins.

How to get there: Take I–89 out of Concord and follow exit 12 to Route 11, to 103B in Sunapee. Or take I–91 out of Springfield and follow exit 8 to Claremont, New Hampshire, to Route 103. The turn to the inn is marked by a sign 200 yards south of the intersection of 103 and 11. The inn is about 1½ miles off Route 103.

※

E: *The three pet Scottish Highland cattle are really great. They look like big, shaggy dogs, and they adore the apples guests feed them in the fall.*

Olive Metcalf

Shelter Harbor Inn
Westerly, Rhode Island
02891

Innkeepers: Jim and Debbye Dey
Address/Telephone: Route 1, 10 Wagner Road; (401) 322–8883
Rooms: 24; all with private bath and television, some with fireplace and private deck.
Rates: $68 to $86, single; $78 to $96, double; EPB. Children under 12, $15; 12 and over, $20.
Open: All year.
Facilities and activities: Lunch, dinner, Sunday brunch, bar. Private ocean beach, 2 paddle tennis courts with night lighting, hot tub, croquet court. Nearby: golf, boat-launching area, tennis, Block Island ferry, Mystic Seaport and Mystic Marinelife Aquarium (16 miles), Newport (32 miles).

If you would like a 3-mile stretch of uncluttered ocean beach located just a mile from a lovely old country inn, find your way to Rhode Island and the Shelter Harbor Inn. When you and the children are not playing in the ocean surf, there's a salt pond near the inn for you to explore.

Eight of the guest rooms are in the restored farmhouse, and ten more are located in the barn. The rest of the rooms are in the carriage house, which is a lovely addition to the inn. Some rooms are ideal for a family, with a queen-size bed, twins, and a sofa bed. There is a large central living room in the barn that opens onto a spacious deck—how ideal for families. There is also a library with comfortable leather chairs where you can relax with a book.

The menu reflects the location of the inn, and at least half the items offered are from the sea. ☛ The finnan haddie is specially smoked in Narragansett. If your children aren't fond of seafood, the menu also includes beef, chicken, veal, and duck. And if all else fails, the kitchen staff will be happy to make a peanut butter and jelly sandwich. You can choose your place to eat, from the formal dining room, the small private dining room with a fireplace, or the glassed-in terrace room. The sun porch has been turned into a pub bar. There is a delightful old wood stove to warm you, and Debbye's plants are everywhere. If weather permits, take a drink out to the secluded terrace.

If you can tear yourself from the beach, there is much to see around here. You are about halfway between Mystic and Newport. The ferry to Block Island leaves from Point Judith. It is an hour-long ride, and when you arrive on Block Island you will find it a super spot for bicycling. You can charter boats for fishing, or stand at the edge of the surf and cast your line into the sea. And then you can come back to the inn to unwind in the hot tub.

How to get there: From I–95 north, take exit 92. Follow Route 2 south a short distance to Route 78. From I–95 south, take exit 1 and follow Route 3 south several miles to Route 78. Follow Route 78 east to the traffic lights. Turn left onto Route 1, going north, and go 4 miles to the inn on the right.

Mountain Top Inn
Chittenden, Vermont
05737

Innkeeper: Bill Wolfe
Address/Telephone: Mountain Top Road; (802) 483–2311
Rooms: 33 rooms and 22 cottage and chalet units; all with private bath, chalets with kitchenette.
Rates: $76 to $148, per person, double occupancy, MAP. Children under 2, free; 2 to 6, 35 percent of adult rate; 7 to 16, 50 percent. Inquire about packages.
Open: All year.
Facilities and activities: Lunch, bar, lounge. Recreation room, sauna, whirlpool. Boating, windsurfing, canoeing, fly fishing, hand trap shooting, horseback riding, swimming in lake or heated outdoor pool, mountain bikes and designated trails, pitch-and-putt golf course, lawn games, cross-country skiing, ice skating, tobogganing, sledding, sleigh rides, maple sugaring. Nearby: Killington and Pico alpine ski areas, complimentary membership at Centre Sport fitness facility.

Mountain Top Inn is just beautiful, with views that no money can buy. At a 2,000-foot elevation, it overlooks crystal-clear, 650-acre Mountain Top Lake, which is surrounded by fantastic mountains. When you enter the inn, you are in a very inviting living area with a large fireplace. Ahead of you is the view and a spectacular ☞ two-story glass-enclosed staircase that leads to the dining room. The food served here is superb, beginning with appetizers like scallops sautéed with chutney and Dijon mustard, and moving on to such entrees as split rack of lamb broiled with a Roquefort and herb coating and served with a light tomato sauce. There are many interesting choices, but what makes parents especially happy is that there is a children's dinner menu as well. Children will enjoy being able to choose their own appetizer—perhaps cheese and crackers garnished with grapes and sliced oranges, or celery sticks with peanut butter and raisins. Children's entrees come with potato and vegetable and include a fried chicken dinner, hamburger, grilled ham steak with pineapple garnish, broiled fillet of scrod, or grilled cheese sandwich.

The rooms, most overlooking the lake and mountains, are large and luxuriously furnished. All have spacious baths. Some rooms have two double beds or a queen-size bed and a sofa bed. Large families especially enjoy the chalet units, most of which have two or more bedrooms, a kitchen or kitchenette, living room, dining area, fireplace or wood stove, and one or two baths.

The inn has an excellent ski touring program. With over a thousand acres to ski on, the ☞ views are awesome. The sugar house, a wooden structure, is well located near several of the inn's ski touring trails. It has been turned into a ski-warming hut where skiers (and others) in the spring have the added bonus of watching the ☞ sap boiling-down process firsthand. There are two other warming huts on the property. The inn has a ski shop with instructors and all the latest equipment. Ice skating and toboggans also are fun, and downhill skiing is nearby at Pico and Killington.

Summertime guests find many activities to keep them well occupied from morning until night, and in the fall the color show of the trees is breathtaking.

How to get there: From Rutland, head north on Route 7. Pass the power station, turn right on Chittenden Road, and follow it into Chittenden. Follow the signs up to the inn.

The Inn on the Common
Craftsbury Common, Vermont
05827

Innkeepers: Penny and Michael Schmitt
Address/Telephone: P.O. Box 75; (802) 586–9619 or (800) 521–2233
Rooms: 18 in 3 buildings; all with private bath, 5 with fireplace or wood stove. Pets by advance arrangement at $10 per pet per visit.
Rates: $90 to $130, per person, double occupancy, MAP. Children up to 6, free; 6 to 12, $45 to $60. EPB rates and package plans available.
Open: All year.
Facilities and activities: Guest kitchenette, lounge with Betamax and 300 films. Heated swimming pool, tennis court, English croquet court, hiking and cross-country skiing trails. Mountain bike and canoe rentals. Near many lakes for fishing and boating.

  It is a long way up here, but it's worth every mile you travel to be a guest of the Schmitts.
  There are three buildings that make up the inn. The north annex is on the common with a lovely picket fence around it. All of its rooms are beautifully appointed. The wallpapers are ☛ Scalamandre reproduction from a South Carolina historic collection. The sheets throughout the inn are brand new and Marimekko. There's a very unusual sofa, an English knoll; try and figure how the arms go down. Two of the bedrooms in the north

annex have a fireplace. One of the bathrooms has such a cute, tiny bathtub. There's a lovely canopy bed in one room. In the main house itself there are three new luxurious rooms, and Penny loves to show them off.

Across the street is the south annex. The guest lounge has a fireplace, comfy sofas, a large television, and ☞ Betamax. The north annex also has a Betamax. There's a library of over 300 films on tape, so even in bad weather there is something to do.

In the main house is the dining room with a glass wall overlooking the rose gardens. All the gardens are lovely. Penny has green hands and is a faithful gardener. The dining room has the perfect atmosphere to savor the sumptuous food, and a five-course dinner is served at 8:00 P.M. The innkeepers provide baby-sitter service for children under six during the dinner hour, as they are not permitted in the dining room at this time. This makes for a much more relaxing evening for Mom and Dad, and the children are sure to have more fun, too. You can use the guest kitchenette to prepare their supper.

A staff of naturalists runs a sports complex near the inn. One hundred and forty acres include lake swimming, sculling, canoeing, cross-country skiing, nature walks, and bird watching. There is a summer walking map of Craftsbury, with walks along the appropriate ski trails, logging roads, and back roads. Come on up. There is something for everyone.

How to get there: Follow I–91 to St. Johnsbury, take Route 2 west, and at West Danville take Route 15 to Hardwick. Take Route 14 north to Craftsbury, and continue north into the common. The inn is on the left as you enter the village.

E: *The solar-heated swimming pool has a little waterfall to let the water in. It disturbs nothing in its peaceful location behind the south annex. Sam, the inn dog, enjoys watching it.*

Highland Lodge
Greensboro, Vermont
05841

Innkeepers: Wilhelmina and David Smith
Address/Telephone: R.R. 1, Box 1290; (802) 533-2647
Rooms: 22 rooms and cottages; all with private bath.
Rates: $125 to $165 (including 15-percent service), double occupancy, MAP. Children under 2, free; 2 to 3, $20; 4 to 8, $35; 9 to 15, $40.
Open: All year except April 1 to May 25 and after foliage season to mid-December.
Facilities and activities: Lunch. Beer and wine license only, setups available. Television in living room, playroom, supervised play program for children ages 4 to 9 in July and August, swing set. Swimming, boating, fishing in Caspian Lake; cross-country ski touring center; sledding. Nearby: Working dairy farm, golf.

When the snow starts falling up here, it has to be one of the most beautiful places in the world. And you can bet that it's popular with cross-country skiers. There is a complete ☞ ski touring center with daily instruction, ski shop (sales, ski rentals for all ages, and repairs), guided tours, marked trails, and skier's lunch. All this is at an altitude of 1,500 feet, where there are miles of ski touring through the wonderful scenery. The inn even has a baby sled to be pulled by a cross-country skier. When children tire of skiing, there's a good sledding hill and sleds to use.

Greensboro, Vermont

Winter isn't the only fun time of year to be here. Caspian Lake, with the lodge's own beach house, is just across the road for swimming, canoeing, and sailing. The inn has rowboats, paddle boats, and canoes to be used for free, and a small sailboat to rent. Fishing is good in June and September until mid-October for salmon, lake trout, rainbow trout, and perch. And if you want to show the children a working farm, take advantage of Vermont's Host Farm program to visit a nearby dairy farm.

Any inn that sends its chef to ☞ France to train for the kitchen surely gets my nod. The food has always been outstanding here, and now it is even better. The menu is inventive and they have their great grilled ☞ black Angus sirloin steaks to prove it. I love the dessert menu. They have great names, and taste equally great. Ishkabibble is a brownie topped with ice cream and homemade hot fudge. Forgotten Dessert is a meringue with ice cream and strawberries. It's nice to find these old favorites on a menu.

Parents can hire a baby-sitter for their children during the dinner hour, if they want to eat by themselves, and accompany their children to a special dinner at 6:30 P.M. A simple children's menu is available, offering hamburger, cheeseburger, hot dog, salad, or a child-size portion of dinner specials.

It's nice to come here in July and August when the innkeepers hire a play lady for the four-to-nine set (if there are enough children). While the children are happily occupied, the lounges and library remain free and quiet for you.

Many of the rooms can sleep three people, with a double bed and a twin bed. In addition, there are one-, two-, and three-bedroom cottages, all of which have living rooms. Some have kitchens, which are very handy when you're traveling with a family.

This is the place to get away from it all. The views and utter peace are so wonderful, they are hard to describe. Come and enjoy.

How to get there: Greensboro is 35 miles northeast of Montpelier. Take I-91 to St. Johnsbury and follow U.S. 2 west to West Danville. Continue west on Vermont 15, to intersection with Vermont 16 about 2 miles east of Hardwick. Turn north on 16 to East Hardwick and follow signs west to Greensboro, at the south end of Caspian Lake. Highland Lodge is at the north end of the lake on the road to East Craftsbury.

The Vermont Inn
Killington, Vermont
05751

Innkeepers: Judd and Susan Levy
Address/Telephone: Route 4; (802) 773–9847 or (800) 541–7795 (outside Vermont)
Rooms: 16; 12 with private bath.
Rates: In summer, $45 to $70; in winter, $50 to $80; per person, double occupancy, MAP. No children under 5; over 5, $40 to $50 in summer; $50 to $60 in winter.
Open: All year except mid-April to Memorial Day and end of October to Thanksgiving. Restaurant closed Mondays for dinner.
Facilities and activities: Game room with bumper pool, television, board games; sauna, hot tub, bar. Shuffleboard, badminton, tennis court, swimming pool. Nearby: Killington and Pico for downhill skiing, alpine slide, golf course, summer theater, gondola ride; Norman Rockwell Museum; Rutland Farmers' Market.

You may be greeted at the door of this friendly red house by a companionable bichon frise named Harry. Judd and Susan are always here, and a nicer couple you'll have to travel a long way to find.

The Vermont Inn is well known locally for the fine food served in the lovely dining room. As a matter of fact, the restaurant

Killington, Vermont

was once again ☞ awarded the three-diamond rating from AAA. Just a sample of the food is tenderloin of pork, so different, sautéed with fresh mushrooms and flavored in sherry wine with cream. Steak teriyaki is excellent, as is their good selection of fish dishes. They have cultivated ☞ a fine wine cellar to enhance the good food. Steak, fish, chicken, and pasta dishes are available for children. Breakfast during the summer is a delicious continental buffet, and in the wintertime don't miss Judd's special French toast.

The inn's guests are a mixed bag. You'll run into young professional people from Boston or New York, a grandparent or two, families, anyone from honeymooners to golden oldies.

This old house has sturdy underpinnings. Some of the original beams still have the bark on them, and how the rocks of the foundation were ever put in place I cannot imagine. Everything was changed around, the old dining room became a lounge to make the inn cozier, so take advantage of the beautiful view of Killington and Pico straight ahead across the valley. There is also a room with a view that houses a hot tub, exercise machines, and lots of plants. It's a beauty and is ideal for anyone who wants to unwind after a day on the slopes or hiking.

I always love inn dogs, as you know, but Harry is really special to me because he's a bichon frise. I have one, too, so I know what wonderful pets they are. Mine is named Muffin. Harry's "Instructions to Guests" on how he is to be treated should be on the *must* list for every inn dog. They are tacked up at the desk. Drop in and read them, then stay awhile.

How to get there: The inn is 6 miles east of Rutland, via Route 4. It is also 4 miles west of the intersection of Route 4 and Route 100 north (Killington Access Road).

E: There is a secluded stream, so quiet, just right for meditating, or, if you are brave, to put a foot in.

The Village Inn
Landgrove, Vermont
05148

Innkeepers: Jay and Kathy Snyder; Elsie and Don Snyder
Address/Telephone: P.O. Box 215; (802) 824–6673
Rooms: 20; 16 with private bath.
Rates: In winter, $55 to $65, per person, double occupancy, MAP. In summer, $44 to $68, per room, EPB. Children age 5 and under, $5 in summer, $20 in winter; 6 and over, $15 in summer, $30 in winter.
Open: All year except April 1 to May 22, and October 20 to mid-December.
Facilities and activities: Dinner daily except on Wednesdays in summer. Lounge. Playroom with Ping-Pong and bumper pool, whirlpool spa. Heated swimming pool, pitch-and-putt golf, two Plexipave tennis courts, volleyball, hiking and cross-country skiing trails into National Forest, ice skating, children's play equipment. Nearby: downhill skiing at Bromley, Stratton, or Magic mountains; alpine slide at Bromley; summer theaters.

This is a family-run inn that welcomes families. Your children will be well entertained, and so will you. Indoors is a fun game room, and outside are play things, a heated swimming pool, two Plexipave tennis courts, and a four-hole pitch-and-putt golf facility. A hike through the National Forest is unbelievably scenic, and summer theater and an alpine slide are nearby.

Landgrove, Vermont

Winter means snow, and there is plenty of it. It's only a short hop by car to Bromley, Stratton, and Magic mountains. Cross-country skiing begins at the inn's door, or try your skills at snowshoeing or ice skating. After a long day revive yourself in the whirlpool spa, and then enjoy the fireside warmth in the Rafter Room lounge.

The architectural style of the inn is peculiar to Vermont, with one building added onto another building. It turns out to be charming. The first part was built in 1810. It has been an inn since 1939. The rooms are spick-and-span, spacious, and very comfortable.

Especially nice for a family is a two-room setup that has a double bed in one room, two twin beds in an adjoining room, and a shared bath. There also are rooms with a double bed and a twin bed and enough remaining space to add a cot.

Dinners are good but not fancy, with entrees like fillet of sole baked with lemon and wine, topped with julienned vegetables; sautéed chicken breast; and a vegetarian stir-fry. If the children prefer, they can order from their own menu.

The common rooms, dining room, and just everything about this quiet spot are relaxing. And the Snyders, who are cordial and welcoming innkeepers, make you want to return year after year.

How to get there: Via I–91, use exit 6 at Rockingham. Take Route 103 to Chester, then Route 11 to Londonderry. Continue past the shopping center for approximately a half mile, and turn right on Landgrove Road. Go 4 miles to the Village of Landgrove. Bear left after crossing the bridge and continue 1 mile to the inn, on your right.

From Manchester, take Route 11 past Bromley Ski Area, and turn left into Peru Village. At the fork in Peru, bear left and continue 4 miles through the National Forest to the crossroads in Landgrove. Turn left toward Weston, and the inn will be on your right.

❈

E: *From horse-drawn sleigh rides in winter to the blueberry pancakes, this is a nice place to be.*

39

MID-ATLANTIC AND CHESAPEAKE REGION

by
Brenda Boelts Chapin

Since 1984 Brenda Boelts Chapin has visited more than 200 inns for each edition of Recommended Country Inns, traveling by car, plane, boat, train, and four-wheel drive. In her quest to present the best, she has hiked, canoed, and ridden horses; she has dined late into the night at romantic hideaways and quizzed chefs about their culinary philosophies (while savoring their specialties). She found historical colonial inns in Virginia, upstate New York inns in the "great camp" style, elegant historic homes in Delaware and Maryland, romantic inns in the lush countryside of West Virginia, and Victorian hostelries and Italianate mansions on Chesapeake Bay. As Brenda says about the perfect country inn: "Their hallmarks are warmth, hospitality, and sweet memories. Beyond this, there is only one generalization that can be made about country inns—no two are alike." She selected 173 of them to recommend in the third edition of her inn guide.

Brenda is a travel journalist whose work has appeared in many magazines and newspapers. Her lectures and slide shows on mid-Atlantic country inns are well received. She lives in Maryland on the Chesapeake Bay with her husband, Charles Chapin, an emergency physician.

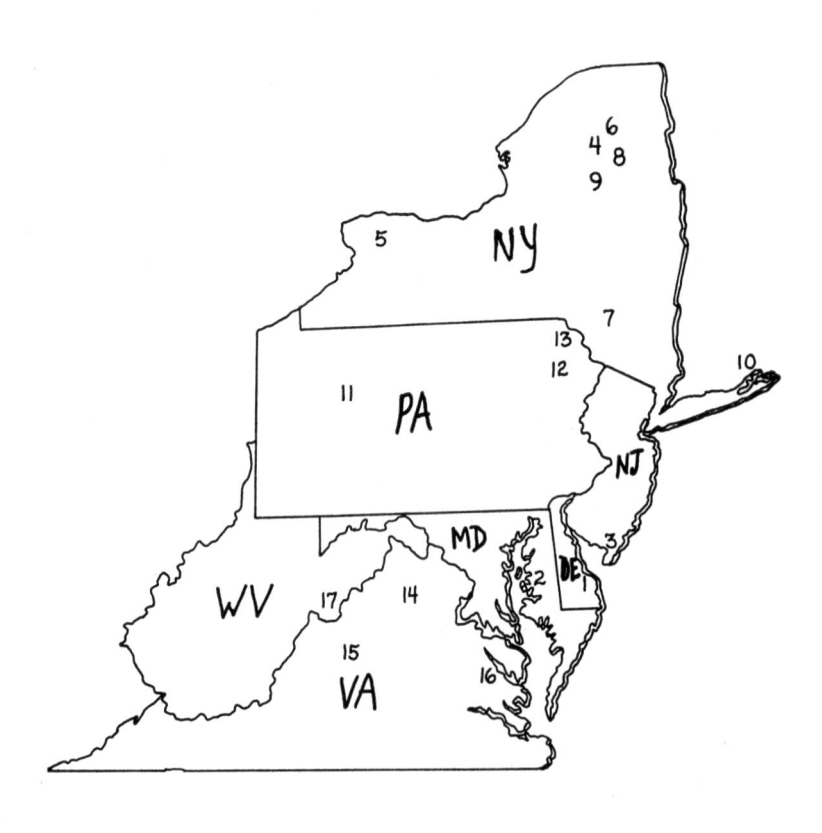

Mid-Atlantic and Chesapeake Region

Numbers on map refer to towns numbered below.

DELAWARE
1. Rehoboth Beach, The Corner Cupboard Inn 44

MARYLAND
2. Easton, The Tidewater Inn 46

NEW JERSEY
3. Cape May,
   The Chalfonte 48
   The Queen Victoria 50

NEW YORK
4. Blue Mountain Lake, The Hedges 52
5. Clarence, Asa Ransom House 54
6. Keene, The Bark Eater Lodge 56
7. Lew Beach, Beaverkill Valley Inn 58
8. North Hudson, Elk Lake Lodge 60
9. North River, Garnet Hill Lodge 62
10. Ram's Head Island, The Ram's Head Inn 64

PENNSYLVANIA
11. Cooksburg, Gateway Lodge 66
12. South Sterling, The Sterling Inn 68
13. Starlight, The Inn at Starlight Lake 70

VIRGINIA
14. Stanley, Jordan Hollow Farm Inn 72
15. Steele's Tavern,
    The Osceola Mill Country Inn and Mangus House 74
16. Williamsburg, The Williamsburg Inn and Colonial Houses 76

WEST VIRGINIA
17. Petersburg, Smoke Hole Lodge 78

olive Metcalf

The Corner Cupboard Inn
Rehoboth Beach, Delaware 19971

Innkeeper: Elizabeth G. Hooper
Address/Telephone: 50 Park Avenue; (302) 227–8553
Rooms: 18; all with private bath and air conditioning. Pets allowed, charge.
Rates: Memorial Day weekend to mid-September: $140 to $225, double occupancy; $110 to $200, single; MAP. Rest of year, $70 to $110, double occupancy; $65 to $95, single; EPB. Children in off-season, $25; in-season, $75.
Open: All year, except Christmas and New Year's.
Facilities and activities: BYOB. Reservations a must. Beach is 1½ blocks. Nearby: tennis, bicycling, golf, historic town of Lewes (15 minutes).

A good reason for taking the family to The Corner Cupboard Inn is the beautiful ocean beach, which is a very short walk from the inn. If you like swimming in the ocean and playing on the beach in the summer, or walking on the beach in the winter, you will like being here.

Then return to the inn at the end of the day and relax. The sun filters through the tall, old shade trees onto the inn's ☛ cozy patios and creates a mood of total leisure. You mix yourself a drink on the cocktail patio and chat.

Around dinnertime on a summer Saturday night, your waiter opens a fine wine, the one you brought in a little brown bag. The ceiling fans turn. Dinner begins: crab imperial with just a touch of green pepper, or beautifully fried soft-shell crab, homemade bread, and more. Children's portions are available. After dinner go for a moonlit stroll on the 🖝 beach.

This is a year-round inn in a lovely residential neighborhood. You find comfortable parlors and sun porches. I do like the former attic room with an appealing private patio nestled in the treetops. "Eastwind" is a small cottage with a private brick patio. Each room is different. One is small, with white walls, green-and-blue curtains, and green iron beds.

The rooms change according to the season. During summer the inn is floored with grass mats, which are exchanged for oriental carpets in winter. In the inn some rooms have antiques and wooden or iron beds.

Elizabeth's decorating is a tasteful homey blend of family heirloom and eclectic furnishings. The antique corner cupboard is in the living room. The long porch room, called the hat room for all the straw hats on the wall, is paneled and breezy in summer. A good selection of magazines and newspapers and games for children lines the parlor tables.

In the winter, guests return from a brisk walk on the beach and meet around the fireplace, sipping brandies, and discussing everything but what they do for a living. Here, the cares of the world are washed away.

How to get there: From Route 1, exit onto Rehoboth Avenue and follow it to the dead end. Make a U-turn, go 1 block, and turn right on First Street. Cross over bridge, turn right, then left on First Street. Go 3 blocks to one-way Park Avenue, and the inn is on the left.

The Tidewater Inn
Easton, Maryland
21601

Innkeeper: Jerome E. Nicolosi
Address/Telephone: Dover and Harrison streets; (301) 822-1300
Rooms: 119, including 7 suites; all with private bath, air conditioning, television. Pets allowed.
Rates: $79 to $94, double occupancy, EP. Children under 18, free.
Open: All year.
Facilities and activities: Breakfast, lunch, dinner, taproom. Swimming pool. Nearby: boating, fishing, hunting, tennis, golfing, bicycling, St. Michael's Chesapeake Bay Maritime Museum.

As pretty as she is rich, Talbot County's 602 miles of shoreline allure hunters, fishermen, boaters, bicyclers, and bench sitters to her shores. The county seat is Easton, where the Tidewater Inn stands landlocked in the midst of more than one hundred historic buildings.

The handsome, brick, colonial hotel-inn was built in 1949, shortly after the original inn burned. The street opposite the inn is a row of diverse shops selling chic clothing, American crafts, and waterfront estates. Enter the inn, and to the right is an elegant jewelry shop. Don't get the idea this is a snooty inn. It's not. It's large, which allows for privacy.

Easton, Maryland

If you arrive during the annual 🖝 Waterfowl Festival in November, the inn will be bursting at the seams, like the town. The highlights are the auction of antique decoys and exhibits by the world's foremost bird carvers. The inn makes no small mention of its local carvers in its decorations. In the Decoy Tavern a large photograph shows a local carver at work.

Talbot County is on the Canada geese flyway. During hunting season there's a 4:30 A.M. breakfast for early risers. The dining room dress code obviously stretches at this hour to include camouflage.

The menus offer traditional meat entrees and a long array of 🖝 Eastern shore specialties that include backfin crab imperial, broiled fresh fish, crab cakes, and soft-shell crabs. At breakfast grits and scrapple are available as well as malted waffles made with walnuts, corned beef hash, and smoked salmon. Available on request is the "Heart Healthy Menu," which includes whole wheat breads, lemon chicken breast, and a fresh fish of the day. Children's portions and special requests like grilled cheese or peanut butter and jelly are no problem.

The rooms are decorated with traditional fabrics and wallpaper that rises from the rust-colored wainscoting. Wooden blinds hang at the windows.

There are many wonderful things to do in this area, from sailing to historical sights. You might come for the log-canoe races, an old-time specialty on the bay. You should take the family to the St. Michael's Maritime Museum for the entire day. It's one of the finest museums on the entire Chesapeake Bay.

By evening, when everyone is craving some physical action, you can walk or drive one-half mile to the city park. You might run into Jerome Nicolosi, who often takes his children there to play on the contemporary wooden jungle gym. Weaving around the park is a fine walking path. The inn also provides access to the local YMCA, which has a large swimming pool, numerous courts, and even baby-sitters.

How to get there: From Route 50 south of the Chesapeake Bay Bridge, take the second Easton exit, turn right on Dover, and the inn is on the right at the intersection of Harrison.

The Chalfonte
Cape May, New Jersey 08204

Innkeepers: Anne Le Duc and Judy Bartella
Address/Telephone: 301 Howard Street; (609) 884–8409
Rooms: 103; 11 with private bath.
Rates: $73 to $116, double occupancy; $50 to $60, single; MAP. Children 14 and under, $3 to $5. Two-night minimum on weekends. 25 percent discount off-season.
Open: Memorial Day through September, October weekends.
Facilities and activities: Tavern. Beach 2 blocks. Wine-tasting weekends, evening theater, and musicals. Concerts by Candlelight, Victorian House Tours, bicycling, tennis, golf, boating, swimming, U.S. Coast Guard Station, bird watching.

    In Cape May the seasons impinge themselves on you. Summer has arrived when the crowds swell, the heat changes all manner of dress and pace, and the Chalfonte opens its doors as it has for more than one hundred years. It has been the site of many a family vacation.
    On the veranda and in the hallways a cool ocean breeze blew the afternoon of my arrival. The air conditioning is "natural." The inn is 2 blocks from the shore, but the wide residential street promotes the breezes as far as the Chalfonte's summer guests.

Each season when the Chalfonte reopens and on other special occasions, a rare opportunity awaits you. Guests are invited to stay gratis in exchange for painting, wall papering, carpentry, or whatever this historic building needs. ☞ Work weekends are so popular they are no longer advertised, but you can request information. Older children with skillful hands can contribute and appreciate the value of historic preservation.

Helen Dickerson is as much a part of the Chalfonte as its familiar rocking chairs on the porch. For more than thirty-five years she's prepared ☞ Southern home cooking for the inn. She fixes American traditionals: roast beef, country ham, southern-fried chicken, crab cakes, broiled bluefish, spoonbread, bread pudding, apple pie, and strawberry shortcake. All is fresh and delicious. You are seated with other guests, and dinner is accompanied with good conversation.

Men are requested to wear jackets to dinner. Children under seven dine in their private dining room served by a staff all their own. That's a splendid practice.

The rooms have wooden floors, and many have marble-topped antique dressers. Most are white walled, and all are simple and very basic.

The energetic innkeepers sponsor a variety of ☞ summer entertainments. Request the brochures before you go. The Concerts by Candlelight might be your cup of tea, or maybe you prefer wine-tasting parties. Ask about plays, music, or comic revue. A watercolor workshop was about to begin the day I arrived. I was fortunate to meet the artist. Those are the kinds of things that happen at the Chalfonte, a summer hotel for the whole family.

How to get there: From the Garden State Parkway, which merges into Lafayette Street in Cape May, go to the first stoplight and turn left on Madison. Proceed past 4 streets and turn right on Sewell, which dead-ends at Howard. The inn is on the corner of Howard and Sewell.

The Queen Victoria
Cape May, New Jersey
08204

Innkeepers: Dane, Joan, and Elizabeth Wells
Address/Telephone: 102 Ocean Street; (609) 884-8702
Rooms: 13, including 2 suites; 9 with private bath, some with air conditioning and television.
Rates: $64 to $125, double occupancy, suites $133 to $203; EPB; parking, beach towels, and passes included. Children $10. Three- and four-night minimums during busy seasons and holidays. Two-night minimum weekends. Special off-season packages.
Open: All year.
Facilities and activities: Walking distance to beach and restaurants. Historic tours of Cape May, bicycling, bird watching, fishing boats. Seasonal events: Christmas Decorations Workshop, touring Christmas inns, Dickens Extravaganza.

Christmas reigns at the Queen Victoria. Guests join Joan and Dane Wells and daughter, Elizabeth, for the annual ☛ Christmas tree decorating weekend (early December). With friend and fellow Victorian expert, Connie Hershey, the hosts relate turn-of-the-century Christmas customs and folklore. The inn is a festive family scene that's interlaced with delicious foods and light humor. A fascinating plan underlies the occasion.

Three trees are beginning to take shape. The small table top represents the early Victorian era; it's hung with popcorn chains and foods expressing symbolic meanings. In the hallway stands the craft-oriented tree (middle era), receiving small token handmade gifts hung directly on the tree. And the grandest of all is the 1890s (late period) parlor tree that appeared during the Industrial Revolution. Beneath the trees, youngsters discover the gifts that excited children of former times.

Joan Wells was executive director of the Victorian Society and Dane an economist before they chose Cape May as their home. The innkeepers treat their guests to insights on the life-style that surrounded the Victorians. Children will learn how the Victorian children lived, dressed, and behaved.

The parlor of the Queen Victoria is filled with an impressive collection of ☞ "arts and crafts" furniture. It's as unusual as it is comfortable. If you simply want to lie about in late twentieth-century fashion, there are an informal wicker room and the porch for summer reading.

Family activities in the area include days at the beautiful beach, bicycle riding, a motorized trolley tour of historic Cape May, and outdoor summer concerts at the town's bandstand. In the evenings a wide range of restaurants are within walking distance from the inn; movie and live theaters are a short drive.

In the rooms you'll find history blends with contemporary comforts. The Queen's cottage suite has a fully equipped kitchen, a fireplace with gas log, a sun porch, and a TV. Whatever the season, you'll appreciate the pleasant convenience of common areas and the one-block walk to the beach.

Breakfast is served buffet style in the dining room. There are ample portions of homemade granola, muffins, and dishes of hot egg and cheese casseroles. You might also enjoy a baked pineapple or a zucchini frittata along with fruit dishes, juices, and freshly brewed coffee. Around a large table guests have a chance to visit while the summer breeze wafts through from the ocean and Christmas is still a happy memory at the Queen Victoria.

How to get there: From the southern end of the Garden State Parkway, continue straight into town (more than 1 mile) to merge with Lafayette Street. At second stoplight, turn left onto Ocean Street. Go 3 blocks and inn is on the right.

The Hedges
Blue Mountain Lake, New York
12812

Innkeeper: R. J. Van Yperen

Address/Telephone: Hedges Road; (518) 352–7325

Rooms: 11, including 1 suite; all with private bath; 14 cottages.

Rates: $55 to $65, per person; MAP. Children up to age 14, $18. Weekly rates, $2 less per person per day. 10 percent gratuity suggested. No credit cards.

Open: Mid-June through mid-October.

Facilities and activities: No alcoholic beverages in lounges or dining room. Swimming, canoeing, and fishing in Blue Mountain Lake. Tennis court, volleyball, horseshoes. Ping-Pong, hiking. Adirondack Museum a 5-minute drive.

The Hedges is the former ☞ "Adirondack Camp" of Colonel Hiriam Duryea on the shores of ☞ Blue Mountain Lake. It's surrounded by tall trees and striking views, and the summer activities are convenient and satisfying to all ages. Children can canoe, swim, hike, and play to their heart's content.

The colonel was a demanding builder. In the tradition of the "great camps," the construction is superb. The bark exterior of the main lodge is a lovely texture. In the stone house near the main lodge the woodwork is polished annually. The new wallpaper

Blue Mountain Lake, New York

selections in brown and gold prints enhance its traditional look. The innkeepers care for their treasured "camp" and decorate in a style consistent with the Lodge.

Here's how a day at The Hedges might unfold: 8 A.M.: Family breakfast begins in the dining room. 9 A.M.: Everyone drives five minutes to the Adirondack Mountain Museum to learn about the area. Noon: Lunch with busy discussion on afternoon's activities. 1 P.M.: Canoe to an island in the lake. 3:30 P.M.: Return in time for swimming and a short walk before an evening shower. 6:30 P.M.: Dinner is served. Afterward you walk to a movie in town. 9:30 P.M.: Cookies and hot chocolate in the game room. 10:30 P.M.: Exhausted, everyone falls contentedly to sleep.

There's a nice little library filled with westerns and children's books, a busy Ping-Pong room, and big comfortable ☞ Adirondack-style furniture everywhere for enjoying the lake views. In the library sits a rustic music stand made by a guest. Music is a spontaneous evening event. If the guests are in the mood, they sing and play the piano. The woodland animals probably enjoy it.

Meals are served at your reserved table in the dining room, where an Adirondack canoe hangs on the wall. One entree with vegetables, homemade breads, and salads are the fare served upon a map of the lake. Saturday nights it's buffet style. Between 9:00 and 11:00 P.M. the hot chocolate and coffee appear with cookies, cakes, and fresh pastries for a nighttime snack.

You're not roughing it here. You have daily maid service, and although the activities aren't organized, there's plenty to do. I think an afternoon of lake fun ranks high on the list of priorities. You can sit on the porch in big Adirondack chairs and revel in the view of Blue Mountain Lake.

How to get there: From I–87 take Route 8 west. At Weavertown take Route 28 north to Blue Mountain Lake. At junction of Routes 28 N, 30, and 28 proceed 1 mile west on Route 28 to the Hedges Road. The inn is on the right hidden in the trees.

❀

B: *In the summertime, when it's hot in the city, a lakeside inn is the place to be.*

Asa Ransom House
Clarence, New York
14031

Innkeepers: Bob and Judy Lenz
Address/Telephone: 10529 Main Street; (716) 759–2315
Rooms: 4; all with private bath and air conditioning.
Rates: $75 to $100, double occupancy; $65 and up, single; EPB. Children under 2, free; 2 and over, $10. No smoking. Checks preferred.
Open: Closed January 2 to early February, Christmas, occasional holy days, and every Friday and Saturday.
Facilities and activities: Lunch on Wednesday, and dinner Sunday through Thursday. Taproom, library, gift shop. Nearby: antiquing, golf, sports, winery tours, artpark in Lewiston, opera in Lancaster, Niagara Falls (40 minutes).

On Main Street in Clarence, you turn in at the red railing for some really fine food and a ☛ handsome inn named for Asa Ransom, the founder. You'll marvel at the size of Asa's original inn that warmed travelers around the hearth. The little taproom is wood from ceiling to floor. It must have been very reassuring after a few days in the wilderness. It still is.

The library, with a cozy fireplace, is just the right size for reading or visiting. An unfinished jigsaw puzzle awaits your attention, or you may have a casual browse through the gift shop

Clarence, New York

off the library. Your frame of mind can't be other than ☞ relaxed and receptive in this warm inn.

Upstairs the rooms are furnished stylishly in Early American. One has marvelous American bald eagles stenciled around the ceiling. Each room has good reading lamps and sparkles with cleanliness. King- and queen-size beds are available. One room has a fireplace.

The area is rich with activities but foremost on your schedule should be a day's touring of ☞ Niagara Falls. This classic American vacation is a perennial family favorite. Afterwards you can return to the inn for a walk. A mere four doors away is the Clarence Town Park with slides, swings, pool, tennis courts, and a pond with duck families in residence.

Dinner is delicious. Children's menus arrive in the form of toys. Girls are handed a Raggedy Ann doll, which is printed with the children's fare, and boys read their selections from the sail of a sailboat. Judy came up with that innovation. The soup arrives in a hot bucket and is ladled out to suit your appetite. Then walnut spice muffins and breads arrive with three flavors of butter, followed by salmon pie, a rich savory dish perfectly seasoned. There also are vegetarian selections. Afterward, the divinely rich walnut pie came with real home-brewed coffee in a silver pot.

In your room are radio cassette tapes. You can listen to "The Shadow," "Fibber Magee and Molly," and others.

After the children are sound asleep in their beds, you feel comfortable descending the stairs for a cup of herbal tea in the library. You are seconds from their door, yet the two of you can have a moment to yourselves.

Can you tell? The innkeepers have children of their own.

How to get there: From I-290 take Exit Route 5 to Clarence. The inn is on the right in the city limits, 1 block before the park. Fly-in, Buffalo International Airport. Amtrak, will pick up.

※

B: *When you see the inn, you're not surprised to find out that Judy has an art background. She designed the ice-water bottles that are brought to the table in this consistently excellent inn.*

55

olive Metcalf

The Bark Eater Lodge
Keene, New York
12942

Innkeepers: Joe Pete Wilson and Harley McDevitt
Address/Telephone: Alstead Mill Road; (518) 576-2221
Rooms: 13; 4 with private baths; 1 cottage.
Rates: From $45 to $55 per person, double occupancy, MAP. Children under 6, free; 6 to 11, 50 percent of adult rate; 12 to 15, 75 percent. 13 percent gratuity. Two-night minimum on weekends. No credit cards.
Open: All year.
Facilities and activities: Picnic lunches by advance request. Bring wine for dinner. Stables, horseback riding, and trails. Cross-country and hiking trails. 200 acres, pond. Nearby: Lake Placid with Olympic sites, downhill and more cross-country skiing. Inn-to-inn ski touring can be arranged.

The Bark Eater is a harbor of alpine friendliness, a classic country inn of the Adirondacks—skiers by the fire, hikers on the summer porch, horseback riders in the woods.

Years ago Joe Pete's parents opened their farm-inn, a 150-year-old stagecoach stop, to guests. Joe Pete and Harley have taken it over, created a cross-country ski-touring center and horseback-riding center and rekindled the country inn spirit in a lush valley setting that sends your spirits soaring.

Keene, New York

The innkeepers bring strong talents to The Bark Eater (a Mohawk word for the Algonquins, which white men initially and inappropriately applied to the mountains). For ☛ professional ski tips there is no one more qualified than Joe Pete Wilson. He's an Olympic skier who's competed nationally in the biathlon, cross-country skiing, and bobsled. He's written a book on cross-country skiing and has got a sense of humor to boot. Harley was a New York executive and gourmet cook before marrying Joe Pete.

Throughout the day you'll find them taking time to visit with guests, giving hiking and touring suggestions, hugging daughter Katie, handing out skis, and saddling horses with the help of a friendly young staff. Meanwhile, Miss Charmer, Katie, hosts the inn children and willingly shares her dog.

The ☛ stables now accommodate fifty horses. You can gallop into the woods and emerge at the meadow pond (near a zip line once used by Outward Bound).

The inn is an old-fashioned blend of comforts, with a stone fireplace and a diverse collection of family pieces. The adjacent Carriage House rooms are handsomely remodeled with a stylish country look.

Evening meals are ☛ scrumptious affairs around community tables. You may want to arrive early, pour yourself a glass of wine, and take a look in the open kitchen, where you'll see the fine art of cuisine. Dinner might begin with Anadama bread (molasses and corn meal) or an herb or buttermilk braided bread, served with a Senegalese soup containing curry, apples, bananas, potatoes, leeks, and tomatoes blended into something indescribably good. As the fresh salad course enters, the conversation begins rolling. "Ahhs" accompany the grilled-beef-and-shrimp shish kebab, or perhaps Norwegian salmon fillet with fresh dill sauce, or boneless chicken with raspberry sauce. Several hearty punch lines later, and the chocolate mousse in pastry tulip appears. For children the chef adapts as needed, so that they can dine on simpler fare. Over coffee everyone is savoring the companionship, thinking food this fine was never so much fun.

Your night, like every night in a classic country inn, becomes one of life's favorite memories.

How to get there: Take exit 73 from I–87 north and go north (toward Lake Placid) to Keene. 1 mile past Keene bear right on Alstead Hill Road at the inn sign. Inn on the right.

Beaverkill Valley Inn
Lew Beach, New York
12753

Innkeepers: Christina and Timothy Dennis; Laurance Rockefeller, proprietor

Address/Telephone: Lew Beach; (914) 439–4844

Rooms: 20; 12 with private bath. Smoking only in card room. Handicap access.

Rates: $110 to $165, per person; $155 to $215, single; AP. Children 2 and under, 50 percent of adult rate.

Open: All year, with some exceptions.

Facilities and activities: Victorian bar, ice cream parlor, billiard room, Ping-Pong room. Swimming pool, hiking and cross-country ski trails, 6 miles of Beaverkill stream for fly-fishing, 2 tennis courts, pond.

Rich in the lore and the history of trout fishing in America, Beaverkill Stream is the premier experience for the art of fly-fishing. The inn, owned by Laurance Rockefeller, is located in the Catskills wilderness along 6 miles of the renowned stream, but you need never have cast a rod to appreciate discreet charms and natural beauty.

Cross the bridge over the Beaverkill, and the American flag sways gently in the breeze above the inn's country porch. Like a tiled oasis shimmering in the sunlight, the blissful enclosed swimming pool can be just glimpsed. What you can't see next to the pool: the ☛ self-serve ice cream parlor where you may delve at will into the cool, creamy goodness of Häagen-Dazs. Around the corner, a sumptuous locker room for pool changing resembles a posh health club.

There's plenty of room for everyone, inside and out. A shady porch winds around the inn filled with wicker; a sun deck off the Victorian bar looks out to the meadow and the stream. There are a country parlor and card room (each with fireplace), a billiard room, and a Ping-Pong room.

The cozy bedrooms have handmade quilts on the beds and are prettily wallpapered; on the nightstand sit a copy of *The Catskills* and a nature conservancy magazine.

Every evening guests gather around square oak tables in the dining room. Chef Christina Dennis (whose oak kitchen is as lovely as the dining room) creates delicious country foods, serving one or two entrees from what is fresh and available. You might begin with an endive and grapefruit salad, then Canadian wild rice, pork tenderloin seasoned with basil and garlic, and for dessert tangy orange-custard tart or rich and light hazelnut praline cake. Breakfast is buffet style; an array of hot and cold dishes compose the selections. Occasionally the chef prepares an early dinner especially for all the children.

Near the inn are conference rooms, which are occasionally opened for the children on a rainy day. Every piece of electronic equipment you might request is available. One family staged a family reunion with films and slides they'd collected through the years and happily added to their repertoire with a vacation along the secluded Beaverkill.

How to get there: Directions sent with reservations.

Elk Lake Lodge
North Hudson, New York
12855

Innkeeper: Peter Sanders
Address/Telephone: North Hudson; (518) 532–7616
Rooms: 6, all with private bath; 7 cottages, several with fireplaces and lake-view decks.
Rates: $90 to $100, per person, AP. Children under 2, free; 2 to 6, 50 percent of adult rate, 7 to 12, 75 percent. 15-percent gratuity. Two-day minimum on weekends. No credit cards.
Open: May through November.
Facilities and activities: BYOB including wine. 12,000-acre private forest preserve located directly on Elk Lake and Clear Pond. Canoes, rowboats, swimming, fishing, hiking, mountain climbing, bird and animal watching.

Elk Lake is a ☛ wilderness lake to behold. From the shore you can see the peaks of Boreas, Colvin, Nippletop, Dix, and Macomb. You can climb the high peaks and follow woodland trails to pristine (100-foot deep, 2-acre wide) Clear Pond. You can canoe to tree-filled islands and beaver ponds. And walk the shore in the moonlit silence, recognizing stars in familiar formations. Each time I return, the beauty of this ☛ 12,000-acre preserve overwhelms me.

North Hudson, New York

The lodge is covered with weathered shingles and is the only dwelling group on the lake. You enter the "great camp" style ☞ common room, where the log beams glisten and the fire burns in the great stone fireplace. Animal skins hang on the walls near a fishing basket. The Stickley furniture is covered in dark-brown leather. In the corner are two "aesthetic rustic" cupboards made by a friend of Peter's. They are unusual and were once borrowed for display by the Adirondack Museum.

Every year the National Audubon Society presents an ornithology workshop at Elk Lake. In addition to the lake there are 600 acres of inlets, islands, bays, and open waters to explore by canoe or rowboat and 40 miles of trails. Children and parents might catch brook and lake trout and landlocked salmon.

The meals at Elk Lake are all-American. Betty Hebert has been the backbone of the kitchen for twenty years. She prepares thick pork chops, tender pot roasts, beef Stroganoff, and chicken in every style deliciously imaginable. Desserts range from homemade berry pies to cheesecakes and ice cream. Often guests request a ☞ picnic lunch and bring a small pack so they can lengthen their day in the woods.

The rooms in the inn are small, pine paneled, and have linoleum floors with small rugs. The cottages are similar but larger, and several have fireplaces and wonderful lake views. Everything is clean.

One family began coming to Elk Lake Lodge long ago. First, it was the two of them. Next they brought the baby. Then the toddler and the new baby. Now it's a family tradition, and all seven of them look forward to their wilderness outing. One day, perhaps, these children will favor their children with an experience in nature.

How to get there: From I–87 North take exit 29, or U.S. Route 9 at North Hudson. Go west toward Newcomb for 4 miles, turn right at the sign, proceed 5 miles to inn on private road.

☙

B: *The expression, "great outdoors," bears significance here.*

Garnet Hill Lodge
North River, New York
12856

Innkeepers: George and Mary Heim
Address/Telephone: 13th Lake Road; (518) 251–2821
Rooms: 26 in 4 buildings; 21 with private bath.
Rates: $50 to $65, per person, double occupancy, MAP. Children 10 and under, $18. Two-night minimum on weekends, 3 nights on holiday weekends.
Open: Closed 2 weeks early June, 2 weeks before Thanksgiving.
Facilities and activities: Nonsmoking dining room. Located on Thirteenth Lake. Cross-country ski center, telemarking, rafting, hiking, swimming, canoeing, fishing, tennis courts. Nearby: downhill skiing at Gore Mountain, tour garnet mine, Adirondack Museum, boat cruises, caving, bird watching, scenic plane rides.

This is a gem of an inn. In fact, there are gems everywhere. Garnets sparkle from the ☛ exquisite fireplace in the Manor House, and minuscule garnets gleam from the gravel as you walk between the buildings that compose Garnet Hill.

Indoors and out this inn is a pleasure. Cross-country skiers follow the trails that lace through the mountains. You can ski from the top of Gore Mountain to Garnet Hill, all 10 miles. The day I arrived there was a nighttime ski trip across the frozen and

North River, New York

snow-covered Thirteenth Lake. What an experience! The moonlight and the stars over the lake and then back to the lodge for hot mulled wine.

April and May is white-water rafting season on the nearby Hudson River Gorge. During summer you can walk the mile to Thirteenth Lake and swim or go boating. George has prepared a good year-round map for hiking and skiing and created a nature trail. Should the weather turn momentarily inclement, the lodge's dining-room tables become convenient game centers. A small television room and a tour of the nearby garnet mine should be kept in mind for such occasions.

The Log House dates from 1936. The rooms here are the smallest of all and beautifully paneled in a rich pine. A short distance away is the Birches, with large rooms and private baths. The Manor House has seven rooms and four baths, which are rustic beauties with spectacular views. The new Tea House has the luxury suites, priced a bit higher. All choices are good ones. The Ski Haus has a loft, ideal for families.

There's a beautiful ☞ lake view from the lodge picture window. Picnic tables fill the room, and the logs that form the walls are as sturdy as the day the lodge was built.

Saturday-night smorgasbords are served during skiing and rafting seasons. Come with a big appetite. There are plenty of vegetables, various homemade breads, and a selection of several entrees such as roast beef, poached salmon, and shellfish. Children—even the most fussy eaters—will delight in the wide selection of foods.

George is an avuncular innkeeper with a subtle sense of humor. He also has a lot of overshoes. He'd loaned out every last pair to guests and was wearing his street shoes through the snow the day we arrived.

How to get there: From I-87 exit onto Route 9 north. After Warrensburg take Route 28 west to North River. From Weverton it's 11.5 miles to the left turn onto 13th Lake Road and the inn's sign. Follow this road 5 miles to the inn.

The Ram's Head Inn
Ram's Head Island off Shelter Island, New York 11965

Innkeepers: Linda and James Eklund
Address/Telephone: Ram Island Drive; (516) 749–0811
Rooms: 17, including 4 suites; 12 with private bath.
Rates: $80 to $110, double occupancy; $165, suite for 4; off-season: $75 to $145; continental breakfast. Children, $15.
Open: May 6 through third week of October.
Facilities and activities: Dinner, bar. Sailing, 800 feet of beachfront, tennis, 6 moorings. Nearby: bicycling, golfing, swimming, boating, fishing, hiking.

The inn is located on the clear waters of Coecles Harbor.

You'll go home with tales of sailing on a summer's afternoon, meandering on the island roads and seeing osprey nests atop the telephone poles, and dining on fine foods by candlelight. You'll whisper the words, "perfect little waterfront inn." You want to keep it a secret. But a wonderful summer holiday can't be kept a silent memory; it must be shared.

☛ Two 13-foot O'Day sloops sit dockside. In seconds you're off to explore the shores of the island sanctuary of unspoiled beauty. Literally one-third of the island is a nature conservancy.

You can also have fun exploring the island by land. Bicycle

Ram's Head Island off Shelter Island, New York

riding on the island's paved roads is feasible for older children, accompanied by parents. Lunch isn't served at the inn, so you'll find the village to be one important place to spend some time. Nighttime brings games in the lounge, which also discreetly serves as a family bar. You might want to bring along some toys, books, and life preservers for the children. Young guests at this inn tend to be in the age of under three and over ten, but they are easily accommodated.

The inn is a large, weathered-shingle, center-hall colonial, built as an inn in 1929. It is light and airy. The rooms are simple and have carpeted floors, white curtains, and maple furniture. The favorite "end" water-side rooms are reserved one year in advance.

There's a slate patio with flowers abloom in heavy clay flowerpots. Everything is conducive to "settle-back summer" fun. There are a hammock and two swings. A child's play set is mounted at the edge of the expansive lawn. Two paths to the water wind around either side of the tennis court.

Dinner at the inn is a saucy event with ☛ sophisticated fare that might include tuna steak in parchment with ginger butter and julienne vegetables, rack of lamb with a honey and pine nut glaze and a port wine sauce, or boneless pheasant covered with raspberry sauce and creamy morels. There are no children's portions or special menus. Either a separate meal is ordered or dishes are shared for an extra plate charge. The desserts have a touch of panache, like the dinners. You might try frozen hazelnut terrine with chocolate truffle in the center or ☛ strawberry gratin sabayon baked with a lovely meringue top. When you spoon it to your mouth, it's gooey and pulls reluctantly from the dish. It's the only time you'll need perseverance to capture your satisfaction at the Ram's Head.

How to get there: Take Route 114 through Sag Harbor to the ferry. On Shelter Island take Route 114 north to the traffic circle and continue straight on Cartright Road to stop sign. Turn right on Ram Island Drive and go right over causeway to the inn.

☼

B: *A ram's head hangs in the entryway. No one knows the origin of the name, Ram's Head Island. A ram has never been seen in these parts, and the island has no such configuration.*

Gateway Lodge
Cooksburg, Pennsylvania
16217

Innkeepers: Joseph and Linda Burney
Address/Telephone: Route 36 (mailing address: P.O. Box 125); (814) 744–8017
Rooms: 7; 3 with private bath; 9 cabins. Dogs allowed in cabins, $8 per day.
Rates: $50 to $60, double occupancy; $65, cabin sleeping 4; EP. Children must be of age to sleep in own room if in lodge.
Open: All year except Thanksgiving and Christmas.
Facilities and activities: Breakfast, lunch Tuesday through Saturday during summer only, dinner Tuesday through Saturday. Tavern. Indoor swimming pool, cross-country skiing from inn, skis available. Fishing, hunting, golfing, bicycling, theater, Clarion River for canoeing and tubing, near 2,500-acre Cook Forest State Park. Hiking.

Gateway Lodge is a wooden jewel in the forest. Step a foot inside the door, and the charisma of the front room lures you the rest of the way. Massive hemlock timbers compose the walls; the ceiling is pine, hemlock, and chestnut. The flooring is oak, and the trim is chestnut. It is lovely.

Summer, winter, spring, and fall, the stone fireplace always has a blazing fire. Even in summer it can get cool at night. Around twilight the lanterns are lit, and the wood gleams from the flame's reflections. The mood is one of pure contentment.

A circle of couches and chairs surrounds the fireplace, a guitar sits casually to one side, and there's an ornately refinished piano. Jars of lemon candies sit within easy reach.

I like coming here for many reasons: the ☞ beauty of the lodge, the outdoors, and the casual relaxed style of the innkeepers. You feel as if they did away with all the pressures of the world. Behind it all they are working very hard, but they make it look effortless. You also feel as if you're entering the forest primeval. There is a wide range of outdoor activities, but should the weather turn to rain, the indoor pool makes a splendid haven.

Joseph and Linda decorated the inn together. The petite and cozy country inn rooms have beige ruffled curtains, print wallpapers, little chests, and bookshelves. Linda keeps ☞ thick quilts on the beds all summer long and exchanges them for "haps" or much heavier quilts for ski season. They are the real thing, handmade from old woolen clothes. They'd keep you warm through a blizzard should you be so lucky as to get "trapped" here.

Families stay in the small cabins across the road from the lodge. After a busy day of hiking, skiing, or tubing on the river, you should celebrate with dinner at the lodge.

Everything is ☞ homemade, from the creamy mashed potatoes to the relishes, jams, breads, and the sweets. Three entrees are served nightly from a weekly selection of thirteen. Request the brochure, which includes the menu. The entrees are ☞ family recipes of Linda's and include plump, stuffed chicken breast, moist and crisp; stuffed pork chop; savory sauced barbecued spareribs; sirloin steak with stuffing; trout; prime rib; and baked Boston scrod. Among the desserts is a chocolate-lover's delight. I'd order with abandon; you'll not have regrets afterward.

How to get there: From I–80 take Route 36 north. The inn is on the right just before the park. Fly-in, Clarion County Airport.

❋

B: *Steps from your room is the enclosed pool beautifully designed by Joe and heated by a wood-burning stove.*

Olive Metcalf

The Sterling Inn
South Sterling, Pennsylvania 18460

Innkeepers: Ron and Mary Kay Logan
Address/Telephone: South Sterling; (717) 676–3311
Rooms: 60 in the inn and cottages, all with private bath; 12 suites, 8 with Franklin stoves.
Rates: $65 to $75, per person; $75 to $90, per person, suite; AP. Children under 5, $15 midweek, $20 weekends; 5 to 16, $32.50 to $45, depending on parents' accommodations. Two-night minimum on weekends, 3 nights on holidays.
Open: All year.
Facilities and activities: Hiking and cross-country trails, 9-hole putting course, tennis court, swimming pond, ice skating, tobogganing, ski rentals, sleigh rides.

The Sterling Inn is surrounded with rhododendrons and mountain laurel. In spring the tulips, daffodils, hyacinths, lilacs, and flowering apple trees blaze your path around the grounds. A special wildflower hike is taken to welcome the warblers back to the Poconos.

In winter call ahead to reserve your cross-country skis and a lesson. In the evenings Mary Kay might show a ski film, so you can practice in your sleep. Ron will direct you to the 6 miles of

South Sterling, Pennsylvania

☛ ski trails that weave through the inn's 103 acres. Ice skating and sledding are nearby.

The Sterling Inn makes special events out of holidays. At Easter, the Easter Bunny is an invited guest; on July Fourth there are barbecues and dancing; and at Christmas, stockings hang above the hearth.

The guest lounges are large with a TV and games to keep the little ones busy on a rainy day. They have stone fireplaces. The newly remodeled suites have a fresh country look. Yours might have a four-poster rice bed, a matching armoire, and a pair of oriental tables beside the sofa. The suites are nice for a family.

Dinner at the inn offers a diverse choice for everyone. While youngsters might select chicken or roast beef, their parents might be more enticed by fresh salmon baked in a light puff pastry; thick, beautiful tournedos of beef; soft-shell crab in season; or tender chicken breast with rosemary and a savory glaze. You may request low-cholesterol or other diet-conscious dishes. Expect homemade breads and fresh seasonal vegetables. Desserts include the exotic rich chocolate Bourbon cake. Fortunately, amidst this ☛ gourmet feasting, the inn hasn't lost its perspective. The inn's honest-to-goodness local fruit and berry pies continue to be served. We're never too sophisticated to appreciate a large slice of blueberry or blackberry pie adorned with a dollop of vanilla ice cream.

This is an ☛ inn for all ages with plenty of room to spread out. Whether you're coming for a honeymoon or a golden anniversary or somewhere in between, there are the mountains to roam, the seasons to enjoy, and the mix and match of all the ages.

How to get there: From I–84 take Route 507 South through Greentown. In Newfoundland take Route 191 South. It's 4 miles to the inn.

B: *The inn's horse-drawn sleigh ride is a glimpse into the past.*

The Inn at Starlight Lake
Starlight, Pennsylvania 18461

Innkeepers: Jack and Judy McMahon & Family
Address/Telephone: Starlight; (717) 798–2519
Rooms: 27; 24 with private bath.
Rates: $110 to $140, double occupancy, MAP. Weekly rates and single rate available. Children under 7, free; 7 to 12, $37. Two-night minimum stay high season.
Open: All year except first two weeks of April.
Facilities and activities: Lunch, bar, game room. Spring-fed lake, 18 miles of cross-country ski trails, ski shop, canoeing, small sailboats, rowboats, tennis court, swimming, and hiking. Nearby: 140 more lakes, golf courses, Upper Delaware trophy trout fishery, riding stables, downhill skiing at Mt. Tone and Elk Mountain.

This is a ☛ quaint and beguiling lakeside inn in the northeastern lake district of Pennsylvania. It's on a quiet little road that fronts Starlight Lake, where boats float gently along the docks. You enter to a busy and friendly lobby. In cold weather two woodburning stoves crackle and burn. Through the glass doors is a busy game room with pool, Ping-Pong, and plenty of children's toys to keep the young ones occupied.

Starlight, Pennsylvania

During the winter there's a professional ski instructor on the staff, and a ☞ ski shop forms part of the inn. In the taproom hangs a cross-country-ski map, and your day on snow begins on the frozen lake. In the summertime you might take a sail on the lake, swim, go into the woods for a hike, row a boat, go horseback riding, or play tennis. Adirondack furniture sits along the porch and on the lake dock.

The rooms are country simple and pleasant. My preference is lakeside rooms with remodeled baths. Prints are on the walls, and magazines are in the large racks. Keep in mind the inn dates from 1909. The sounds of the inn blend in with the frogs and the silence outdoors. It's the way you might imagine "ye olde" little country inn.

More than ten years ago, Jack and Judy and their four children came from New York City to the inn. Jack left the recording business, and Judy brought her theatrical talents that she had honed at the Yale Drama School. Their love of music permeates the inn. A collection of albums is easily accessible, as is the grand piano stacked high with song sheets.

It's nothing short of wonderful to have a fine meal with Starlight Lake for a view. For the children, there's a special menu with simple fare that's perfectly suited to their young tastes. But for those with a gourmet interest in foods, the lusty steak au poivre is sautéed in crushed peppercorns with brandy and cream. For a light mood try the veal sautéed in white wine and lemon juice. The chef also prepares fresh local rainbow trout. I do like it when you can order freshly brewed coffee with dessert. The ☞ chocolate walnut pie satisfies the appetite perfectly. Afterward you can take a lakeshore stroll in the fresh evening air with the stars lighting the way.

How to get there: From Route 17 in New York, take exit 87 and go into Hancock, New York. Take Route 191 across the Delaware to Route 370 and turn right. Follow the signs to the inn.

Jordan Hollow Farm Inn
Stanley, Virginia
22851

Innkeepers: Marley and Jetze Beers
Address/Telephone: Route 2, Box 375; (703) 778–2285
Rooms: 16; all with private bath and air conditioning.
Rates: $75, double occupancy, EPB. Children 16 and under, free; over 16, $10. No more than 2 children in room with parents.
Open: All year.
Facilities and activities: Lunch, dinner, tavern. Lounge room. Horseback riding, 2-wheel cart rides, and horse boarding for guests' horses. Nearby: swimming lake, fishing, golf, tennis, hiking, canoeing, museums, antique shops, Luray Caverns.

Jordan Hollow began as a single log cabin 200 years ago. A second cabin was added, and around these hand-axed gems the inn has grown. It's ☞ home to twenty-five horses, goats, peacocks, cats, and a Chinese pug named E.T., who affectionately follows Marley about the inn, taking time out to charm the guests. You're also likely to meet Rowe Baldwin, a relative who came to help during the inn's beginnings and pleased the Beerses when she agreed to stay.

Stanley, Virginia

Marley and Jetze met in Monrovia, West Africa. Jetze occasionally speaks his native Dutch as well as German or French with the guests. Their travels are reflected in the art that is displayed in an intimate log-cabin dining room. I found the cheerful carved African mask a good mood setter for Marley's "country continental" cuisine. You might order the roasted quail in wine-and-cream sauce, fresh rainbow trout amandine, juicy broiled chicken breast, or the boneless butterfly chops. A special children's menu offers chicken or pork chops along with soup and salad.

Marley, an accomplished horsewoman, or her experienced assistants lead guests on trail rides. Depending on your skills, you can take a gentle beginner ride or join the advanced treks into the mountains. They may also teach you how to drive a 🐎 pony cart. Driving horses via two- and four-wheeled vehicles is the fastest growing horse sport in the United States, and Marley's carriages are pulled by the oldest breed in the world, the Fjord horse. Parents are required to supervise their children around the horses.

A mere hundred yards from the front porch of the inn is Rowe's Lodge, with cozy modern guest rooms. They are furnished with antiques, country artifacts, and sturdy mattresses and decorated with pretty print wallpapers. Each holds a small bookshelf, which is selectively filled. The rooms open onto a long wooden deck. My favorites are the south-facing rooms overlooking the Shenandoah Mountains.

There are many activities to keep you busy at Jordan Hollow Farm, in addition to horseback riding. A nearby lake offers swimming, Luray Caverns aren't far, and a canoeing outfitter will arrange for a day on the Shenandoah River. Bicycling and hiking are also convenient. For the children, a convenient indoor lounge may be available, and a small game room is adjacent to the country tavern.

Jordan Hollow has a comfortable, relaxed atmosphere. It offers plenty of fresh air and beautiful countryside, and I was happy to hear Marley say, "We are surrounded by national parks; no one can ever take our views away."

How to get there: From I–66 exit onto Route 55 to Front Royal, turn south on Route 340, and continue past Luray for 6 miles to Route 624. Turn left, and signs direct you from here.

The Osceola Mill Country Inn and Mangus House
Steele's Tavern, Virginia 24476

Innkeepers: Kathy and Paul Newcombe, Stephen Boddy

Address/Telephone: Route 56; (703) 377–MILL

Rooms: 11, all with private bath and air conditioning; 1 suite with whirlpool and fireplace. No smoking indoors. Handicap accessibility in Mangus House accommodation.

Rates: $69; $99, suite; double occupancy; EPB. Children $10.

Open: All year.

Facilities and activities: Dinner by reservation, BYOB including wine and beer. Game room, music room, VCR. Swimming pool, swing set, hiking and bicycling. Nearby: antiquing, Skyline Drive (4½ miles), Lexington, Staunton, and Wintergreen (18 miles).

Osceola Mill was a working ☛ gristmill until 1969, with Flavo self-rising stone-ground flour among its products. After extensive work on the mill, the Newcombes, along with their young children, moved into their combined home and country inn. Not even catching their breaths, they walked across the road

Steele's Tavern, Virginia

and up to the Victorian Mangus House, donned their remodeling clothes, and didn't come out until seven more rooms were handsomely finished. Mangus House is for couples, and the Mill accommodates families with children. A small cottage for the romantically or luxury-inclined has a Jacuzzi overlooking the stone fireplace.

Family inn-travelers find a small swimming pool, swing set, special inn toys, and a large-screen TV in the Mill living room, which will keep the children well entertained.

Kathy and Paul have furnished the inn with Pulaski furniture, a contemporary brand of Victorian and country reproductions. Soft, natural, earth tones accent the buildings' exposed beams. In several of the rooms are crafts made by local women.

The Mangus House has a formal parlor; a ☛ music room with piano, organ, and guitar; and a game room set for bridge or puzzles. The furnishings are a blend of antiques and reproductions.

Around twilight you might be alerted to dinnertime by the aromatic scent of ☛ chicken barbecuing on the outdoor grills lining the wooden deck. Meals are served family style around large oak tables in the dining room. Two seatings include an early hour for families with children. One of Kathy's favorite wintertime dishes is a marinated pork tenderloin served with heaping bowls of rice and vegetables. Classic American desserts, like creamy cheesecakes or pecan pies, and cups of hot coffee follow.

During dinner someone usually mentions the dollar bills stuck among the ceiling's wooden beams. Paul placed the first dollar there to silence a childhood dispute and forgot the incident. Guests surreptitiously began adding bills of their own, and it's since been named the "college fund."

After dinner you can have a seat around the wood-burning stove for a songfest or get up a game of Scrabble back in the game room. Should you have selected the fireplace cottage for the evening, then I realize you're filling the whirlpool.

How to get there: From I–81, take exit 54, go 2 miles east on Route 56 to inn on the right-hand side. If you come to the village of Vesuvius, make U-turn and return to inn.

olive Metcalf

The Williamsburg Inn and Colonial Houses
Williamsburg, Virginia 23187

Innkeeper: Russ Cleveland
Address/Telephone: Route 2, Box 152; (804) 229–1000
Rooms: 82, in 26 houses; all with private bath, air conditioning, television.
Rates: $225 to $510, double occupancy, per room, EP. Children, $15. Request package plans.
Open: All year.
Facilities and activities: Breakfast, lunch, afternoon tea, dinner, bar in nearby tavern. All facilities of the Williamsburg Inn: golf, swimming pools, parlors, Sunday recitals, Christmas Yule-log ceremonies. Colonial Williamsburg.

Children are treated to a living-history lesson in Colonial Williamsburg. There are street characters in eighteenth-century dress who tease them about their twentieth-century clothes and refuse to acknowledge inventions beyond 1800. Riding in carriages, eating old-fashioned sugar cookies, and visiting the schoolhouse are all part of a trip here. The busy sights and sounds teach as they inform.

Williamsburg, Virginia

Located in the heart of Colonial Williamsburg are tiny houses, known as the Colonial Houses, which are named for the former owners or for their uses. They are charming comfortable places amidst the ☞ historic district and the archeological dig. You may step out the door of your home to see a shepherdess and her flock going down the street or hear the sounds of guinea hens in the yard next door. In Williamsburg, where authenticity is the byword, colonial life is ☞ nurtured and made a modern pleasure.

The houses are decorated with curtains made from colonial patterns and filled with furniture that are reproductions. Wooden window blinds are hung at the windows, and upstairs the latch doors on the closets remind me it's hard to improve on some old but good inventions.

The Orell House has been so well preserved that it remains in its original state. It was here that the prime minister of Italy stayed when he came to town. You don't have to be a prime minister or even a cabinet member to stay here, but if they're holding an economic summit as they did in 1983, it helps.

Across the street is the Lewis House. It's a lovely reproduction and has a brick patio with a small garden in the back surrounded by a low picket fence.

Families and friends usually share the houses. One family has spent the last seventeen Christmas holidays in their favorite tiny home here.

When you stay in the Colonial Houses, you eat in the old taverns with several offering children's portions and special menus.

How to get there: Directions given by the inn. Fly-in, Williamsburg Airport.

✻

B: Colonial Williamsburg is an intriguing way to relive the past.

Smoke Hole Lodge
Petersburg, West Virginia
26847

Innkeeper: Edward W. Stifel, III

Address/Telephone: P.O. Box 953; no telephone. Please write and include your phone number.

Rooms: 5 double bedrooms (twin beds), all with private bath; 2 dormitories, one sleeps 4 and one sleeps 5.

Rates: First person in each room or dormitory, $90 per person; additional person in same room or dormitory, $45 per person; AP. Children 4 and under, free. 10 percent discount for groups of 8 or more. Two-night minimum.

Open: May 9 through October 31.

Facilities and activites: BYOB. 1,500 acres to explore. River for fishing, swimming, canoeing, tubing. Hiking, bird watching, reading, life planning.

Looking for adventure?

Smoke Hole is a startling contrast in the wilderness, a magnificent cedar lodge that curves around the mountainside. On the lower level a row of handmade rustic rocking chairs line up as if queuing for pleasurable attention. A hammock rests nearby, and an outdoor stone fireplace serves for grilling thick juicy steaks, as well as providing friendly warmth on a cool twilight autumn eve.

Petersburg, West Virginia

Smoke Hole Lodge began in 1876 as a schoolhouse, and additions made it a Stifel family lodge and later a guest lodge. In a 1985 flood, Ed Stifel stood on the banks of the Potomac and watched the entire building be swept down the river. Encouraged by family, friends, and guests, he determined to rebuild. First he consulted flood experts, lumbermen, and a cement company to see if heavy trucks dared travel his one-lane road.

Despite the rustic nature, there are ☛ contemporary hot-water showers and facilities; the beds are twin-sized. The lighting and cooking are gas, and before bedtime Ed carries a gas lantern to your bedside for you to blow out just like your grandmother (or great-grandmother) did.

In this remote setting, you probably won't want to let small children wander a great distance or spend the day without supervision. Older youngsters (over nine) will be in heaven. Bring along games for evening play.

We were seated one evening on the deck far above the river, enjoying cook's delicious chicken à l'orange and rice, vegetables, and salad, when Ed told everyone to look skyward. A bald eagle soared silently up the valley.

Over scrumptious chocolate cake and coffee, the head of the West Virginia Nature Conservacy talked about the rare wildlife around Smoke Hole. A biologist recently arrived (with a $20,000 piece of equipment) searching for an endangered species of bat. Ed's Bob the Cat greeted her by laying that specific bat literally at her feet. After two days of searching she never found another.

☛ Nature lovers, bird watchers, fishermen, hikers, and peace and quiet searchers will be in heaven. A visitor who caught a 17-inch bass within sight of the lodge confided, "It was the best morning I've ever experienced by the side of a river." It's a very special place. I can think of no other so remote, yet so near to the nation's capitol.

How to get there: Meet Ed at Alt's grocery store in Petersburg. Fly in to Petersburg airport and Ed will pick you up. Helicopter from Petersburg airport directly to inn by special arrangement.

✷

B: *Families in search of remote hiking, river swimming, and good fishing will find Smoke Hole Lodge an excpetional experience.*

THE SOUTH

by
Sara Pitzer

In the introduction to the second edition of her *Recommended Country Inns—the South*, Sara Pitzer writes, "Diversity thrills me. I look for it. Visiting inns in the South, I found it in abundance. Southern hospitality is not just one way of behaving. It ranges from thigh-slapping camaraderie at the kitchen table of a rural inn to the white-gloves graciousness of a Mississippi plantation."

A North Carolina–based freelance writer, Sara considers herself, above all, a reporter; and she prides herself on describing what she sees in an objective, accurate manner. In her inn guide, Sara recommends 145 of the best and most interesting inns in ten southern states. There are romantic antebellum plantation mansions, elegant French-style town houses, remote and rustic inns in the Great Smoky Mountains, sprawling country estates, cozy beachfront inns, and peaceful inns near trout streams in the Ozarks.

Sara is the author of Globe Pequot's *Pennsylvania: Off the Beaten Path* and is writing *North Carolina: Off the Beaten Path*. She lives in the country with two dogs, half a dozen cats, and one patient husband.

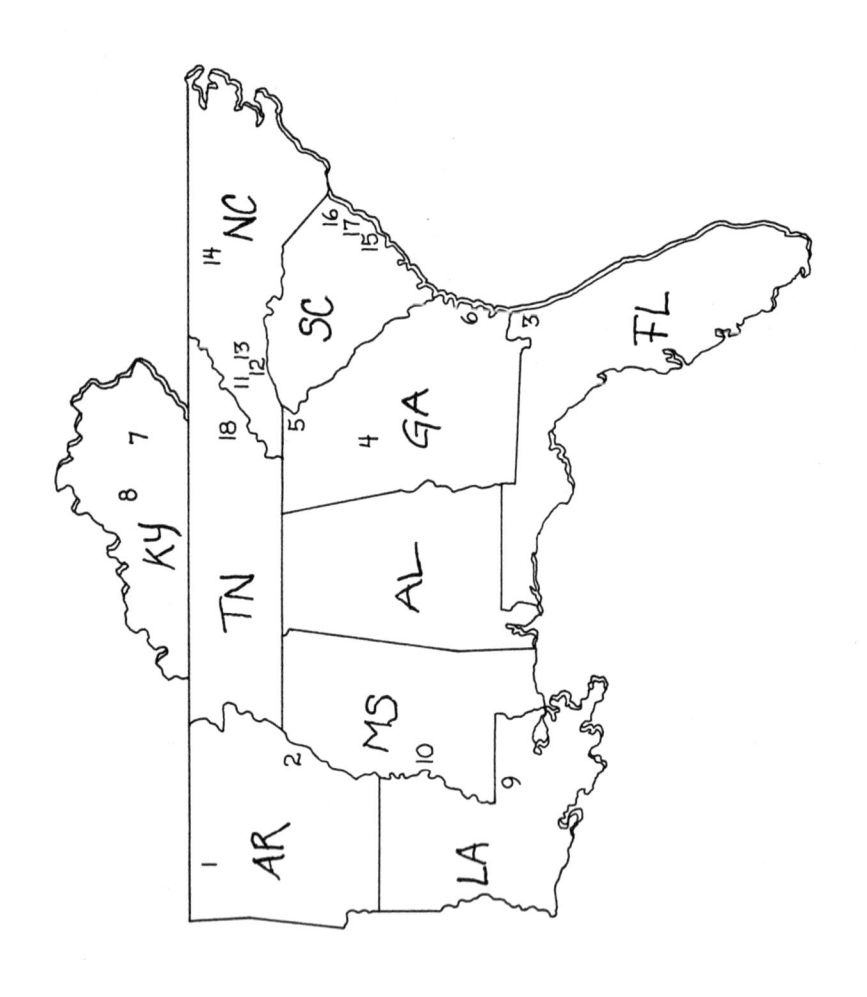

The South

Numbers on map refer to towns numbered below.

ARKANSAS
1. Eureka Springs, Heartstone Inn and Cottages 84
2. Mountain View, Ozark Folk Center 86

FLORIDA
3. Amelia Island, The 1735 House 88

GEORGIA
4. Atlanta, Beverly Hills Inn 90
5. Dillard, Dillard House Farms 92
6. St. Simons Island, Little St. Simons Island 94

KENTUCKY
7. Berea, Boone Tavern Hotel 96
8. Harrodsburg, Shaker Village of Pleasant Hill 98

LOUISIANA
9. Jackson, Asphodel Village 100

MISSISSIPPI
10. Vicksburg, Cedar Grove Mansion-Inn 102

NORTH CAROLINA
11. Bryson City, Nantahala Village 104
12. Cashiers, High Hampton Inn and Country Club 106
13. Pisgah Forest, The Pines 108
14. Winston-Salem, Brookstown Inn 110

SOUTH CAROLINA
15. McClellanville, Village B & B 112
16. Myrtle Beach, Serendipity 114
17. Pawleys Island, Tip Top Inn 116

TENNESSEE
18. Seymour, The Country Inn 118

Heartstone Inn and Cottages
Eureka Springs, Arkansas 72632

Innkeepers: Iris and Bill Simantel
Address/Telephone: 35 Kingshighway; (501) 253–8916
Rooms: 9, 2 cottages; all with private bath, air conditioning, television.
Rates: Rooms, $51 to $70, double occupancy, EPB. Cottages, $59 to $79, double occupancy, EP. Children under 10, $6; 10 and over, $12.
Open: All year except from Christmas through New Year's Day.
Facilities and activities: Inn is in the historic district, within walking distance of restaurants and downtown Eureka Springs tourist activities (country music shows, go-carts, museums, miniature golf, buggy rides, and more). Nearby: horseback riding, canoeing, fishing.

The Heartstone Inn gets its name from a large, flat vaguely heart-shaped stone that the Simantels found on the property. They play with the heart theme, using the phrase "Lose your heart in the Ozarks" and a heart-shaped logo in their brochure. The doors have heart-shaped welcome signs. The stone that justifies it all rests in the front garden, surrounded by flowers.

Children seem to recognize the stone as a heart faster than do their parents. The main house is sufficiently full of knickknacks

Eureka Springs, Arkansas

and pretty decorative items to make you nervous about staying there with children, but the annex, which is equally pleasant and has big rooms, is pretty well childproof and children are welcome there, as well as in the cottages. Eureka Springs has more tourist activities than normal humans can take in during a day. This inn is a good place to walk back to and slow down.

The inn is pretty. It's an Edwardian house, painted pink, with a white picket fence and ☛ lots of bright pink geraniums and roses all around.

Inside, Iris has furnished it mostly with country antiques. In one room a red, white, and blue quilt perks up the bed. Another quilt decorates the wall. Also as decoration, an Edwardian wedding gown hangs out to be admired.

But I think the attractiveness of the inn comes not so much from its pretty artifacts as from what those things reflect of Iris and Bill. For example, in the dining room I admired a ☛ Pennsylvania Dutch hex sign in which tulips and hearts make up the pattern. Iris said that the sign stands for everything they believe in and explained the symbols for faith, hope, charity, love of God, and smooth sailing. Then she kept the moment from getting too solemn by pointing to a print of yellow irises on the other wall. She said, "That's so I remember who I am in the morning."

When Iris was talking about the elaborate breakfasts they serve in the large and sunny breakfast room, she said that guests feel pampered by breakfasts including ☛ strawberry blintzes, coffeecake, and several kinds of fruit. As part of making breakfast special, she said that they dress up in long prairie dresses to serve it. "Well, Bill doesn't wear a prairie dress," she said. "That would be too special."

How to get there: From the west, take the first 62B exit off Route 62: From the east, take the second 62B exit. Follow 62B through town until it becomes Kingshighway.

*

S: *Families enjoy staying in the roomy cottages, where they can cook their own meals, but they have the option of purchasing the inn's scrumptious breakfast if they want a perfect start to their day.*

Ozark Folk Center
Mountain View, Arkansas 72569

Innkeeper: June Burroughs
Address/Telephone: Mountain View; (501) 269–3871
Rooms: 60; all with private bath and air conditioning. Wheelchair access.
Rates: $40, single and double, EP but free coffee in recreation room. Children 12 and under, free; over 12, $5. Inquire about winter discounts.
Open: Lodge open all year. Attractions and restaurant open May through October.
Facilities and activities: Breakfast, lunch, dinner. Swimming pool, craft-demonstration area, gift shop, music auditorium, outdoor stage, conference center. Located in the Ozark Mountains, close to fishing, hunting, and hiking. Near Blanchard Springs Caverns.

The only thing worse than traveling with a bored child is traveling with several children of different ages—all bored. The beauty of the Ozark Folk Center is that it offers so much to do and see, all of it historically and culturally significant, and all of it interesting to people of any age who have a spark of curiosity. The center is set up with families as the main concern, and there are lots of nice little procedures to help you know exactly what's going on and how to get to it.

Mountain View, Arkansas

When I checked in, the woman at the desk gave me a map showing where the craft demonstrations and music auditorium are, drew paths on it with her pen to make sure I knew how to get from my room to the activities, and then drew by hand another little map to show me where I could find mountain music the night that none was performed at the auditorium. Before I left the office, I heard her rearranging the room assignments of two families traveling together so that they'd be in adjoining rooms and closer to the swimming pool.

The rooms are in octagonal cabins that are built from native cedar and are scattered around the grounds, looking a lot like huts. Inside they are comfortably simple. If you'd rather not have air conditioning, ☞ you can open three sliding glass doors to let in the breeze, or you can just open the draperies for a wide-screen view of the trees. The only decorations are locally stitched samplers and quilt panels on the walls.

Quilting is just one of the mountain crafts that local people demonstrate in the folk center. If you plan to visit, you should write for a schedule of events because, in addition to daily demonstrations of wood carving, making apple dolls, playing stringed instruments, and so on, ☞ the center offers a summer full of workshops on everything from basketry and weaving to clogging. These crafts and activities are taught by people who live in the area. Many of the workshops are suited for children and adults equally, making this a real opportunity for family members to see and do together. Staying one night would give a family a great taste of the Ozarks, but you could stay lots longer without anyone's getting bored.

You don't have to worry too much about feeding finicky eaters, either, because the dining room serves traditional Southern cooking, which is typically geared to family tastes—you know, all that fried chicken, mashed potatoes, and biscuits.

How to get there: Follow the signs from State Road 9 at Mountain View to Spur 382. The signs lead you directly to the main parking lot of the center.

The 1735 House
Amelia Island, Florida
32034

Innkeepers: Gary and Emily Grable
Address/Telephone: 584 South Fletcher; (904) 261–5878
Rooms: 6 suites; all with private bath, air conditioning, television, and some with kitchenette.
Rates: $55 to $70, single; $65 to $70, double; continental breakfast. Lighthouse: $95, single; $105, double; continental breakfast. No children under 6; age 6 and over, $5.
Open: All year.
Facilities and activities: Cooking and laundry facilities. Beachfront location. Near restaurants and downtown historic Fernandina Beach shopping and sightseeing; boating from the marina.

You don't find many places like The 1735 House at the beach these days. It's a Cape Cod–style inn, directly facing the ocean, furnished with antiques, wicker, neat old trunks, and some bunk beds just right for kids. Three suites in the inn include efficiency kitchenettes, which are nice for a family. All suites have access to the inn's kitchen and laundry facilities.

If you want to give your family a unique vacation, reserve the ☞ lighthouse for your stay. About 2 blocks from the inn, it is four stories high and has two bedrooms, two baths, and a full kitchen.

Amelia Island, Florida

Its walls are covered with navigation maps. As you enter, you can either step down into a shower-and-bath area or take the spiral stairs up to the kitchen. A galley table and director's chairs make a good spot for playing cards, chatting, or ocean gazing, as well as eating. The stairs keep spiraling up to a bedroom and bath, and finally up to an enclosed observation deck, which is the ultimate spot for ocean gazing.

All the accommodations are right on the beach, so you and the children can get down to the surf without even crossing a road. The beaches in this area are smooth, flat, and clean, with no rugged drops or rocks. The ideal way to spend time on them is alternating sunning, bathing, and occasional trips back into your rooms for a rest or a new bottle of tanning lotion or another sand pail.

The kids will get a hoot out of the way breakfast is served. The night before you tell the staff what time you want breakfast, which is rolls, buns, juice, and beverages. In the morning it will be delivered right to your room in a wicker basket.

The staff are full of helpful recommendations about good eating places, of which there are many on Amelia Island, too. The Down Under Seafood Restaurant, under the Shave bridge on A1A, is in keeping with the nautical mood of the inn and the lighthouse. The seafood is all fresh from the Intracoastal Waterway. There's a boat ramp with a dock, and the atmosphere is correspondingly quaint. You can enjoy cocktails and dinner.

If staying at The 1735 House gets you in the mood for more inns, you're welcome to browse through a large, well-used collection of books about inns in the office.

How to get there: Amelia Island is near the Florida/Georgia border. Take the Yulee exit from I-95 onto Route A1A and follow the signs toward Fernandina Beach. The inn is on A1A.

Beverly Hills Inn
Atlanta, Georgia
30305

Innkeepers: Lyle and Bonnie Kleinhans
Address/Telephone: 65 Sheridan Drive N.E.; (404) 233-8520
Rooms: 12 rooms, 5 suites; all with private bath and air conditioning, 14 with small kitchen.
Rates: $59 to $90, singles, double and suites; continental breakfast and complimentary wine. Children, $5.
Open: All year.
Facilities and activities: Close to restaurants, shopping centers and department stores, art galleries, museums, theaters, and historic sites.

Here's an inn that seems almost to have been invented for the sole purpose of making it easy to travel with children in the city, because you can handle them pretty much as you would at home, keeping snacks in the kitchen, and tolerating a little noise, knowing it won't irritate other guests.

At the Beverly Hills, the interior walls are brick, 🖝 so thick you couldn't hear the Cleveland Symphony if it were playing Beethoven in the next room. That's because the building was originally an apartment complex. When Lyle and Bonnie converted it to an inn, they kept the little kitchens in the rooms and decorated the rooms with antiques, oriental fabrics, and sunny colors.

Atlanta, Georgia

I liked the larger-than-usual space with room for a couch or extra chairs. It felt bright and attractive and ☞ very private. The kitchens don't call you to cook, really (no visitor should bother to cook in a city as full of fine restaurants as Atlanta), but it's great to have a place to warm a baby bottle, to chill a bottle of wine, or brew a cup of tea.

Lyle says that he enjoys breakfast with the guests more than anything else. In the winter, breakfast is served in a sunny white-brick room decorated with plants and overlooking a garden patio. ☞ In good weather, breakfast moves right out to the patio. Guests sit around in the sun, talking with Lyle, reading their papers, and striking up conversations with one another. It's friendly and casual. In chilly weather, a pleasant solarium brings sunshine to your morning paper.

After breakfast, take a minute to look at the collection of Civil War memorabilia Lyle is building. I was amused to notice that it has a decided Yankee slant, something I'd lay odds you won't find anywhere else in Atlanta.

At the end of the day, you can spend some time chatting or reading in the library, hoping, if you're no more talented than I, that someone will play the baby grand piano for a while. As dinner time approaches, Lyle will ask you what kind of food you like and whip out his copy of *Cuisine Atlanta* to help you decide which of the ten restaurants within walking distance or the scores more a short drive away will be exactly what you're in the mood for.

How to get there: From downtown Atlanta, drive north on Peachtree for about fifteen minutes. Turn right onto Sheridan Drive. From I-85 south, take the Peachtree exit. Turn left. Continue going about 15 minutes to turn right onto Sheridan. The inn is about ½ block on the right.

⁂

S: *An authentic London taxicab ferries guests around the city. What a kick for kids!*

Dillard House Farms
Dillard, Georgia
30537

Innkeeper: John Dillard
Address/Telephone: Highway 441 (mailing address: P.O. Box 10); (404) 746–5349, (800) 541–0671
Rooms: 10 in the original inn with shared baths; 56 motel rooms, all with private bath; 2 cottages; 2 suites with Jacuzzis. Air conditioning, television. Pets accepted; $5. Wheelchair access.
Rates: $30 to $69, rooms; $125 to $145, cottages; $100, suites; double occupancy, EP. Children, $2.
Open: All year.
Facilities and activities: Breakfast, lunch, dinner, no bar service. Swimming pool, tennis, horseback riding, farm-animal zoo, country-music performances and magic shows in season. Nearby: fishing, hiking, white-water canoeing and rafting, antiques, craft activities, golf, skiing.

If anybody had told me twenty-five years ago that families would go to farms like the one I grew up on and call it a vacation, I'd have been skeptical. If they'd told me that *I* would do it, I'd have said they were flat nuts. But then, how was I to know about Dillard House Farms and North Georgia?

The people in Dillard say that ☞ they are country people and

Dillard, Georgia

proud of it. And like most country people, they're more proud of their food than practically anything else. About a hundred years ago, the Dillards started taking in boarders. Although things are a lot fancier now, the feeling is the same. You sit down to a meal served family style at one of the big tables in the dining room with whomever else shows up and quickly learn the meaning of "boarding-house reach."

I said, "What's for dinner?" as I walked into the dining room and could hardly believe the answer.

☛ Dinner was barbecued pork, Brunswick stew, fried chicken, country ham, corn on the cob, green beans, parsley potatoes, squash casserole, carrots, and biscuits. Oh, and peach cobbler for dessert. Virtually everything had been produced right there on the farm.

☛ Not only is there a lot for kids to do, it's also a nice opportunity for them to learn that milk doesn't originate in square boxes and chicken wasn't always plastic-wrapped on a Styrofoam tray in the grocery store.

Because of all the activities available, they call Dillard House Farms a resort now, but the feeling is still as down-to-earth and homey as it must have been back when the Dillards first started taking in boarders.

In the original inn, the wood-paneled walls and hardwood floors covered with braided rugs are like those of any old-time farmhouse. The bedrooms in the original inn are very simple, furnished in a style that I call "basic summer camp." If your taste inclines toward something more elaborate, you may prefer a room in one of the other buildings on the farm. You might want to stay in the cottages with your family. One is large enough for six people, while the other is good for a maximum of eight.

How to get there: Dillard House is on Highway 441 between Franklin, North Carolina, and Clayton, Georgia. You can see it from the road, and a large sign in the field directs you to the drive onto the property.

Little St. Simons Island
St. Simons Island, Georgia
31522

Innkeepers: Laura and Ben Gibbens
Address/Telephone: P.O. Box 1078; (912) 638–7472
Rooms: 2 in main lodge with private bath; 4 in River Lodge, all with private bath; 4 in Cedar House, all with private bath; 2 in Michael Cottage share bath.
Rates: $175 to $275, single; $275 to $375, double; AP. No children under 5; 5 and over, $50. Ferry service included. Minimum 2-night stay. Inquire about special family packages in summer and longer-stay and off-season discounts.
Open: February to November.
Facilities and activities: Dinner includes wine. Bar in lodge. Ocean and pool swimming, birding, naturalist-led explorations, horseback riding, beachcombing, shelling, fishing, canoeing, hiking, wind surfing, horseshoes.

This is truly a special place. It is a ten thousand-acre barrier island ☛ still in its natural state except for the few buildings needed to house and feed guests. You can get there only by boat.

When my husband and I visited, we felt welcomed as though we'd been visiting there for years.

I still marvel at how much we did in a short time. The

St. Simons Island, Georgia

permanent staff includes 3 naturalists. One of the naturalists loaded us into an old pickup truck and drove us around the island to help us get oriented. We walked through woods and open areas and along untouched ocean beaches. I saw my first armadillo. I gathered more sand dollars than I've ever seen in one place before. We saw deer, raccoons, opossums, and more birds than I could identify. Serious birdwatchers plan special trips to Little St. Simons to observe the spring and fall migrations.

We rode horseback with one of the naturalists. I was scared to death because I'd never been on a horse before, but they got me up on a mild-mannered old mare, and she plugged along slowly. By the end of the ride, I almost felt as though I knew what I was doing.

We canoed out through the creeks. When a big wind came up, I had a notion to be scared again, but the naturalist directed us into a sheltered spot where we could hold onto the rushes until the weather settled; then we paddled on.

When we weren't out exploring the island, we sat in front of the fire in the lodge, chatting with the other two guests and inspecting the photographs on the walls. They're standard hunting-camp pictures; rows of men grinning like idiots and holding up strings of fish, hunters with rifles grinning like idiots, and people climbing in and out of boats grinning like idiots.

This is a wonderful spot for children. Just think of the Robinson Crusoe aspects of the place. Imagine, as a child, seeing beaches that have never known a boardwalk or a hotdog stand. Imagine the thrill for them of adventuring in the wild, while you have the reassurance of careful, competent guidance from the naturalists.

How to get there: When you make your reservations, you will receive instructions on where to meet the boat that takes you to the island.

S: *The Gibbens have added such creature comforts as nice bathrooms and handy ice machines, but these all rest lightly and inoffensively in the natural scene.*

Boone Tavern Hotel
Berea, Kentucky
40404

Innkeeper: J. B. Morgan
Address/Telephone: CPO 2345, Berea College Campus; (606) 986–9358 or 986–9359
Rooms: 57; all with private bath, air conditioning, television. Pets accepted. Wheelchair access.
Rates: $37 to $67, single and double, EP. Children under 12, free.
Open: All year.
Facilities and activities: Breakfast, lunch, dinner. No bar service. Swimming pool, golf course, tennis courts, and craft shop. All Berea College campus facilities and activities.

I felt privileged to be at the Boone Tavern Hotel on the campus of Berea College. For years I'd been hearing about the college's outstanding work-study programs, the high quality of work and service offered by the students, and the overall good feeling you get from being around a place where people are implementing a good idea that works. Of Berea's 1,500 students, 80 percent come from Appalachia. They are chosen for their academic ability and financial need. They all work at least ten hours per week, and they pay no tuition.

It all comes together at Boone Tavern. Although instructors

and hired professionals provide management and direction, ☛ the inn and restaurant are mostly staffed by students. The rooms are furnished with furniture handmade by students. Students make the craft items in the gift shop. Students guide tours of the historic campus for guests. They do it all well.

A student took me on a tour of many of the inn's guest rooms, each of which is decorated differently with furniture ranging from formal settees to Early American–style pieces. Each room was comfortable and immaculately clean.

I think this is an ideal place to go when you begin to want to show your children what college campuses are like, because this one, unlike most, makes the full facilities of the campus available to guests of the inn.

The dining room, also, is easy for families with children because it is geared to them, rather than to a crowd that likes two or three drinks before dinner.

As for the food, which is ultimately what matters in a dining room, I talked to the chef, Ken Schad, as he was preparing Pork Loin Sarah Jane, a boned pork loin stuffed with prunes and served with fried apples and a sage-and-corn-bread dressing. All dinners are served with ☛ Boone Tavern Spoonbread, which everyone assured me is "world famous." They're so proud of it that they've got the recipe printed up on 5-by-7-inch cards for those of us who ask for it. One of the secrets is using white rather than yellow cornmeal. One of the most popular desserts is the Jefferson Davis Pie, a caramel-based pie that is a little lighter than chess pie. They also serve homemade ice cream with homemade sundae sauces, and that's my idea of a perfect dessert.

How to get there: The inn is on the college campus. Berea is 40 miles south of Lexington, Kentucky, on I–75, midway between Cincinnati and Knoxville. Take exit 76 at Berea and follow Kentucky Highway 21 to the inn.

Shaker Village of Pleasant Hill
Harrodsburg, Kentucky
40330

Innkeeper: Ann Voris
Address/Telephone: 3500 Lexington Road; (606) 734–5411
Rooms: 73 (in 14 buildings); all with private bath, air conditioning, television. Pets accepted by special arrangement.
Rates: $34 to $65, single; $44 to $80, double; EP. Children under 18, free. Inquire about special winter packages. No credit cards.
Open: All year except Christmas Eve and Christmas Day.
Facilities and activities: Breakfast, lunch, dinner. No bar service. Cruises on the *Dixie Belle* riverboat. Shaker craft and farming demonstrations.

Shaker Village preserves twenty-seven original nineteenth-century buildings as they were used by the community of Shakers living in the village. Staying here provides a rare opportunity to show children what life was like for people with nonmaterialistic values and no electricity. The lesson starts as soon as you enter a guest room, as I learned when I toured here.

"That's the closet," Ann Voris said. We were in one of the guest rooms and she was pointing to a strip of heavy pegs along the wall. The Shakers hung everything, from their clothes to their utensils and chairs, on such pegs. ☞ Guests at Shaker Village do the same.

The rooms are furnished in the same sparse, simple style of the Shakers: rag rugs; streamlined, functional furniture; trundle beds; plain linens. Only the modern bathroom, telephone, and television set in each room make it different than it originally would have been.

Like other communities of plain people, the Shakers made up in the bounty of their table for what they lacked in knickknacks. The Shakertown menu, which says, "We make you kindly welcome," does the same. Shakers, wherever they lived, adopted the food of the area. In Kentucky, this means fried chicken, country ham, fried fish, roast beef, and large sirloin steaks. Fresh vegetables (some from the garden on the premises) and salads are passed at the table, as are breads from the bakery. ☞ The smell of baking bread distracts you much of the day at Shaker Village. And for dessert, Shaker lemon pie tops off everything. It's an unusual lemon pie, made with a double crust and whole sliced lemons, plus eggs and sugar, because the Shakers didn't waste anything—not even lemon peels.

Although the meal is bountiful, the dining rooms in the old Trustees' House resemble the guest rooms in their simplicity. The wood floors are polished and clean but unadorned. The tables and chairs are typical, functional Shaker design, and the place settings are plain white dishes. For me it added up to a fascinating, almost-insider's view of unusual people whose way of life is almost gone except in this re-creation.

How to get there: The entrance to Shaker Village is off U.S. Route 68, 7 miles northeast of Harrodsburg and 25 miles southwest of Lexington. Signs mark the drive clearly.

❃

S: *Many special events, including weekends of Shaker music and dance, are held during the year. You can write for a yearly calendar to help you plan a trip according to your family's interests.*

Asphodel Village
Jackson, Louisiana
70748

Innkeeper: Owen Couhig Kemp
Address/Telephone: Route 2, Box 89; (504) 654–6868
Rooms: 20; all with private bath, air conditioning, television, and 6 with fireplace. Limited wheelchair access.
Rates: $50 to $70, single and double, EPB. Children under 6, free; 6 to 12, $5.
Open: All year except Christmas Day.
Facilities and activities: Lunch, dinner, full bar. Swimming pool, volleyball, croquet, hiking trails in the woods, horseshoes, antebellum mansion open for tours, gift shop. Near many plantations and historic mansions open to tourists.

"People wonder what they're going to do with the children while they're here," Owen Kemp said, "but the way it usually works is that they open the door, the kids are off to the woods and the creek, and nobody hears a peep from them until it's time to leave."

Asphodel Village is an assortment of buildings in the woods on a 500-acre plantation. Over a span of about twenty years, the buildings have been moved in or built to meet various demands. Now that guest rooms are no longer in the old mansion, the place

Jackson, Louisiana

works even better for families, because everyone has more room and more privacy.

The swimming pool and other game facilities are nice to know about, but Owen is right in observing that the real entertainment here is nature's own—the woods.

The guest rooms are spacious, simple, and furnished with good antiques (some of which are for sale) and good, firm beds. My room had two doors; the back door opened onto a little deck looking into the woods.

Just a few steps away, the oldest building in the village houses the restaurant. I walked over for dinner a little before dark and ☞ sat on the porch, which seemed more popular than the indoor dining rooms that night. Amazingly, I didn't see a single bug or mosquito.

On the advice of the couple at the next table, I started with a cup of corn-crab soup. It was thick and spiced with an ingredient I liked but never did identify. We all had fun discussing it. The waiter would say only that it was ☞ "cook's magic."

He wouldn't say much about the bread, either. When he brought it to my table, he said, "One good thing about eating alone, you don't have to share the bread." He put down a loaf that would have been enough for three people. It was feather-light, almost like cake, and creamy colored. The waiter said it was "Asphodel bread"; the cook had been making it for years from her own special recipe and magic, and it always turned out right.

The sweet, cakelike nature of the bread makes it a great favorite with children, as does the notion that it's made from magic. The menu includes some scrumptious items, such as barbecued shrimp kebab—wonderful for mommies who don't have time to cook like that at home—but there are also enough more familiar items such as chicken so that picky eaters don't have to be a problem.

How to get there: Asphodel is between Baton Rouge and St. Francisville on State Route 68. From Baton Rouge, take the Natchez exit off I–110 onto U.S. 61. Go north 12 miles, turn right on State 68. The inn is 8 miles on the left. From St. Francisville, follow 61 south to Highway 964. Turn left and go to the intersection of 68. Turn left on 68 and continue 4 miles to the inn.

Cedar Grove Mansion–Inn
Vicksburg, Mississippi 39180

Innkeepers: Ted and Estelle Mackey
Address/Telephone: 2200 Oak Street; (601) 636–1605 or (800) 862–1300 from outside Mississippi
Rooms: 7 in the mansion, 2 in the pool house, 8 suites in Little Tara; all with private bath, air conditioning, television. Limited wheelchair access.
Rates: $75 to $120, double occupancy, EPB. Tour of mansion and complimentary glass of wine or soft drink on arrival included. No children under 6; 6 to 12, $15; 12 and over, $20.
Open: All year.
Facilities and activities: Pool and Jacuzzi. Four acres of formal gardens. Nearby: Mississippi River, historic sites, restaurants.

The trouble with taking children to many plantation homes is that they quickly lose interest in hearing about the old furniture and silver. An antebellum mansion doesn't mean much to them because the Civil War doesn't have much reality to them. Just stepping into the parlor changes all that at Cedar Grove. I still remember my first impressions. I saw the cannonball lodged in the

Vicksburg, Mississippi

parlor wall. I saw a patch in the door. I saw a ragged hole in the parlor floor that had been framed and covered with heavy glass so you could see through to the rooms below.

What *is* all this?

"Union gunboat cannonball, from the Civil War," the innkeeper said. "It came through the door and hit the parlor wall. Mrs. Klein, the owner of the house, insisted on leaving it there as a reminder after the war."

And the hole?

"War damage. After the fall of Vicksburg, Grant slept here for three nights. He turned the servants' quarters down below into a Union hospital for his soldiers. The Kleins were in residence at the time."

☛ The innkeepers' familiarity and personal fascination with the history of the house give them little stories to tell about every room of the mansion. Listening to them and knowing that the house is largely furnished with its original antiques adds a human note to the Civil War that I've never gotten from reading plaques in museums or touring military memorials. They even know that what I thought was a goldfish pond out in the yard actually, back in 1885, had been a catfish holding pond to keep the fish lively until it was time to eat them.

Their hospitality is as good as their history. I've seen many styles of Southern hospitality. I like Cedar Grove's style: ☛ helpful, low key, undemanding. If you have a mint julep, it's made from an old house recipe. Your full plantation breakfast will be served graciously in the formal dining room.

The innkeepers have menus from favorite local restaurants to help guests decide where to go for dinner. Tuminello's, which has been operating at the site of the old Marine Hospital since 1899, is just a half block away, if you prefer walking. Just a few miles away by car, the Delta Point serves continental cuisine.

How to get there: From I-20, take the 1A Washington Street exit. Go north about 2 miles. Turn left onto Klein.

Nantahala Village
Bryson City, North Carolina 28713

Innkeeper: Ragan B. Walker
Address/Telephone: Highway 19 (mailing address: P.O. Drawer J); (704) 488-2826 or (800) 438-1507
Rooms: 14 in lodge, 8 motel apartments, 35 cabins; all with private bath and television, most with air conditioning.
Rates: $35 to $60 single and double rooms, $40 to $100 cabins. Highest rates are in summer. Children under 6, free. Inquire about special off-season discount plans.
Open: April 1 to October 31.
Facilities and activities: Breakfast, lunch, and dinner. BYOB. Swimming pool, tennis courts, volleyball court, Ping-Pong, horseshoes, badminton, hiking trails, antique-and-craft shop. Rafting, fishing, horseback riding. Activities director on premises June, July, August.

Nantahala Village is ☛ one of my favorite places. The lodge is pleasant and unpretentious, not the kind of place where you worry about knickknacks getting broken by frisky children, and the cabins are a nice alternative when you've got several offspring in tow.

This place was a popular mountain retreat before white-water rafting in the Nantahala Gorge became a big attraction. Although you see lots of rafters around the inn and in the dining room and there's an outfitter's store across the road, the rafting culture doesn't dominate the scene. Many people still stay just for the pleasure of some cool days in the mountains or to be close to all the other opportunities of the Great Smokies.

The food is tasty down-home American, Thanksgiving-everyday cooking, served up in generous proportions. I was at the inn without children, but I thought as I ate that mine would have appreciated the absence of strange and exotic flavors and would have enjoyed the good, familiar tastes offered.

I declined an appetizer because I knew full well that I was going to want to indulge in some ☛ cinnamon rolls the next morning. I had roast turkey with mashed potatoes and dressing, turnip greens, steamed carrots, cranberry sauce, yeast rolls, and I made a trip to the salad bar. I ordered regular cheesecake for dessert. Sometimes they serve chocolate cheesecake, and that is my favorite.

As I savored bite after bite of this huge feast, I was watching the mountains through the dining-room windows and planning all the activities I wanted to try the next day. Whatever I planned, I knew I'd stop in the lobby for a cup of coffee before breakfast. Then I'd walk a couple of miles down an abandoned old road that winds along the mountainside. And after that I'd have a big breakfast with homemade jam to stoke up energy for whatever I would do the rest of the day. To my mind, it adds up to a perfect vacation.

How to get there: The inn is 9 miles southwest of Bryson City on Highway 19.

❉

S: *I took home a jar of homemade strawberry-rhubarb preserves from the Simple Pleasures gift shop. Delicious.*

High Hampton Inn and Country Club
Cashiers, North Carolina 28717

Innkeeper: Will McKee
Address/Telephone: Cashiers; (704) 743–2411
Rooms: 32 in main lodge, 98 in annex cottages; all with private bath. Limited wheelchair access.
Rates: $73 to $85, single; $62 to $80, per person, double occupancy; AP. Children under 2, free; ages 2 to 6, $34 to $42; over 6, $43 to $50.
Open: April until after Thanksgiving.
Facilities and activities: Breakfast, lunch, dinner. No bar service; BYOB in private tavern. No pets in rooms, but a kennel is available on the grounds. Golf course, tennis courts, hiking and jogging trails, 3 lakes for swimming and boating. Fishing. Badminton, shuffleboard, Italian lawn bowling, croquet, archery. Golf-and-tennis pro shop. Many outdoor and folklore workshops, retreats, and programs.

The folks at High Hampton Inn and Country Club like to call their place "plain and rustic," but don't get the idea that you're only a step above tenting in the wilderness. Over the years, the McKees have carved out a broad swath of civilization at 3,600 feet above sea level in the Blue Ridge Mountains of Western North Carolina.

Cashiers, North Carolina

The lobby gives you a good sense of the inn. It seems to stretch on forever, has ☞ a stone chimney with four fireplaces in the center, and smells faintly of newly sawed wood. The furniture is square country-style, mountain-crafted pine, with cushions in beige-and-rust tweeds and plaids. There's a lot of it. I counted two dozen couches and love seats, grouped with chairs. People sat in small groups all around the lobby, talking, working jigsaw puzzles, and just reading.

The dining room extends off the lobby and looks to be about the size of a football field, with two long buffet tables in the center. You're assigned a table when you check in, and that's your table for as long as you're at the inn. All meals are served buffet style, and the volume of food is in direct proportion to the size of the dining room. I had a nice supper of roast pork loin cut in thick slices, stewed apples, summer squash, candied sweet potatoes, and an assortment of raw vegetables from the salad bar. The dessert table held several different kinds of cake, including strawberry shortcake. Many guests had more than one dessert!

After dinner, some people who were participating in a spring conservation retreat at the inn spent some time ☞ singing in the side yard. Among them I saw a couple with a baby, several elderly people, and many children. It occurred to me that High Hampton Inn is one of the few inns I've visited where ☞ people of all ages seem equally welcome and comfortable and where there are activities appropriate for all ages.

As active as the place had been all day, it got quiet almost immediately after nightfall, and by 11 P.M. you couldn't hear a soul or even see a light anywhere on the grounds. I think everybody was worn out from a day full of play.

How to get there: The inn is 2 miles south of Cashiers on Route 107.

S: *When you come here with your family, you might want to consider staying in one of the inn's six vacation homes, which hold up to six people, have a kitchen and a TV, and are rented on the European plan.*

The Pines
Pisgah Forest, North Carolina
28768

Innkeepers: Tom and Mary McEntire
Address/Telephone: 719 Hart Road (mailing address: P.O. Box 7); (704) 877-3131
Rooms: 22 in inn, cabins, and cottages; most with private bath.
Rates: $48, single; $58, double, EPB. Children up to age 1, free; age 1 to 12, $12. Stays of 7 or more days, 10 percent discount.
Open: May 1 through October 31.
Facilities and activities: Dinner Wednesday through Saturday. BYOB. Hiking, swimming, fishing in Pisgah Forest. Near restaurants, golf, and the Brevard Music Festival.

At The Pines, families can vacation in the country in the kind of setting we used to think of as "Grandma's" before most of the Grandmas went into condos. The kids can taste the kind of food Grandmas used to cook before we all started counting calories.

These days Mary tries to limit her cooking to breakfast for guests, but she says emphatically that it's "a big breakfast, with our famous cheese grits and eggs to order, fruit, hot biscuits, and pancakes." No way Mary will ever serve up a doughnut out of a box and coffee in a Styrofoam cup and call it breakfast. I asked about the secret of the grits. She said it's easy. She cooks the grits

Pisgah Forest, North Carolina

in a double boiler and, when they're tender, adds butter and lots of Colby cheese.

The inn is a big old farmhouse, supplemented by two 🐾 real log cabins and three cottages, on Hart Mountain. "Taking care of the mountain" is fully a family project.

But, if you're a casual observer, you'd have trouble sorting out who is related and who's just acting that way. For instance, annual flowers bloom everywhere because one of the guests plants them every spring. The beds are weed free because several other guests bring their garden gloves and weed every morning during their stay.

A honeymoon couple planted a tree, but an extremely cold winter killed it, so on their tenth anniversary, they planted laurel at The Pines.

The iron porch furniture is sparkling and rust free because a guest paints it each year.

Admire the needlepoint cushions and pictures; guests made them. Notice the match-stick bird cage in the corner; a guest built it sitting right there on the floor.

Families who come to The Pines enjoy the place as a spot for the children to run among the hills, gawking at the cows and climbing trees, and as a base from which the entire family can go hiking and swimming. Add a little sightseeing and some supper at one of the family-style restaurants in nearby Brevard (or at the inn on Wednesday through Saturday nights), and by the time everyone gets home at night, the children are too tired to do much more than sleep in the mountain air while visions of the Waltons float in their wee little heads.

How to get there: From midtown Brevard, bear right on Old Hendersonville Highway. Turn right at the power plant, then right on Hart Road. Ask for a brochure with map when you make reservations.

☼

S: *It was raining the day I showed up at The Pines. Mary came out to the car with an umbrella to get me.*

Brookstown Inn
Winston-Salem, North Carolina 27101

Innkeeper: Deborah Bumgardner
Address/Telephone: 200 Brookstown Avenue; (919) 725-1120
Rooms: 52; all with private bath, air conditioning, television, and some with whirlpool tubs, some with private sitting rooms. Wheelchair access and 2 rooms equipped for the handicapped.
Rates: $69 to $85, single; $79 to $95, double; continental breakfast and evening wine and cheese party. Children under 12, free; 12 and over, $10.
Open: All year.
Facilities and activities: Restaurants nearby. Meeting facilities. Touring historic Old Salem, local colleges and universities, galleries and museums.

As an inn, this old building is in its fourth incarnation. It was built in 1837 by the Moravians to be a cotton mill. Then it became a flour mill and later a storage building for a moving company. The mill was restored as an inn and a complex of specialty shops and restaurants in 1984. It's listed on the National Register of Historic Places.

This is the kind of place that offers advantages to a family both in its proximity to Old Salem, where you can easily spend a couple of days touring the old buildings and watching the demonstrations of old ways, and in its own intrinsically interesting design. These days, when so much of our time is spent in modern buildings that have no surprises or secrets, Brookstown Inn is a sort of playground for adults and their children.

As often happens in building within an existing large structure, the new spaces are larger than average, with spectacularly high ceilings, surprising twists and turns, nooks and crannies, and a wealth of visual interest in exposed beams, old brick, and historic artifacts.

More specifically: On the fourth floor, in what originally was a dormitory for girls who worked in the cotton mill, renovators found and have preserved behind glass ☞ a plaster wall full of graffiti. The old factory boiler visually dominates Darryl's Restaurant. In guest rooms ☞ architectural features of the original building, such as brick buttresses, unusual roof slopes, and interesting spaces, have been incorporated into the design of the room.

The decor throughout the inn is Early American, appropriate to the building and its Old Salem connection, without being oppressive. Quilts decorate lobby walls; country touches like hand-woven baskets, pieces of pewter, and silk flowers are scattered throughout the public areas. The ☞ huge open spaces keep it from feeling at all cluttered. In the guest rooms, furnishings are reproductions appropriate for the period set off with Wedgwood-blue stenciling around the windows.

In the breakfast room, which has brick floors and comfortable club chairs around round tables, your continental breakfast is absolutely appropriate: Moravian buns, sugar cake, and fresh fruit. If you visit Old Salem during your stay, you can pick up recipe cards for these famous Moravian delicacies.

The old Moravians were famous for their hospitality. Old Brookstown Inn is doing a remarkably good job communicating spirit as well as offering the modern creature comforts you expect from a first-class hostelry.

How to get there: Coming from the west on I–40, take the Cherry Street exit. Turn right when you come to the light at the top of the ramp, onto Marshall Street. Follow the inn signs, turning left onto Brookstown Avenue. The inn is on the right. Coming from the east on I–40, take the Cherry Street exit. As you come to the light coming off the ramp, turn left onto First Street. Go 1 block, turn left on Marshall. Follow the inn signs, turning left on Brookstown.

Village B & B
McClellanville, South Carolina 29458

Innkeeper: Cheri George
Address/Telephone: 333 Mercantile Road; (803) 887–3266
Rooms: 1 with private bath and air conditioning. No smoking in room. No unmarried couples.
Rates: $40 to $55, single or double, continental breakfast. Children under 4, free; 4 and over, $5. No credit cards.
Open: All year.
Facilities and activities: Restaurant nearby (closed Sunday and Monday). McClellanville is a fishing village. Boating, near national forest trails, hunting, between Charleston and Georgetown.

Midway between Charleston and Georgetown, I stumbled upon a wonderful little town with a tiny inn that is perfect for a family traveling with young children. The place has lots and lots of outdoor play room; the innkeepers have a young child of their own; and the village offers a chance to see what a real (rather than touristy quaint) fishing community is like.

Village B & B, only about a mile from Route 17 on an unpaved road, lies in the middle of a ☞ large lawn with woods behind and with fields edged with live oaks and their requisite Spanish moss across the road.

McClellanville, South Carolina

It's the smallest inn I've ever visited, but it definitely *is* an inn. The room is 20 feet by 20 feet in a wing completely separate from the owners' house. The pale floor, sanded and finished old southern pine, is so striking it practically stands up and says hello. The teal wallpaper complements the floor without being too dark because of all the ☞ big white-curtained windows that let light in and let you look out at the rural countryside. A large bath and dressing area extend to the rear.

The antique iron beds, dressed in fluffy white and peach covers, had been in Cheri's family for three generations. When she decided to open the inn, she hauled them from the barn and had them blasted and painted white. It's a special pleasure to be able to take children into a place that is really pretty but not so fragile you're afraid they'll break something just by moving. And the room is so huge, you don't feel one bit crowded having the children in it with you.

For kids, it's a special treat, too, having breakfast brought right to them in the room. At a round table near the door, Cheri serves your breakfast: blueberry or honey bran muffins, fresh ambrosia, and coffee or tea. The overall effect is amazingly relaxing.

While Cheri chatted at the table, I studied the large watercolor seascapes on the walls and wondered where she'd found such nice art, intending to ask her about it before I left. Before I got around to it, she made an offhand mention of ☞ "Matthew's paintings" and indicated a bin of some for sale I'd somehow overlooked in the corner. In his spare time, her husband, Matthew, paints local outdoor scenes, birds, flowers, and shells.

I don't claim to be an art critic, but I have to tell you, I was so taken with Matthew's work that it took me an hour to narrow the choices down to five favorites and then another half-hour to decide on the two I just had to have.

How to get there: From U.S. 17 turn at McClellanville at the caution light. Follow the signs to the inn.

☼

S: *McClellanville was originally a village of summer homes for plantation owners. Many old homes still remain.*

Serendipity
Myrtle Beach, South Carolina 29577

Innkeepers: Cos and Ellen Ficarra
Address/Telephone: 401 71st Street North; (803) 449–5268
Rooms: 12; all with private bath, refrigerator, air conditioning, television.
Rates: $58 to $82, single or double, EPB. Children, $10. Inquire about fall and winter rates.
Open: March 1 to November 30.
Facilities and activities: Heated pool, Jacuzzi, shuffleboard, Ping-Pong, bicycles, gas grill. Nearby: ocean beach (1½ blocks), restaurants, golf courses, tennis courts, outlet shopping, fishing.

    Serendipity is a breath of good taste in a resort area much given to glitz and pink-plastic dinosaurs. Staying here, rather than at one of the more standard motels, is not only more appealing to your senses, but it also offers a chance to show your children the differences among styles of living without lecturing.

    The inn itself is *very* pretty, *very* clean, *very* comfortable. That's not always true of lodgings in vacation centers.

    The furnishings and decor are several notches above beach standards for artistic interest and aesthetic appeal. The Ficarras are knowledgeable collectors of fine antiques and art, and even though they don't spread a lot of that really good stuff around the

Myrtle Beach, South Carolina

inn, I think ☞ the level of their taste still affects the look of the grounds and guest rooms.

In the Oak Room, for instance, two antique lion's head oak chairs from Pawleys Island dominate; in one smaller room, Holly Hobby wallpaper is lifted beyond cliche by a quilted bedspread and a signed Norman Rockwell print.

But, as Ellen is quick to point out, the furnishings are all chosen to stand up to a little beach sand and salt water, so that you don't have to worry about a damp suit ruining fine upholstery.

All the rooms have good reading lights and chairs and, just in case you didn't bring a book, you may choose one from what Ellen and I laughingly called the "trashy novel" selection of paperbacks in the common room. Guests leave books they've finished and take others, and Ellen adds those she's read, so the collection is ever-changing. To me, places that are ☞ set up for readers rank high.

Likewise, ☞ Ellen's breakfasts are a cut above the usual B & B continental because, instead of going for the near-ubiquitous croissant, she serves breads baked by a local German friend, along with hard-boiled eggs, cereal, bagels and cream cheese, and her own specialties, differing from day to day. When I was there she had prunes stewed with apples and spices that were so good I tried to duplicate them when I got home. Other guests raved about her warm brown Betty.

As for dinner, Cos and Ellen recommend two places that are as special, in their own ways, as Serendipity itself. Mrs. Frances' Kitchen at Prince's Place is a plain little place where black cooks prepare authentic soul food without pretensions for about $5 a meal. Villa Roma, an Italian restaurant whose proprietors come from Rome, offers fresh hand-cut veal, fresh pasta, and breads made on the premises. The Ficarras eat there themselves whenever they can.

How to get there: Take Highway 17 (King's Highway) to 71st Avenue North. Turn east toward the ocean. The inn is just off the highway, behind hedges.

Tip Top Inn
Pawleys Island, South Carolina 29585

Innkeeper: Sis Kelly
Address/Telephone: P.O. Box 1278; (803) 237–2325
Rooms: 30; all with private bath.
Rates: $50 to $65 per person, MAP (midday dinner). Children under 4, free; 4 to 9, $15; 10 to 15, $30; 16 and over, $35. EP rates from April to second week of May and in October. Single-night stays $5 extra. Priority and discount given to stays of a week or longer. No credit cards.
Open: April 1 to November 1.
Facilities and activities: BYOB. Beachfront location, swimming, fishing. Crab dock in marsh.

Sis Kelly, a blue-eyed dynamo in her early sixties who could run circles around many people half her age, is as much a part of your experience at Tip Top Inn as the sand, sun, and water. ☛ It doesn't take her long to learn all about you, and she doesn't forget from year to year. She remembers whether you like dark or light turkey meat, that you don't eat anything with onions, and that you drink decaffeinated coffee.

Sis supervises the kitchen at every meal. She's proud of her staff and the food. One cook has been at the Tip Top for nearly twenty years, and an assistant has been here for nearly fifteen years. Their cooking has changed some in that time. Like many of us, they've learned to use less fat and not to overcook vegetables. Everything, from the hot biscuits to the pecan pie, is homemade.

The day I visited, dinner, served at 1:30 P.M., began with she-crab soup, and went on to fried chicken with real (not instant) mashed potatoes, okra, and succotash made of fresh limas, corn, and tomatoes. With a meal like that in the middle of the day, most people don't want much for supper, but you can keep food in the guests' refrigerator if you want to make an evening snack, prepare a picnic, or charcoal-grill a steak.

Sis says the guest rooms are done in "early marriage furniture" that kids, salt, and sand can't hurt. The floors are weathered board and covered with braided rugs. The curtains are blue-and-white ticking.

It's only a few steps from the inn down to a gloriously wide beach, the kind with soft sand that's good for burying each other in, and the surf is gentle enough that you can feel safe about letting the children play in it while you watch. And, horror of horrors, should you have a rainy day, the common room is well suited to relaxing and chatting with other guests while the children amuse themselves. Summer furniture blends with pine-paneled walls and a brick fireplace. Two sets of tables and chairs make a good place for playing cards, working puzzles, or writing. And on the porch, more tables and summer furniture get you closer to the ocean.

An earlier proprietress kept a sign proclaiming the hours from 2 to 4 P.M. "quiet time." Sis framed it and included it in a grouping of pictures on one wall in the living room. People honor it. Having an official quiet time, with lots of quiet activities available, can help tremendously in keeping your children from getting cranky and argumentative because they are too tired.

How to get there: From Route 17, turn at the Pawleys Island sign onto the connector road. Go to where you must turn either left or right. Turn left and go ¼ mile. The inn is on the right.

The Country Inn
Seymour, Tennessee
37865

Innkeeper: Annette Christenberry
Address/Telephone: Route 3, Chris-Haven Drive; (615) 573–7170 or 577–8172
Rooms: 13; all with private bath and air conditioning. Limited wheelchair access.
Rates: $35, single; $45 to $65, double; continental breakfast and greens fee. Children under 12, $5; 12 and over, $10. Inquire about biking vacations.
Open: March 1 through November.
Facilities and activities: Beer and setups available. Fast food available at the golf clubhouse. Restaurants nearby. Hot tub. Next to Bays Mountain Golf Course, which has a swimming pool and tennis courts. Bicycle rentals. Nearby: downtown Knoxville, Gatlinburg, and Pigeon Forge, and Great Smoky Mountain National Park.

If you're going to spend time at Pigeon Forge, taking in the myriad rides, tourist attractions, and restaurants that line the highway there, you might use The Country Inn as a kind of cooling-off place to get the kids unwound afterwards. They'll like the pool and would probably be glad to swim while you get in a little golf or tennis.

In spite of its name, this inn, settled among the fields of this farming community, takes you by surprise. Both the inn and the neighboring golf course are on part of the farm, Chris-Haven, that used to belong to the grandfather of Annette's husband. Annette designed and furnished the inn with an intimate sense of what is appropriate for the country setting. The building is stone and stucco, with a stone-walled patio curving across the front and around one side. Spruce trees flank the front entrance, and the building is surrounded by oaks that have been here a long time.

Annette created the same sense of quiet country inside with ☛ two bay-window seats and a ☛ stone fireplace in the lobby, wildlife art on the walls, and touches in the guest rooms such as a wicker vanity and a nicely worn leather chair. Until now, the golf course has been the main attraction for guests, but Annette has begun offering special biking vacations, in association with an East Tennessee bicycling organization, ranging from short rides to "rambles" of two or more days.

You can bring your own bike, helmet, and other equipment, or rent them at the inn. The packages include trail planning and guides if you want them. It's great riding because the ☛ scenery is lovely, and about the only traffic you'll encounter is grazing cows and horses and maybe an occasional fisherman along a stream. The bike trips are a special passion of Annette. Ever since she took her first one in New England, she has wanted to open up the possibilities of such fun for as many people as she can.

Whether you golf or bike or just bum around, it's nice to be back for late-afternoon snacks and beer or tea on the back porch. This is when guests really get to know one another. And come dinnertime, in keeping with the quiet pleasures of the inn, Annette likes to send guests to Ye Olde Steak House, a restaurant in an old log building down the road, where you can order salad, potato, and what Annette swears is about the best steak you've ever tasted.

How to get there: The inn is about a twenty-minute drive south of Knoxville off U.S. 441. Coming from the north (Knoxville), take 441 south to Burnette Station Road. Go 3 miles and turn right at the inn's sign. If you are going north on 441 from Pigeon Forge, take a left onto Burnette Station Road.

THE MIDWEST

by
Bob Puhala

Bob Puhala is well acquainted with inns that are suitable for families. He has done his research for both editions of *Recommended Country Inns—the Midwest* with his family—his wife, Debbie; their daughters, Kate and Dayne, now aged three and one respectively; and sometimes his parents. As Bob puts it, "Kate and Dayne were country-inn veterans from the time they were two months old."

Bob traveled 15,000 miles to research the two editions of the guide. In the second edition, he describes 175 of the best and most interesting inns in eight midwestern states. There are enchanting inns hugging the banks of the Mississippi, Victorian farmhouses-turned-inns, rustic lodges overlooking the northern lakes, historical turn-of-the-century wayside inns, European-style romantic retreats, and island inns reached by boat and horse-drawn carriage.

Bob is a Chicago journalist and author. He has been writing a weekly travel column for the *Chicago Sun-Times* for seven years, and he belongs to the Society of American Travel Writers, the nation's top organization of professional travel journalists.

The Midwest

Numbers on map refer to towns numbered below.

ILLINOIS
1. Eldred, Hobson's Bluffdale 124
2. Galena, Log Cabin Guest House 126

INDIANA
3. Middlebury, Das Essenhaus Country Inn 128

IOWA
4. Dubuque, The Redstone Inn 130

MICHIGAN
5. Arcadia, Watervale Inn 132
6. Mackinac Island, Grand Hotel 134
7. South Haven, Old Harbor Inn 136

MINNESOTA
8. Taylors Falls, Historic Taylors Falls Jail 138
9. Wabasha, The Anderson House 140

MISSOURI
10. Lesterville, Wilderness Lodge 142

OHIO
11. Coshocton, Roscoe Village Inn 144

WISCONSIN
12. Elkhart Lake, Siebken's 146
13. Kohler, The American Club 148
14. LaPointe, Woods Manor 150
15. Mitchell, Silver Springs Inn and Resort 152
16. Portage, Bonnie Oaks Estate 154
17. Sturgeon Bay, Bay Shore Inn 156
18. White Lake, Wolf River Lodge 158

Hobson's Bluffdale
Eldred, Illinois
62027

Innkeepers: Bill and Lindy Hobson

Address/Telephone: Hillview Road; (217) 983–2854

Rooms: 8, with 3 two-room suites; all with private bath and air conditioning.

Rates: $50 per adult, AP and all activities. Children up to 13, $23 to $35. Week's farm vacation: $295, adults; $130, children under 4; $175, ages 4 to 8; $210, ages 9 to 13; AP. EPB rates available. Three-night minimum Memorial Day, July 4, and Labor Day. Two-night minimum on all other weekends, June through September.

Open: All year for B&B; farm vacations, March 1 to December 1.

Facilities and activities: Horseback riding and trail rides (children 9 and over), cart rides, swimming in heated pool, hot tub, canoe day trips, hiking through private wooded bluffs, arrowhead hunting, wild-blackberry picking, fishing in private pond or Illinois River, hayrides, square dancing, ice cream socials, bonfire roasts; workshops in forestry, archeology, pottery, ceramics, wildlife, and more. Baby-sitters available.

What a deal for kids! Bluffdale, a 320-acre farm (soybeans, corn, wheat, and a few pigs) run by the Hobsons, offers kids a chance to become junior farmers during their stay, as they are given the opportunity to help with regular farm chores.

Eldred, Illinois

☛ Feeding chickens and pigs, gathering fresh eggs from the henhouse, bottle feeding calves, herding geese, picking fresh blackberries, and harvesting vegetables from the two-acre garden is so much fun for little ones.

Especially if they're mini–city slickers.

The farm has been in Bill's family since 1828. His great-great-grandfather named it for the spectacular bluffs that run through the property.

Lindy is the chef of the family, and her contribution is down-home, country cooking at its best. Meals, served family-style, may include eggs, French toast, pancakes, and home-baked breads for breakfast; maybe a picnic lunch that can be eaten during a break as families hike through private wooded bluffs; and supper-table specials like barbecued pork chops, pot roast, or baked ham, topped off with oven-fresh sweets and homemade ice cream.

Overnight rooms are spartan, but comfortable enough, done in bandana red and blues. You don't come to Bluffdale for room-side splendor; there's far too much to do. The flexible schedule includes: ☛ Saturday-night square dances; Sunday ice cream socials; Monday family baseball games; Tuesday-afternoon cookout picnics at Greenfield Lake; Friday-night bonfire sing-alongs; and lots more.

How to get there: From St. Louis, take Missouri 367 north to Alton, Illinois. Continue north on U.S. 67, then head north on Illinois 267. Turn west at Illinois 208 and continue to Eldred. At Eldred–Hillview Road (at the bottom of a hill, opposite the Standard gas station), turn north, and proceed just over 3½ miles to the farm.

❧

B: *A special country getaway.*

125

Log Cabin Guest House
Galena, Illinois
61036

Innkeepers: Linda and Scott Ettelman
Address/Telephone: 11661 West Chetlain Lane; (815) 777–2845
Rooms: 3 authentic 1800s log cabins, 2-room historic Servant's House; all with private bath, air conditioning, television. Wheelchair access to cabin.
Rates: Cabins, $50 to $85; Servant's House, $45; double occupancy, EP. Children, $5. Two-night minimum (Friday and Saturday) during summer season.
Facilities and activities: Very private location; near old barn, fields, woods. A short drive to historic attractions, specialty shops, museums, and restaurants of Galena.

Kate, my three-year-old, gave me her stamp of approval for the Log Cabin Guest House when she climbed up to the expansive sleeping loft, jumped on one of the rope beds, pointed to a small pioneer-style corner crib, and said excitedly, "Look, a bed for Daynie, too!" (Her sister, "Baby Dayne," is one year old.)

Kate didn't know just how lucky she was, visiting an authentic log cabin built in 1865 by a Civil War veteran who came to the then-booming lead-mine frontier town of Galena to make his fortune. Two additional cabins on the grounds date to 1850–

Galena, Illinois

1860; Linda and Scott discovered them north of Platville, Wisconsin, dismantled them, then reassembled and restored the buildings on their historic homestead.

The main room of the soldier's cabin is dominated by a huge stone hearth, ☛ perfect for cooking marshmallows on chilly evenings. A massive stone floor provides some coolness even on the warmest days. Logs are whitewashed inside to give the cabin a bright, happy feeling, unlike many dank historic cabin homes. An antique spindle bed is tucked into the room's far corner. Kids love the sleeping loft; it makes them feel like pioneers themselves.

No food is served here, but it's just a short drive to all the restaurants and attractions in historic Galena, often called "the town that time forgot." Its Civil War architecture is largely intact; specialty shops make it a browser's paradise; and the Farmers' Home Hotel is a good spot for hearty family-style breakfasts, while the Kingston Inn remains the town's premier dinner spot.

More for kids: run along the Galena River in Grant Park; tour President Ulysses S. Grant's home; visit the Stockade used during the 1832 Black Hawk War; walk through historic Vinegar Hill Lead Mine; hike along the ridges of Mississippi Palisades State Park.

Or go 12 miles northeast to Charles Mound, the highest elevation in Illinois (1,235 feet), which boasts a panoramic view of three states (Illinois, Iowa, and Wisconsin).

How to get there: Take U.S. 20 west through Galena to Chetlain Lane and turn left. Go ¼ mile and you'll find the farmstead on the left.

B: *With its split-rail fence and stone path leading to the cabins, we feel like we're in a private, history-laden village that's all our own.*

Das Essenhaus Country Inn
Middlebury, Indiana
46540

Innkeepers: Bob and Sue Miller, owners; Wilbur and Rosalie Bontrager, managers
Address/Telephone: 240 U.S. 20; (219) 825–9447
Rooms: 32, including 5 suites; all with private bath, air conditioning, television. Wheelchair access.
Rates: $49 to $95, single; $60 to $95, double; includes continental breakfast Sunday only. Children under 12, free.
Open: All year.
Facilities and activities: Large enclosed porch, game room, kids' playground. Renowned restaurant, Das Dutchman Essenhaus (also owned by Millers), across the street. Villagelike setting, with specialty and country stores a short walk away. Located in heart of Indiana Amish country. Lots of Amish quilt-and-crafts shops throughout Crystal Valley. Also near Shipshewana, Amish town where numerous festivals are celebrated during year.

This inn resembles a huge Amish farmhouse—not surprising since it's located in the heart of Indiana's Amish country. My kids were fascinated by the clip-clopping of horses' hooves as they pulled black buggies down main highways. And three-year-old Kate couldn't understand why little girls wore long black dresses and prayer bonnets in the heat of the summer.

"Didn't their Mamas buy them any shorts?" Kate asked me.

If you like pure country styling, the inn will quickly become a favorite. Its handcrafted pine furnitue is made by Amish craftsmen in nearby Nappanee, another Amish settlement. And every available open space is graced with country crafts.

The main floor resembles a huge great room that's open to the rafters high above. High-back sofas, chairs, and rockers give it a homey feel. I especially like the silver-plated potbellied stove.

The second floor resembles an open country meadow, complete with a white picket fence around the balcony and a ☛ white clapboard, one-room country schoolhouse that is a hit with children. It's complete with desks, blackboards, books—the works.

Guest rooms are elegantly country, boasting pine four-poster beds; quilts and spreads are done by local artisans.

☛ As inn guests, you may make reservations at Das Dutchman Essenhaus, the popular Amish-style restaurant that normally seats on a first-come, first-served basis. Family-style fare means huge platters of heartland meats, potatoes, dressing, heaping bowls of vegetables, steaming loaves of bread, and desserts like old-fashioned apple dumplings.

Families should consider exploring the side roads of the surrounding Crystal Valley, where they'll find Amish quilt shops, bakeries, and craft stores. The inn also offers three-hour guided tours of Indiana's Amish heritage; you'll visit a cheese factory, buggy shop, furniture factory, hardware store, and the new Menno Hof Center in Shipshewana.

How to get there: From South Bend, take U.S. 20 east to the inn in Middlebury.

The Redstone Inn
Dubuque, Iowa
52001

Innkeeper: Debbie Griesinger
Address/Telephone: 504 Bluff Street; (319) 582–1894
Rooms: 15, with 5 suites; all with private bath and air conditioning.
Rates: Single, $55 to $130; double, $68 to $160. Continental breakfast with junior and deluxe suites. Children free.
Open: All year.
Facilities and activities: Afternoon teas, luncheons and dinners for guests and other visitors. Nearby: downhill skiing, Mississippi riverboat cruises, riverboat museum, Cable Car Square (specialty shops in a historic location), cable-car rides.

Dubuque may be located in the middle of America's corn belt, but it's also a bustling Mississippi River town that celebrates its long-ago history as a port of call for riverboat stern-wheelers. And it boasts a surprisingly wide variety of additional attractions that should fascinate kids and parents alike.

The ☛ paddle wheeler *Spirit of Dubuque* plies the Mississippi, resembling a vision out of Mark Twain's riverboat tales; day and evening cruises are offered.

Landlubbers can walk the decks of the side-wheeler *William M. Black* and immerse themselves in the exhibits of the F. W. Woodward Riverboat Musuem.

Dubuque, Iowa

At Cable Car Square, watch the eyes of little ones grow big as quarters when their cable car climbs up the side of a 189-foot bluff; the reward is a spectacular vista of three states—Iowa, Illinois, and Wisconsin.

There are also a Civil War shot tower; Eagle Point Park; Mathias Ham Museum, with its historic twenty-three-room limestone mansion open for touring; and ☛ Crystal Lake Cave (5 miles south of the city), a 3,000-foot-long underground trek boasting glittering rock formations.

Another link to Dubuque's past is The Redstone Inn, an 1894 Victorian mansion restored to its original splendor.

Children like to page through the color-photo portfolio that holds pictures of all guest rooms; no two are alike, so select your favorite.

During my last visit, I stayed in a third-floor room (no elevators, but about forty steps) furnished in the inn's opulent Victorian style—antiques and reproductions, balloon curtains, period lighting fixtures, and more. It also had a whirlpool (great for touring-tired Moms and Dads) and a fireplace with free logs.

Junior and deluxe suites rate breakfast in the downstairs formal dining room; count on homemade caramel rolls, croissants, and bagels. Parents should enjoy afternoon teas that might feature dainty finger sandwiches, English truffles, and gingerbread cherry pie, an inn specialty.

For dinner, the Ryan House, an 1873 Italian-style villa, often visited by Ulysses S. Grant, offers some of the town's best food; consider beef Wellington, shrimp Creole, and *Coq au Vin Rouge*, just some of its specialties.

How to get there: Whether entering Dubuque from the west via U.S. 151 or east on U.S. 20, pick up Locust Street at the bridge and proceed to University. Turn left and drive to Bluff, then turn left again. The inn is on the street's left side.

❀

B: *Victorian elegance, rivertown style.*

Watervale Inn
Arcadia, Michigan
49613

Innkeeper: Dori Noble Turner

Address/Telephone: Watervale Road; (616) 352–9083; winter mailing address: 20265 Cottagewood Road, Excelsior, MN 55331; (612) 474–8558

Rooms: 20, all with shared bath; 12 cottages, all with private bath.

Rates: Rooms, $50, adults; $25, age 9 and under, with 2-day minimum, MAP. Small cottage, $500 per week. Other weekly rates available. No credit cards.

Open: May through October.

Facilities and activities: Tennis courts. Located on lake; rowboats, canoes, sailboats, and sailboards available. Nearby: woods and high sand dunes; short drive to Sleeping Bear Dunes National Lakeshore.

The Watervale Inn is ☛ one of Michigan's best-kept secrets. The main lodge (a historic boarding house for lumberjacks) and its outlying cottages (homes for loggers with families) make up the entire historic 1880s logging town of Watervale, which hugs Lake Lower Herring and Lake Michigan among spectacular shorelines of high bluffs and sand dunes.

It's now a haven for families who truly want to get away from it all, a ☛ secluded lakeside paradise that has the feel of a private retreat.

Arcadia, Michigan

First a little history: When the local lumber company went bankrupt in 1893, the town was abandoned. Dori's Uncle Oscar later bought the town and began restoration work.

Today the handsome, pale-green clapboard boardinghouse, with its long veranda hoarding cool lake breezes, is a special place. Guest rooms are cozy and quaint, recalling its boardinghouse heydey with iron-rail beds, chenille spreads, and comfy chairs.

Many of the historic cottages, rented by couples and families, boast fireplaces, too.

Hearty pancake breakfasts and scrumptious dinners are served in the old boardinghouse dining room. I doubt that lumberjacks feasted on such meals as duck à l'orange or chateaubriand.

Families have many spots to explore nearby. You can still see some pier posts peeking out from under the waves at one end of the inn; that's where schooners once loaded cut timbers off a long wharf built into the lake.

Mount Baldy is at the end of the road. The dune is a tough climb, but the reward is a breathtaking view of rugged Lake Michigan shoreline not often viewed by the casual visitor.

And ☛ Sleeping Bear Dunes National Lakeshore is a short drive north on Michigan 22; it boasts one of the Midwest's most incredible shorelines, with wind-sculpted dunes hundreds of feet high. Kids love to roll down these massive hills of sand.

How to get there: From Detroit, take I–75 north to U.S. 10 and go west. At Scottville, take U.S. 31 north to Michigan 22 and continue north to the Total gas station/general store. You've gone too far! Turn around and count six telephone poles to Watervale Road. Turn right and then turn right again at the tennis courts to the inn.

Grand Hotel
Mackinac Island, Michigan
49757

Innkeeper: R. D. Musser, manager
Address/Telephone: Mackinac Island; (906) 847–3331
Rooms: 275; all with private bath, some with air conditioning.
Rates: $115 to $200 per person, MAP. Children, $15 to $60.
Open: Mid-May to early November.
Facilities and activities: Main dining room, Geranium Bar, Grand Stand (food and drink), Audubon Bar, Carleton's Tea Store, pool grill. Baby-sitter service available. Swimming pool, private golf course, bike rentals, saddle horses, tennis courts, exercise trail. Carriage tours, dancing, movies. Nearby: museums, historic fort, and other sites, guided tours; specialty shops. There are no motor vehicles allowed on historic Mackinac Island; visitors walk or rent horses, horse-drawn carriages and taxis, and bicycles.

It would be difficult for a child to become bored at the Grand Hotel. This historic and elegant haven, on timeless Mackinac Island, offers a magnificent swimming pool, movies, bike rentals, horseback riding, tennis courts, a golf course, exercise trail, horse-drawn carriage tours. . . . You get the idea.

Built in 1887, the Grand Hotel has been called one of the last remaining great hotels of the railroad and Great Lakes–steamer era. Its location high on an island bluff provides magnificent vistas over the Straits of Mackinac waters.

Its incredible, many-columned veranda measures 880 feet long (claiming to be the longest in the world). Many adult guests simply sit here in a rocker to capture cool lake breezes, sip on a cocktail, and admire the hotel's endless acres of finely manicured lawns and flower gardens.

Inside, services are legion and include complimentary morning coffee, concerts during afternoon tea, dinner dances, and more. ☛ It seems the pampering never stops.

Guest rooms are subtly elegant, and several have terrific lake views. Breakfast and dinner, included in the room rate, offer superb dining. Kids will love a special dessert treat—the Grand pecan ball with hot fudge sauce.

☛ No motor vehicles are allowed on the island, so touring is done by foot power, horsepower, or bike power. A "can't miss" attraction is historic Fort Mackinac, a restored eighteenth- and nineteenth-century British and American military outpost with fourteen original buildings. Interpretive guides wear period costumes, and visitors are treated to daily rifle and cannon firings, a Redcoat muster, craft demonstrations, and dramatic reenactments of historic island events.

How to get there: From either Mackinaw City from the Lower Peninsula or from St. Ignace on the Upper Peninsula, a 30-minute ferry ride brings you to Mackinac Island. Dock porters will greet your boat. There's an island airstrip for chartered flights and private planes.

❈

B: Simply one of the "Grand"-est inns imaginable.

Old Harbor Inn
South Haven, Michigan
49090

Innkeeper: Shirley Tubner, supervisor
Address/Telephone: 515 Williams Street; (616) 637–8480
Rooms: 12, with 3 suites; all with private bath, air conditioning, television, and 8 with kitchenette.
Rates: Rooms: $40 to $100, single; $50 to $110, double; suites: $120 to $160; MAP. Children up to 13, free.
Open: All year.
Facilities and activities: Located on Black River, near Lake Michigan. Nearby: restaurants, boating and water sports, North Beach.

South Haven is a ☛ Lake Michigan village boasting an atmosphere that closely resembles a California beach town.

If you don't believe me, just go to North Beach during the height of the summer season. (The kids will instinctively head here anyway.) It literally teems with outrageous bikinis, loud surfer shorts, volleyball games, Frisbee players, and tiny sandcastle builders.

Consider making the Old Harbor Inn your headquarters during your South Haven stay. The inn sits on the banks of the Black River in a re-created New England fishing village. It's fun to stroll along cobblestoned walkways, on boardwalks that skirt the water, and through colorful "beach" shops with names like Bahama Mama's and Flying Colors.

The inn also overlooks village docks where charter fishing boats offer Coho challenges on Lake Michigan; or your family can take up more sedate pursuits, like leisurely sailboat cruises.

Guest rooms are spacious and contemporary. All the rooms face the village or the water. My favorite is Number 6, with a massive indoor hot tub from which you can also soak up river views through a long bank of windows that span two walls. It also boasts a mini-kitchen, which is very handy for the capricious appetites of little ones.

And the ceramic-tile fireplace is a virtual requisite for nightly ghost tales just before bedtime.

Kids love to dine on the *Idler*, an authentic Mississippi riverboat that offers fine cuisine. It is a special treat that may be too expensive for a large family. I also suggest Clementine's, a Phoenix Street favorite that serves some of the best burgers (and sandwiches) in town.

How to get there: Exit I–196 at Phoenix Street. Continue for 3 stoplights, then turn right to the inn.

Historic
Taylors Falls Jail
Taylors Falls, Minnesota
55084

Innkeeper: Helen White
Address/Telephone: 102 Government Road; (612) 465-3112
Rooms: 1 guest house for up to 4 people, with private bath and kitchen.
Rates: $60 per person, double occupancy; EPB (ingredients). Children, $5.
   Optional third night at no extra charge. No credit cards.
Open: All year.
Facilities and activities: Part of the Angels Hill Historic District overlooking the St. Croix River. Nearby: St. Croix National Scenic Riverway, the falls, canoeing, fishing, other sports.

After a long ride with a car full of children, you might be tempted to put the little ones behind bars. But with a jail so charming as the Historic Taylors Falls Jail, why not consider throwing the entire family in the slammer?

The old jail, located high on historic Angels Hill, overlooks the rushing St. Croix River. ☛ Children are fascinated the minute they step up to the front door; that's because the jail's original, full-size iron grate still swings over the entryway. No doubt it prevented plenty of escapes in the past.

Taylors Falls, Minnesota

After walking inside the historic building, you may never want to leave.

There are pine floors throughout, with a potbellied Montana Queen wood-burning stove in a spacious living room, complete with a richly colored Navajo rug.

A sleeping loft is reached by an attractive staircase; its bed is graced with hand-quilted bed coverings. A sofa bed downstairs accommodates more overnighters.

Breakfast food is provided for guests. Just mosey to the jail's kitchen, and help yourself to a variety of foods, including 🖙 locally produced cheeses, farm-fresh eggs, and maple syrup especially bottled for the jail. A grocery store is nearby, so you can stock up on lunch and dinner foods if you don't want to eat out. If you want time off from cooking, ask Helen for suggestions of area restaurants.

A drive through the Angels Hill Historic Distric, a cluster of well-maintained and restored nineteenth-century buildings, is a good way to start your touring day. But most families will want to head for the St. Croix National Scenic Riverway just across the river in St. Croix, Wisconsin. The displays at its Visitor and Interpretive Center are a fascinating way to get oriented to area geography, and the falls are exciting for everyone.

And there are plenty of canoeing and fishing opportunities all along the river.

How to get there: Take Minnesota 95 to Taylors Falls. At Angels Hill, go west 1 block to Government Road and the jail.

☼

B: *What kind of criminals were jailed here? Here's a local newspaper report from June 30, 1876: "Archy Cummings of Dodge County came down on one of the drives, and after getting a little full, concluded he weighed about four tons, and very loudly proclaimed the fact that he could whip anybody in town. Marshal Peter Trump took the young man to the calaboose. Next morning he paid $10 and costs, $14 in all, for his drunk."*

The Anderson House
Wabasha, Minnesota
55981

Innkeepers: John, Jeanne, and Gayla Hall

Address/Telephone: 333 North Main Street; (612) 565–4524, (800) 862–9702 in Minnesota, (800) 325–2270 outside Minnesota

Rooms: 54, including 2 suites; 37 with private bath, some with television, all with air conditioning. Wheelchair access. Pets OK in certain rooms.

Rates: $39 to $49, shared bath; $49 to $73, private bath; $81 to $95, suites; EP. Children, $5. Midweek traveler's special and numerous packages.

Open: All year except Christmas Day.

Facilities and activities: Breakfast, lunch, dinner, ice-cream parlor. Can arrange for baby-sitters. In winter, ice fishing, skating, boating. About 30 miles from 3 ski resorts. Right across the street from Mississippi River and fishing, boating. Also area antique shops.

It seems as if all little kids love pussycats. They like to pet them, cuddle them, talk to them, get licked by them.

Now they can do all that and go on vacation, too.

That's because The Anderson House actually ☛ "rents" pussycats to overnight guests. In fact, fifteen cats are on daily call and will be more than happy to purr your family to sleep and make them feel at home. Once you've come and met a favorite cat, you can call ahead to reserve it for your next visit.

The Anderson House is the oldest operating hotel in Minnesota, dating to 1856. The rambling red-brick inn, which takes up a block of the town's Main Street, traces its roots back to Pennsylvania Dutch country. In fact, Grandma Ida Anderson, who ran the hotel at the turn of the century, earned her reputation for scrumptious meals conjured up in the hotel's kitchen.

The tradition continues under great-grandson John, whose stewardship marks the fourth generation of family ownership.

Not only is the hospitality hard to beat, but so is the cooking. Get ready for cheese soup, chicken with Dutch dumplings, bacon-corn chowder, *kugelhopf, limpa,* pork tenderloin cooked in sauerkraut, Dutch beer—and if you're lucky, fresh shoofly pie for dessert.

Guest rooms are delightful, with antique beds and handmade quilts and bedspreads; some afford glimpses of the Mississippi River, just across the street.

The surrounding bluff-country landscape is spectacular, especially farther north as you near Lake City and Red Wing.

And just an hour's drive west is Northfield, where you can tour the bank robbed by Jesse James and his gang—a botched attempt that signaled the beginning of the end for the notorious outlaw. Northfield's colorful Jesse James Days, held in September, is a fun-filled festival that reenacts Jesse's no-good deed and shouldn't be missed.

How to get there: U.S. 61 and Minnesota 60 go right through town. The inn is located right on North Main Street.

Wilderness Lodge
Lesterville, Missouri 63654

Innkeeper: Stephen Apted
Address/Telephone: Box 90; (314) 637-2295, toll free from St. Louis 296-2011
Rooms: 40 rooms and riverside suites, 4 cottages; all with private bath and air conditioning.
Rates: Rooms and cottages, $54; riverside suites, $67; per person, MAP. Children under 5, free; ages 5 to 12, $41 to $53. Two-night minimum required. Special package rates.
Open: May 1 through November 30.
Facilities and activities: Dining room, bar. Archery, shuffleboard, volleyball, horseshoes, Frisbee-golf course, walking trails, tennis courts, platform tennis, children's playground, swimming pool, hot tub (cold weather only), hayrides, canoeing, tube floats. Horseback riding nearby.

It's always exciting to drive into the Ozark foothills, especially when our three-year-old, Kate, entertains us with tales of her favorite Disney character, Goofy, exploring the woods à la Davy Crockett.

With that in mind, the Wilderness Lodge is a perfect "frontier" getaway. Located on 1,200 rolling acres near the bank of the crystal-clear Black River, the lodge offers some of the best country-style fun imaginable.

Lesterville, Missouri

A group of young canoers were excitedly telling their parents about their afternoon's adventures as we entered the Main Lodge. It's the oldest building on the property, a heavy log-and-timber construction with tan pitch that ☛ made me feel like a pioneer in the wilds.

Outside, kids can frolic in a swimming pool that offers panoramic views of lodge surroundings. Inside, a game room promises all kinds of family fun, while a crackling fireplace warms chilled evenings.

The lodge's rough-hewn country-style furniture is just what you'd expect. Especially interesting are ☛ American Indian–style rugs displayed on the walls, animal trophies, and the obligatory rifle hanging above a manteled hearth.

I've rarely seen guest cabins so complement the beautiful Ozark countryside. Especially attractive is the use of ☛ native rock, peeled logs, pine siding, and porches built right into the landscape. Country-antique furniture and Indian artifacts add to the woodsy ambience; many rooms feature large fireplaces and high loft ceilings.

Family-style breakfasts and dinners are lodge specialties. Morning menus include eggs, pancakes, and beverages; dinner platters are heaped high with good country cooking like fried chicken, fresh bread, and sweet pastries.

No doubt the kids will do some "adventure" planning at the dinner table. Let's see, there are tube floats down the river, horseback riding, hayrides, canoeing . . .

How to get there: From St. Louis, take I–270 south to Route 21 and continue south to Glover. Then head west on Route 21/49/72. Near Arcadia, take Route 21 south, then west for about 22 miles to Peola Road. Turn left and continue down the dirt and gravel path, following the signs to the lodge.

Roscoe Village Inn
Coshocton, Ohio
43812

Innkeeper: Carol Wills
Address/Telephone: 200 North Whitewoman Street; (614) 622–2222
Rooms: 50; all with private bath, air conditioning, television. Wheelchair access.
Rates: $66 to $71, EP. Children, $6. Several seasonal weekend packages.
Open: All year.
Facilities and activities: Roscoe Village canal-era town. Amish country nearby. Pro-football Hall of Fame in Canton. Scenic countryside of Ohio River Valley.

Kids' jaws literally drop when they first enter Roscoe Village. The ☛ historic mid-1800s canal-era town, with its narrow street crowded with general stores, blacksmith shop, and costumed guides, transports them back through time.

Horse-drawn wagons move up and down the road, offering tours of the historic village.

And children love to walk the historic Ohio & Erie towpath north from the village to where the *Monticello II*, a reconstructed canal boat, takes on passengers and floats them down to Mudport Basin.

Amid the hubbub of this interesting little village sits the

Roscoe Village Inn, a brick structure that elaborates on the era's gentility and hospitality. Exposed wood timbers, wrought-iron chandeliers, a huge hearth, and wonderful Ohio folk art and crafts reflect the village's canal-era heritage.

Rooms are handsome, with elegant wood furniture hand-crafted by Amish craftspeople in nearby Holmes County. Count on four-poster beds, high-back chairs, and more.

Meals are country tasty. Consider a breakfast of whole wheat griddle cakes; hazelnut, whole wheat waffles; farm-fresh eggs, honey, and sweet butter, along with homemade rolls.

For a glimpse into another bygone era that survives in the twentieth century, head into Holmes County for Amish sights and sounds; it boasts the largest Amish population in the United States.

Always a winner for sports-minded youngsters and adults: the ☞ professional football Hall of Fame in Canton, just a short drive away.

How to get there: From Cleveland to the north, take I–77 south to exit 65. Follow Route 36/16 west into Coshocton. Turn west on Ohio 541, then north on Whitewoman Street to the inn. From Columbus and Indianapolis to the southwest, take I–70 and exit north on Route 60. Then turn east on Route 16 and follow into Coshocton. Next follow directions listed above.

∽≈∾

B: *Don't miss all the antique and specialty stores along Whitewoman Street, which gets its name from the Walhonding River—* walhonding *is the Delaware Indian word for "white woman."*

Siebken's
Elkhart Lake, Wisconsin 53020

Innkeepers: Doug and Pam Siebken
Address/Telephone: 284 South Lake Street; (414) 876–2600
Rooms: 53 rooms, 33 with private bath; 1 lake cottage. Pets OK.
Rates: $52 to $58, weekdays; $62 to $68, weekends; EP. Children free. May and September, deduct $10 from room rates. Two- to four-night minimum during Road America race weekends.
Open: May through September.
Facilities and activities: Breakfast, lunch, dinner. Opera House bar, antique store and gift shop, TV/game room. Water sports, boat rentals, golf course within walking distance; horseback riding, antiquing, go-carting. Road America race track nearby.

Siebken's resembles a favorite uncle's rambling country cottage that children love to visit. That's not surprising, since the turn-of-the-century summer lodge, run by Doug's family since 1916, sits just across the road from Elkhart Lake, is filled with comfy country furniture, is populated by friendly four-legged critters, and serves great family-style meals.

Don't be surprised if your welcome to Siebken's comes with a wet nose. That's because Chelsea, the inn's old English sheepdog, Nigel (an Irish wolfhound), and Farley (a Belgian sheepdog) often usurp the role of official greeters.

They may be big lugs, but they're lovable big lugs.

Guest rooms are comfortable and airy, though some are cozy and small. All are eclectically styled, mostly with country furnishings. Ceiling fans are a nice touch, and hallway radiators provide heat on chilly Wisconsin nights.

Homestyle food is a hallmark of Siebken's. Count on ☛ platter-sized portions of almost everything. I think the roast duck is delicious.

Elkhart Lake is one of the state's oldest summer resort havens. Swimming, boat rentals, and a golf course are within walking distance; kids love horseback riding nearby; you might even try your luck at the local go-cart course.

☛ Road America, an internationally renowned race track famous for its Indy-style and stock-car racing, is a short ride away. The summer racing season fills Elkhart Lake with excitement, and you should try to attend at least one race afternoon for an unforgettable experience. Even if you miss out, you'll sometimes hear the roar of engines revving up the straightaway from Siebken's itself.

And at night, several well-known race car drivers inevitably come to the inn's old Opera House bar to relax and spin stories.

How to get there: Siebken's is about 60 miles north of Milwaukee. Take I–43 to Wisconsin Highway 57 (Plymouth exit). Continue north past Plymouth; then turn left on County Trunk J and right on 67 to Elkhart Lake.

The American Club
Kohler, Wisconsin
53044

Innkeeper: Susan Porter Green
Address/Telephone: Highland Drive; (414) 457–8000, (800) 472–8414 in Wisconsin, (800) 458–2562 in northern and central Illinois, Iowa, Michigan, and Minnesota
Rooms: 160 rooms and suites; all with private bath, air conditioning, television. Wheelchair access.
Rates: $81 to $207, single; $98 to $237, double; EP. Children 10 and under, free; over 10, $12. Two-night minimum on weekends from Memorial Day through Labor Day weekend, and December 30–31.
Open: All year.
Facilities and activities: Six restaurants and dining rooms. Baby-sitter service available. Ballroom. Sports Core health club. River Wildlife, 800 acres of private woods for hiking, horseback riding, hunting, fishing, trap shooting, canoeing. Cross-country skiing and ice skating. Golf course. Nearby: antiquing, lake charter fishing, Kettle Moraine State Forest, Road America (auto racing).

The American Club is such a regal destination that many people tend to think of it only as an exclusive couples getaway. How wrong they are.

Kids love The American Club, still one of Wisconsin's best-kept secrets. It offeres a plethora of things to see and do—from

Kohler, Wisconsin

horseback riding, hiking, and fishing in its private, 800-acre tract of woods (called River Wildlife) to swimming, indoor tennis, and more at the Sports Core, a massive, world-class activity emporium.

There's plenty for Mamas and Papas, too. Especially if they're golfers. The club's 27-hole course, the Pete Dye–designed Blackwolf Run, was named ☞ one of the country's best new golf courses of 1988. I can attest to that; I could only manage a 93 for my eighteen holes.

The inn itself possesses an uncommonly European ambience, with its custom-crafted oak furniture, crystal chandeliers, and shiny brass. In fact, it looks more like a baronial estate than a hostelry.

Built in 1918 as a temporary home for immigrant workers of the Kohler Company (the famous plumbing manufacturer, still located across the street), the "boardinghouse" served as a meeting place where English and citizenship classes were taught—a genuine "American Club."

Today, luxurious guest rooms are a big part of the fun. In both the main building and the new Carriage House, guest rooms boast handsome oak paneling, handmade European comforters, skylights, and more. There are even four fluffy pillows on each bed.

Bathrooms are big attractions here, since they ☞ showcase Kohler products. All contain comforting whirlpools; a few even have four-poster brass canopies over huge marble-lined whirlpool baths.

The ultimate is the saunalike environmental chamber in special suites that offers a pushbutton choice of weather—from bright sun and gentle breezes to misty rain showers.

Gourmet food, offered at The Immigrant, is outstanding; and the pub room is great for family sandwich lunches.

If you ever want to leave the club grounds during your stay (you probably won't), Road America (world-class Indy-style auto racing) is just a short drive away.

How to get there: From Chicago, take I-94 north and continue north on I-43, just outside of Milwaukee. Exit on Wisconsin 23 west (exit 53B). Take 23 to County Trunk Y and continue south into Kohler. The inn is on the right.

From the west, take I-94 south to Wisconsin 21 and go east to U.S. 41. Go south on 41 to Wisconsin 23; then head east into Kohler.

Woods Manor
LaPointe, Wisconsin 54850

Innkeepers: Gail and Woody Petersen
Address/Telephone: P.O. Box 7; (715) 747–3102
Rooms: 6; all with private bath. Pets OK.
Rates: May 26 to October 7, $82 to $94, per room; rest of May and October, $65 to $71, per room; continental breakfast buffet. Children 6 and under, free; over 6, $15.
Open: May through October.
Facilities and activities: Restaurants nearby. Swimming pool, whirlpool, sauna, clay-surface tennis court, private beach. Located on Madeline Island; Robert Trent Jones–designed golf course on island; biking, hiking, cross-country skiing; swimming, boating, sailing, fishing, windsurfing. Baby-sitting can be arranged.

Talk about a kids' kind of place. On my last visit here, the inn's swimming pool, with a great view of Lake Superior, was in overdrive as youngsters beat the heat.

"It's really the only place (on the island) you can swim for any length of time, since Lake Superior is usually so frigid," Gail said.

Woods Manor seems to have been built for the perpetual motion of children, done in an expansive Mediterranean style that's open and airy. Built in 1924 by Woody's great-grandfather as a summer house to "escape those dog days of Nebraska summers," it rests on magnificent shoreline property of Madeline Island, largest of the Apostle Island National Lakeshore.

Guest rooms are quaint, almost spartan in their furnishings; one boasts a big brass bed, another the inn's only private porch. But then, ☞ it's the location that transforms Woods Manor into something out of the ordinary—and its swimming pool, sauna, whirlpool, and clay tennis courts. Its huge grounds transform the surrounding property into a private lakeside park for guests.

There are plenty of island activities away from Woods Manor, too. Madeline Island, an old trapping station for seventeenth-century traders, has its own fur trading post/museum. ☞ Great biking on little-used roads takes you around the island perimeter or into the interior's deep woods.

You can charter a sailboat or take a cruise. And Bayfield, a historic fishing village on the mainland (where you catch the ferry to Madeline), has its own attractions and charms. Kids should love a tour of the historic cooper shop; parents can browse specialty stores; gourmet meals are the province of the renowned Old Rittenhouse Inn; and Gruenke's Inn, a historic eatery right on the waterfront, is a great place to take the family for home-cooked meals.

How to get there: Take the ferry from Bayfield to the island. Off the ferry, turn left on the first island road you come to, then right on County H, then left on the first road you see. That will take you to the inn.

Silver Springs Inn and Resort
Mitchell, Wisconsin
53073

Innkeepers: Larry and Kathy Gentine
Address/Telephone: Silver Springs Lane (mailing address: P.O. Box 562, Plymouth 53073); (414) 893-0969
Rooms: 4 cedar chalets, sleeping maximum of 6 people or 3 couples each; all with 2 private baths, air conditioning, television.
Rates: For one couple: $99, one night; $189, two nights; $279, three nights. For two couples: $198, one night; $359, two nights; $529, three nights. Children under 14, $25 per night. EP. May through October, two-night minimum on weekends. Includes free gear and trout fishing in private trout ponds, streams.
Open: All year.
Facilities and activites: Breakfast, lunch, dinner. Baby-sitters can be arranged with advance notice. Private trout hatchery, 38 trout ponds and streams, hiking, and snowmobile trail edging property. Adjacent to 45,000-acre state forest. Nearby: downhill and cross-country skiing.

On my last visit to Silver Springs Inn, my Pa hooked a three-pound trout while fly fishing at one of the inn's thirty-eight private trout pounds.

Mitchell, Wisconsin

My daughter Kate, then twenty-two months old, held the fish proudly for a few snapshots and talked incessantly for the rest of the evening about "Grandpa's big fishy that goes wiggle, wiggle, wiggle."

Those are the kinds of treasured memories that make Silver Springs Inn so special.

It is 184 acres of tall red and white pines, trout streams, and artesian-fed ponds, nestled in a bowl-shaped valley surrounded by Ice Age hills and swells of breathtaking Kettle Moraine State Forest. The surroundings create powerful impressions. "The scenery is as pretty as anything we just saw out in Colorado," said one guest from Milwaukee.

"There is a magic here people don't soon forget," says Larry Gentine.

That's for sure. ☞ Where else can a child get "private" fly-fishing lessons from the inn's own fish biologist, no less, and choose his own, well-stocked fishing hole to try his luck?

Attractive and roomy guest chalets have decks with floor-to-ceiling windows overlooking the woods and trout ponds, a wood-burning fireplace in the great room, extra-long beds adorned with handmade quilts, and two baths; there's also a sleeper sofa in the living room. ☞ Plenty of space for parents, kids, grandma, and grandpa.

Dinner specials include the best rainbow trout I've ever tasted. That's a good time to talk about the inn's fanciful history, which includes its site as an 1830 Black Hawk Indian War battlefield and as a private fishing club frequented by old Milwaukee Braves' stars Warren Spahn and Joe Adcock.

More kid fun: It's just a short drive to Elkhart Lake swimming; Lake Michigan is less than 20 miles east; and Manitowoc's Maritime Museum, a splendid collection of Great Lakes sea lore, is 30 miles north.

How to get there: From Chicago, take I-94 into Wisconsin. In Milwaukee, continue north on I-43 to I-57 (Plymouth exit). Go north to Wisconsin 23, turn west, then south on County S to the inn.

❋

B: During the winter, take the family cross-country skiing at Greenbush, one of the state's top Nordic spots.

Bonnie Oaks Estate
Portage, Wisconsin
53901

Innkeeper: William L. Schultz
Address/Telephone: 3rd Avenue, RR #3, Box 147; (608) 981–2057
Rooms: Two historic houses; each with private bath and kitchen.
Rates: $60 single or double; EP. Children, $10.
Open: April through October.
Facilities and activities: Huge private estate with rambling grounds; hike the woods, bicycle, fish, picnic, bird watch, float the Neenah Creek, relax. Restaurants about 15 minutes away. Wisconsin Dells 10 minutes away.

Bill rigged an inner-tube tree swing on a tree next to meandering Neenah Creek so a young visitor could sway across the channel and plop into its refreshing waters. The boy swung like Tarzan, emitted the obligatory king-of-the-jungle cry, then gently dropped into the creek with a splash.

It was a scene right out of *Tom Sawyer*.

But here I was at Bonnie Oaks Estate, a secluded, eighty-acre country spread that serves up heaping helpings of country-spun hospitality.

Kids love the turn-of-the-century estate. ☛ They can hike its grounds; visit three Indian effigy mounds; float the Neenah by inner tube or boat; spy on sandhill cranes that populate low-lying fields; or bike on little-used country roads.

Mamas and Papas love Bonnie Oaks, too. The 1872 log house, decorated in antique and country stylings, offers simple but gracious living. The Carpenter's House, once the estate's chicken coop, now is also a comfortable, woodsy getaway. Both have kitchens, so you can cook you own meals. And the Tower House (the old windmill water tower) may soon boast its own guest rooms. Already the third-story tower, reached by an outside spiral staircase that carries you to the treetops, is open to all visitors for study and meditation.

Bonnie Oaks has quite a history. Famed pianist Josef Lhevinne summered here for twenty years; each year he had his grand piano hauled by rail and wagon from his New York City apartment to the first-floor room in the Tower House.

Then his students arrived: Van Cliburn, James Levine, Jan Chiapusso. Even Paul Robeson was a frequent visitor. Imagine his glorious baritone reverberating through the serene countryside.

Don't worry if kids want a change of pace. ☛ Wisconsin Dells, one of the Midwest's premier children's summer-vacation meccas, is only a ten-minute drive away. Its attractions include Indian powwows, water slides, miniature golf, Storybook Gardens, the amphibious "Ducks" tour, and the Tommy Bartlett Water Show.

How to get there: Portage is about 27 miles north of Madison. Take I–90-94 to the Portage exit, Wisconsin 78, and go north to the Wisconsin 127 Dells turnoff. Take 127 to AA in Briggsville, then County X; continue 2 miles, then turn left on 3rd Avenue to the estate.

❋

B: *Like Bill says, Bonnie Oaks is very special. You'll know the moment you arrive.*

Bay Shore Inn
Sturgeon Bay, Wisconsin 54235

Innkeepers: John "Duke" Hanson and Paul Mathias
Address/Telephone: 4205 North Bay Shore Drive; (414) 743–4551
Rooms: 35, located in main lodge, beach and ranch terraces, A-frame chalets, and cottage; all with private bath and television, some with air conditioning. Some rooms can accommodate wheelchair guests, but the inn has no special wheelchair facilities.
Rates: Main lodge weekdays, $49 to $75; weekends, $59 to $95; A-frames, $75 to $95; EP. (Rates change three times during season.) Two-night minimum on weekends. Inquire about AP packages.
Open: May 1 through October 16.
Facilities and activities: Breakfast, lunch, dinner. Children's beach on Green Bay, playground, tennis court, basketball, croquet, horseshoes, bikes, fishing, rowboats, mini-fish sailboats and instruction, canoes, pontoons, and rides on a 22-foot sloop. Nature trails on 20 acres. State parks and maritime museum nearby.

The Bayshore Inn is located at the gateway to beautiful Door County peninsula, amid tall trees, bays, bluffs, and dunes dubbed the "Cape Cod of the Midwest." The inn stands on the shore of massive Green Bay and has a terrific warm-water (for the Midwest) beach, with plenty of shallows so little ones can wander in without unduly worrying their parents.

An expansive playground includes swing sets and tennis and basketball courts—even horseshoes, now apparently a presidential sport. Children can wind through miles of nature trails. And the inn's restaurant serves home-cooked family-style meals that should please even the most finicky eaters.

Since my wife and I often travel and vacation with our two small daughters, we have learned just how important it is to keep the kids happy and occupied. (All parents wish to avoid a remake of "The Lost Weekend"—or worse). The Bay Shore scores big points on both counts.

The rustic main lodge was built in 1921 and has a massive stone fireplace that stretches to the ceiling. But ideally, families will want to rent A-frame chalets or beachfront rooms with easier access to fun activities. Try to make A-frame reservations at least one year in advance to have a realistic chance of securing your first-choice vacation dates.

Innkeeper Paul is proud of the inn's menu. Consider crepelike Swedish pancakes smothered in gooey lingonberries for breakfast, along with homemade breads, jellies, and cinnamon-swirl loaf. Renowned butter-fried chicken, made from cherished Swedish and Norwegian family recipes, is scrumptious dinner fare. And kids love watching the ☛ Door County fish boil, where whitefish, potatoes, and vegetables are boiled in a huge cauldron over a big fire.

How to get there: In Sturgeon Bay, take the Route 42/57 bypass to Gordon Road. Turn west and continue to Bay Shore Drive (3rd Avenue). Then turn north until you reach the inn, located on the shoreline.

B: Simply one of the Midwest's finest family-style inns.

Wolf River Lodge
White Lake, Wisconsin 54491

Innkeeper: James Peters, manager
Address/Telephone: White Lake; (715) 882–2182 or 882–3982
Rooms: 9, with 1 suite; 1 room with private bath.
Rates: $70, weekdays; $80, weekends; per person, double occupancy, MAP. Most reservations are made through weeklong or weekend package rates: winter ski season (Christmas season to mid-March), $130 per person/3 days, 2 nights; spring, summer, fall, $125/3 days, 2 nights; packages include 3 meals Saturday, 2 meals Sunday. Children, $10 per day; $100 for 3-day, 2-night weekend.
Open: Mid-April to October 1; Christmas to March 1.
Facilities and activities: Breakfast, lunch, dinner. Bar, wine cellar, parlor and game rooms, outdoor hot tub. Located on Wolf River, with world-class white-water rapids during high-water periods. River is always runnable, April through October. Trout fishing May and June, cross-country skiing.

What could be a better family way to spend a hot summer day than floating down a cool wilderness river in an inner tube?

That's precisely why hundreds of families come to Wolf River Lodge. A rustic getaway located deep in Nicolet National Forest country of northern Wisconsin, it's perfect for families who want to laze on crystal-clear water among spectacular deep-woods scenery.

Wolf River Lodge also boasts a reputation as ☞ one of the Midwest's premier white-water rapids centers. In fact, during high-water periods of early spring, the Wolf River is a world-class white-water run, with frothing white-water tumbling over boulders and ledges, dropping 12 feet per mile for 25 miles.

The log lodge building, surrounded by tall trees, is hunting-lodge quaint, with exposed logs throughout, comfortable crazy-quilt-arrangement sitting rooms, game rooms, and the obligatory stone fireplace. Guest rooms are small but cozy, with pine furniture, brightly colored quilts, and braided rugs.

Solid "big woods" dining fare includes hearty breakfasts and evening meals of delectable trout, roast duck, or thick steaks.

In between guests are often too busy plying the river to think about lunch. Tubing, rafting, and excellent trout fishing (especially in May and June) are all part of the fun.

And after a long day on the water, kids and adults alike enjoy soaking in the ☞ lodge's outdoor hot tub.

How to get there: From Milwaukee, take I–43 north to Green Bay; then take U.S. 41/141 north to Wisconsin 64. Head west to White Lake. Turn north on Wisconsin 55 and then watch for the Wolf River Lodge signs that direct you there.

B: *Wolf River Lodge is an ideal Christmas or winter getaway for the entire family. Located in the heart of Wisconsin's big woods, it offers great cross-country skiing through a wilderness setting.*

ARIZONA, NEW MEXICO, AND TEXAS

by
Eleanor S. Morris

Eleanor S. Morris is no stranger to inns. In addition to writing *Recommended Country Inns—Arizona, New Mexico, and Texas*, Eleanor has stayed at country inns in such diverse places as Australia, Portugal, Canada, Mexico, and Japan. She says that a country inn is a place where you are never a stranger, no matter how far you are from home.

Eleanor traveled 12,000 miles through Arizona, New Mexico, and Texas to visit inns for the second edition of her inn guide. As she puts it, "This is big country, with an incredible diversity of terrain presenting a wide variety of ecological systems . . . from the mossy reaches of eastern Texas's Piney Woods to the arid deserts of southwestern Arizona." She recommends 149 unique and eclectic inns—prairie-style villas in western Texas, horizon-hugging adobe haciendas, sprawling Texas and New Mexico cattle ranches, historic hotels in ghost towns, Victorian cottages and mansions in the Piney Woods, and mountain-view lodges near ancient ruins.

Eleanor is a freelance travel writer living in Austin, Texas—a "refugee," she says, from the big cities of Houston and Dallas. She has published widely in national newspapers and magazines. When she's not traveling, she is at home in Austin with her husband, working on a novel.

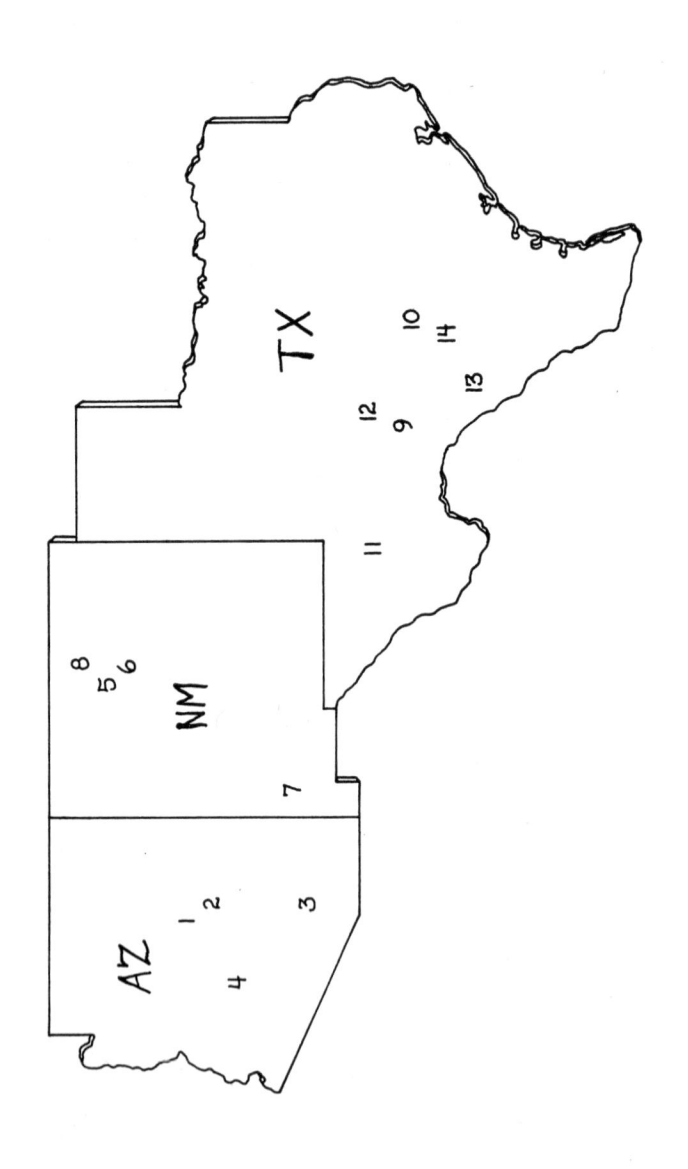

Arizona, New Mexico, and Texas

Numbers on map refer to towns numbered below.

ARIZONA
1. Mormon Lake, Mormon Lake Lodge 164
2. Payson, Kohl's Ranch Resort 166
3. Tucson, Tanque Verde Ranch 168
4. Wickenburg,
    Flying E Ranch 170
    Wickenburg Inn 172

NEW MEXICO
5. San Juan Pueblo, Chinguague Compound 174
6. Sante Fe, Rancho Encantado 176
7. Silver City, Bear Mountain Guest Ranch 178
8. Taos,
    Casa Europa 180
    El Monte Lodge 182

TEXAS
9. Bandera,
    Dixie Dude Ranch 184
    Mayan Dude Ranch 186
    Twin Elm Guest Ranch 188
10. Burton, Long Point Inn 190
11. Fort Davis, Indian Lodge 192
12. Fredericksburg, River View Farm 194
13. San Antonio, Bullis House Inn 196
14. San Marcos, Aquarena Springs Inn 198

Mormon Lake Lodge
Mormon Lake, Arizona
86038

Innkeeper: Betty Jo Davis
Address/Telephone: P.O. Box 12; (602) 774–0462 or 354–2227
Rooms: 7 cabins, including 2 two-bedroom cabins with kitchens. Pets welcome.
Rates: $35 to $75, EP.
Open: All year.
Facilities and activities: Restaurant, country store. Game room with video games and pool table, boating, fishing, horseback riding, stagecoach rides, hiking, cross-country skiing. Elevation 7,500 feet.

Although I found it charming, I almost decided to leave Mormon Lake Lodge out of this book when I was told that the water in the cabins gets turned off in the winter! (Because the pipes freeze.) But I was convinced to include the lodge when I discovered that such a lack of water was no deterrent to the enjoyment of Mormon Lake—the lodge is full, both winter and summer. I leave it up to you when to come.

The small settlement of Mormon Lake is a premium hunting ground for deer, elk, antelope, turkey, bear, and goose. When snow comes, there are ☛ 67 miles of groomed cross-country skiing trails. Then, everyone gathers around the wood stove in the bar, or the big fireplace in the lobby, before toting cans of water to their cabins. (Every cabin has a portable toilet in the rear for winter use, as indoor ones are in use from May 15 to October 15 only.)

Summer, the water supply is normal, and people come to enjoy the lake, the good food, and country-western dances on Friday and Saturday nights. At the Hitching Post, kids can enjoy guided horseback rides; if they take to the hiking trails, they'll see plenty of wildlife—elk, deer, "even skunk and porcupine." Fishing on the lake is easy if you bring a pole—the Country Store has all the bait, hooks, sinkers, bobbers, tackle, and live bait that any young angler could desire.

When the lodge was built in 1924, all guest rooms were upstairs, above the restaurant and lounge. The building burned in the same decade, however, and when it was rebuilt, the upper floor was reserved for dining and meeting rooms, leaving the cabins for lodging.

Years ago, local ranchers had a branding party, burning their brands into the lodge's log walls. (Maybe that's how the early fire started!) There are antiques like old school desks, safes, and sewing machines around the lobby, and the restaurant has cozy red-checked tablecloths and savory odors that satisfy young appetites hearty from the outdoors.

"I love the area," the innkeeper says. "It's a pristine wilderness with variable weather conditions. We can have a lot of snow, but it can be warm enough to ski in your shirtsleeves."

Let's keep it that way. "People from Phoenix come up and mess up my wilderness," local residents complain, but they soften it with a laugh. All the same, if you go, don't mess with Mormon Lake!

How to get there: Mormon Lake is south of Flagstaff, off Lake Mary Road. Turn west when you see the Mormon Lake sign. The lake road circles the lake, and the inn will be on the east side of the road as you come through the village.

Kohl's Ranch Resort
Payson, Arizona
85541

Innkeeper: Blaine Kimball
Address/Telephone: Highway 260; (602) 478-4211
Rooms: 41 plus 8 cabins, all with private bath, air conditioning, and television. Small pets permitted.
Rates: $65 to $125, EP. Children under 12, free.
Open: All year.
Facilities and activities: Restaurant. Swimming pool, video game room, country music on summer weekends. Creek with fishing, horseback riding, hiking. Nearby: Tonto Fish Hatchery, Wood Canyon Lake with boat rental, Zane Grey Cabin and Museum (5 miles).

Kohl's is on Tonto Creek, and the cabins are located on its banks. ☞ "Everybody who stays here wants to stay in a cabin," Blaine says. "But we have only eight, so we've tried to give our newly decorated lodge rooms the effect of being in a cabin." I think they've succeeded: My room had a stone fireplace, a log wall, and plank-patterned carpet! Even the bath was outdoorsy, with plank-patterned vinyl on the floor and shower walls.

"We're in beautiful Zane Grey Country," says Blaine, and the cabin (now a museum) where the author wrote many of his books is not far from Kohl's. The Mongollon Rim, a canyon cut in the rock below Coconino and Sitgreaves national forests, can be seen from the inn.

The countryside is dotted with lakes and streams for fishing and boating around the largest stand of Ponderosa Pine in the world. Canoes and rowboats are for rent at Wood Canyon Lake; but what kids like best, says Blaine, is fishing, with a pole and a string, in the stream on the edge of the property. It's kept stocked with trout by the Tonto Fish Hatchery, another popular spot that kids enjoy visiting.

Kohl's Ranch is over a hundred years old. The old cowboy barn down on the creek has been newly renovated. It's been on the place since way back when, according to Blaine, and now it's a great eating place for the youngsters, who can munch fast foods while sitting on old bar stools. The back windows look right out on the creek. There are menus for children in the Zane Grey Dining Room, too, and now there are two lounges, instead of one, for the grownups, with live country music on summer weekend nights.

The lodge—a long, low L-shaped building with a two-story A-frame center—is a casual, rustic place. Be sure to notice the great stone fireplace studded with amethyst geodes and copper rock in the huge lobby. There's an open stairway in the center of the lobby, leading up to the balcony gift shop, which has souvenirs and knickknacks for kids to browse among. Otherwise, there's nothing for sale for miles around—"We're really rustic," says Blaine.

But your family won't want for anything. There is something for everyone, right down to the platefuls of Kohl's famous barbecue.

How to get there: The lodge is on Highway 260, 17 miles west of Payson.

Tanque Verde Ranch
Tucson, Arizona
85748

Innkeepers: Lesley and Bob Cote
Address/Telephone: Route 8, Box 66; (602) 296–6275
Rooms: 58, including 13 suites; all with private bath, air conditioning, patio.
Rates: $130 to $165, single low season; $180 to $220, single high season; $160 to $195 for two, low season; $200 to $275 for two, high season; AP. Children $45 to $55. American Express.
Open: All year.
Facilities and activities: Special programs for children from May to December. Evening enrichment lectures. Indoor and outdoor pools, tennis, horseback riding, health spa, shuffleboard and horseshoes, children's playground.

Bob Cote calls his ranch a country inn—with horses. "Country inns are a lifestyle all to themselves," he told me. "Actually, I was an educator for many years, and this type of work is not much different. You're involved twenty-four hours, total involvement, the whole focus of your being. It's a complete pattern of life." Bob loves it: He glows, which should give you an idea of life on this ranch. You'll glow, too!

In addition to all the other exercise, a hundred horses are

Tucson, Arizona

ready to be saddled at any time. Evenings, listen to enrichment lectures. "We always have an evening activity to pique people's interest in the Southwest, so that they'll want to return," Bob confesses. "After that, we can't keep them awake. We've tried. If you do my program, you can't stay up!"

Discussions are on Cochina and Hopi Indian legends or "rattlesnake talk" or desert animals, plants, and flowers. That, after a dinner of roast leg of veal with celery-and-olive dressing, broiled filet of ocean perch with creole sauce, or baked Hawaiian pork chops, guarantees you the soundest sleep of your life.

"We have three choices every meal," Bob says, pointing out that ☛ they're four-star in a well-known travel guide. "There's so much food, it suits every palate, even the children's."

Lunch-buffet choices during my visit were Spanish lamb stew, broiled cod with béarnaise sauce, and the Black Forest sandwich of roast beef and Swiss cheese grilled on rye bread. I love soups, and the inn's cream of celery-almond soup was four star with me.

The children's programs are well planned, with counselors overseeing supervised group activities at certain times, away from the adults. Horseback riding, tennis, hikes, and games all keep youngsters happy down on the ranch.

☛ Most of the luxurious guest rooms have fireplaces; all have private patios.

The ranch has a colorful history. It was built in 1862 on a Spanish land grant and is one of the oldest in America being used as a guest facility. Children enjoy hearing the tale of the original owner, rumored to have been hanged in his own parlor because he would not tell bandits where his money was. Bob adds: "The second owner played William Tell and missed. What do you think happened to him? Right! He was sent to jail!"

How to get there: Take Speedway exit off I–10 and drive to the absolute end. The road goes through town and out toward the mountains, so don't give up—it dead-ends at the unpaved road on the left leading to the ranch. There's a sign.

E: *The many Cote children around the ranch make it a great place for youngsters to make new friends while learning western, nature, and Indian lore.*

Flying E Ranch
Wickenburg, Arizona
85358

Innkeeper: Vi Wellik
Address/Telephone: Box EEE; (602) 684-2690
Rooms: 16; all with private bath, air conditioning, refrigerator.
Rates: $155 to $200, double occupancy, AP. Children up to age 2, $25; 3 to 6, $35; 7 to 12, $45; 13 and older, $55. AP. 2-day minimum. Horseback riding extra. No credit cards.
Open: November 6 to May 1.
Facilities and activities: BYOB. Swimming pool, sauna, spa, horseback riding, tennis court, volleyball, basketball, shuffleboard, Ping-Pong. Occasional square dances and impromptu races and rodeos for children.

Innkeeper Vi Wellik and her husband came to the Flying E Ranch in 1948 and 1949 as guests. It took them eight years to make the transition from guests to owners, but not very long to make the Flying E a popular spot. "We tried to think of everything to make guests comfortable," she told me. I was impressed with the results. Rooms are not only inviting, with picture windows and comfortable ranch furniture, they are absolutely immaculate. ☛ There are even electric blankets for chilly evenings, and every room has a sink and refrigerator, though there's not any need—the food in the dining room is as good as grandmother's.

Wickenburg, Arizona

It's informal, too. Breakfast is to individual order, but lunch and dinner are family-style service. The weather is so pleasant, lunch is usually served out on the patio. The coffeepot in the dining room is always on, and the ☞ cookie jar is always full—and often full of little hands helping themselves!

Vi hosts a happy hour in the saloon, providing setups and ice (bring your own bottle) and snacks like nuts and mushroom dip with chips.

"I enjoy people," Vi says. "We have guests who come from all over the world. One summer, guests from Switzerland spent six weeks."

Activities besides horseback riding and swimming include unscheduled surprise events like hayrides, dude rodeos dubbed "dudeos," boot races for the kids, and even britches branding (not with a hot iron!). Breakfast cookouts, lunch rides to scenic spots, and chuck-wagon cookouts are regular events; and if you don't ride horses, you'll still get to the site.

While there are TV and VCR in the lodge, "they are rarely used," says innperson Jane. "There's so much else to do that we don't encourage TV; we don't say, there's the TV, go watch! We have a lot of cookouts; we'd rather the kids go swimming in the pool, use the tennis or the volleyball-basketball court, play Ping-Pong or shuffleboard, or go horseback riding with their parents."

Horses are not included in the tariff, however. One ride a day runs $12; two per day, $18; and an unlimited number per week, $90. If you need lessons, the wranglers are there to help.

Vi is widowed now and runs the ranch with the help of a dedicated staff, some of whom have been with her since she bought the ranch in 1952. "If you like people, it's a very rewarding experience," she says.

How to get there: From the stoplight at the center of Wickenburg, take Highway 60 west through the underpass. After you pass the new Safeway store on your left, you'll see a large Flying E sign, also to your left. The ranch is a short way down the unpaved road, across the cattle guard.

Wickenburg Inn
Wickenburg, Arizona
85358

Innkeeper: Lefty Brinkman
Address/Telephone: P.O. Box P; (602) 684-7811
Rooms: 47 (6 in lodge, 41 *casitas*); all with private bath, air conditioning, television. Pets by prior arrangement. Smoking discouraged.
Rates: $90 to $280, double occupancy, AP. Children under 2, free; 2 to 12, $35; 13 and up, $50.
Open: All year.
Facilities and activities: Special programs geared to children during March and Easter, Thanksgiving, and Christmas holidays. Arts and Crafts Center, Desert Caballeros Western Museum, Wildlife Preserve and natural history program, archery, 11 tennis courts with instruction and clinic, horseback riding, swimming pool.

Try to begin your stay at the Wickenburg Inn on a Sunday night. That's Lefty's get-acquainted-party night. "We get them started immediately, there's so much to do," says Lefty, who positively radiates energy, health, and good humor. Wickenburg Inn is geared to the good family life. It is definitely an outdoorsy place, with enough activities going on daily to fill a cruise ship. Both outdoor and indoor activities keep Mom and Pop and the kids busy from dawn to bedtime.

Outdoors, there's always the lure of the horses, but equally popular are the archery and tennis clinics. The Wildlife Preserve and natural history program, with walks, talks, and slide shows, is a unique endeavor in this resort setting, teaching reverence for life and nature. Indoors, there's plenty of creativity going on in the Arts and Crafts Center, while the Desert Caballeros Western Museum offers minerals and Indian lore along with Wickenburg history from prehistoric times to the present.

Casitas and rooms are cozy, with the former having wet bars, fireplaces, small refrigerators, and stoves. But what guests would want to eat in their rooms? "Our chef is a master with soups; they're dynamite," Lefty says. "And our desserts are more filled with calories than they ought to be!" Which did not stop me from trying out all the flavors on the homemade-cookie tray, as well as a hefty taste of the mud pie.

Food is served buffet style (and occasionally ordered from a menu), and the chicken à la king I helped myself to at lunch was topped with the fluffiest biscuits I've eaten in a long time. "I go through the dining room seeing if everything is OK," Lefty told me as several guests came up to say goodbye and rave about their stay. When I commented on this, he remarked that his staff have their heads on straight and enjoy what they're doing. But their inspiration surely comes from the innkeeper himself. "My motto to them is that they should 'touch' each guest each day in one form or another, get them in a tennis game . . . !"

How to get there: On Highway 89 from Wickenburg, turn right 4 miles past the "Wickenburg Inn" sign high on a hill to your right. The road to the inn will be on your right, marked by an orange-and-green sign.

Chinguague Compound
San Juan Pueblo, New Mexico
87566

Innkeepers: JB (Joan) and Philip Blood
Address/Telephone: Box 1118; (505) 852-2194
Rooms: 3 1- and 2-bedroom guesthouses with air conditioning, fully equipped kitchen, living area with kiva (Indian "beehive") fireplace, and screened porch. Pets by prior arrangement.
Rates: $65 to $125, May 1 to September 30; $65 to $150, October 1 to April 30; EPB.
Open: All year.
Facilities and activities: Library, games, and television. Hiking, bird watching, visiting the pueblo. Indian events in the Eight Northern Pueblos, International Folk Art Museum in Sante Fe.

You pronounce *Chinguague* "ching-wa-yea," which isn't hard at all—my difficulty was in remembering it! Named for the *arroyo* you have to cross to get to this fascinating inn, it means "wide place" in the language of the San Juan Indians.

Before I could cross the *arroyo*, I had to drive through the town of San Juan Pueblo and ask for help in finding it. The obliging switchboard operator at the police station said they often send inn guests on their way with a police escort, but this time she called Philip Blood, who came and got me. (He was coming into town to get the mail, anyway.)

San Juan Pueblo, New Mexico

By now I imagine you've tumbled to the fact that this is an unusual place. ☞ Situated on the banks of the Rio Grande in the midst of the San Juan Indian reservation, Chinguague Compound is an idyllic retreat of individual adobe *casitas*. It's a perfect place for families to experience a different sort of leisure: Guests take long walks along the river, or go fishing or bird watching—"there are plenty of birds," JB says. "In fact, the breezes in the trees and the birds are the only noises around here!" There are hundreds of books to read, classical-music records to listen to, or you can just plain loaf, watching the sunrise and sunset over the Sangre de Cristo Mountains.

JB claims to be on perpetual vacation. Both she and Philip are fugitives from back East, delighted to be in the inn business.

"It's fantastic—we've met people from all over the world. We find bed-and-breakfast people just wonderful. We invite all our guests to breakfast, though they can cook their own, but we've even had a guest with dietary restrictions who would come—she'd just bring her own breakfast!"

It's hard to stay away. Everyone likes to dine on cornmeal pancakes with New Hampshire maple syrup, sausage, homemade granola and coffee cake, and fruit-and-yogurt parfait. ☞ JB and Philip grow their own corn and grind it; they also make apricot preserves and plum or peach honey from their own trees. They even grind whole wheat flour from wheat sent by a friend in Thomas, Oklahoma!

How to get there: Take Highway 285 north to 68 north to the white water tank. Turn left into San Juan Pueblo and ask for help at the police station on the right by the post office. (Or call, and help will be forthcoming.)

✱

E: *At the end of the school year the pueblo has a powwow for the schoolchildren, JB says. "They advertise it in the post office a week before," so it's not easy to catch. But there are other events, such as Indian dances, at each of the pueblos. And, says JB, the International Folk Arts Museum just 30 miles away in Sante Fe is "wonderful for kids from three to one hundred!"*

Rancho Encantado
Santa Fe, New Mexico 87501

Innkeeper: Betty Egan
Address/Telephone: Route 4, Box 57C; (505) 982–3537
Rooms: 22, including suites and cottages; all with private bath and air conditioning, some with television.
Rates: $95 to $300, per room or cottage, depending on season, EP.
Open: March 21 to January 5.
Facilities and activities: Restaurant, cantina, library, recreation room with video games, billiards and pool table. Swimming pool, shuffleboard, tennis and basketball courts, horseback riding, hiking trails. Nearby: Sante Fe and Taos, Bandelier National Monument, Sante Fe National Forest, Spanish mountain villages of Chimayo, Truchas, and Trampas.

The main lodge of today's Rancho Encantado was built in the late 1920s. It was a small country inn with twelve rooms and two separate cottages, all enjoying a view of the Sangre de Cristo Mountains and 168 acres of desert. The Egan family bought the spread in 1968, and old-timers wouldn't know the place now.

The former modest guest ranch is now a luxurious resort, but the inn ambience has remained unchanged. Betty Egan regards her guests as friends, inspiring her staff to maintain the warm and intimate atmosphere of the original inn. ☛ Every guest, young or old, is treated like a celebrity, and those who look familiar probably are—the resort has hosted many famous personalities.

New rooms of adobe, brick, and hand-painted tile are decorated with Indian rugs, wall hangings, and other arts and crafts of the region, and all are true to the traditional ranch style of the original inn.

I walked over a picturesque little bridge to reach the newest *casitas*. More luxurious, they have front porches, fireplaces, sitting areas, large dressing rooms, and such details as ☛ skylights in the bathroom, as well as the gorgeous view afforded the whole ranch.

In the main lodge the dining room and cantina, with adobe walls, tiles, and wood-beamed high ceilings, offer several tiers for dining. Thick, juicy steaks vie with sole meunière or roast duck Montmorency amid whitewashed walls and warm woods. Try guacamole with blue-corn *tostadas* for an appetizer. For the children, the staff is happy to prepare hamburgers, French fries, and *quesadillas*, or anything else young palates prefer (and at sixty-five percent of entree cost).

The whole family will enjoy breakfast, Southwest style, with a burrito of scrambled eggs in a flour tortilla. Then it's off for the summer sports: tennis or volleyball, swimming or horseback riding (children over seven only), or hiking along trails first trod by the conquistadors, who were looking for gold. It almost never rains here, but the Rec Room, with video games, pool table, and TV, can amuse the stay-at-homes.

The ranch is located between Santa Fe and Taos, excellent location for excursions to museums, Indian pueblos, and Indian dances.

How to get there: Take I–84 north from Santa Fe to the Tesuque exit. Take Highway 22 past Tesuque about 2 miles; the inn is on the right.

Bear Mountain Guest Ranch
Silver City, New Mexico
88062

Innkeeper: Myra McCormick
Address/Telephone: P.O. Box 1163; (505) 538-2538
Rooms: 15 (some suites); all with private bath and air conditioning. Pets accepted.
Rates: $48 to $79, AP. No credit cards.
Open: All year.
Facilities and activities: No smoking in the dining room. Bird-watching room, birding being a specialty of the inn, with a full schedule of classes and nature clinic. Gila Cliff Dwellings, prehistoric Indian sites, ghost towns, fishing, rock hunting, horseback riding.

Love of nature and care for her fellow humans mark Myra McCormick and her unique guest ranch. "Tell me your interests," she says, "and I'll plan a tour for you, guided or otherwise." Her list of suggestions is wide, encompassing geology, archeology, caving, white-water rafting, wild-plant seeking, fossilizing, fishing, hiking, birding (a favorite), or just plain "soaking up sun on the front porch."

As for the children, "The children who come here with their

Silver City, New Mexico

parents love the outdoors," Myra says. "We get pretty sensible, well-minded youngsters here, and although their attention span may not last long for classes, they have a pretty good time anyway. Invariably they want to go to the cliff dwellings." Another exciting excursion is to the Glenwood Catwalk: grilled metal rails, elbow height, forming a walk between vertical rock walls on the west side of Gila National Forest.

Peace, solitude, friendliness, and health are the watchwords of Bear Mountain. Myra has a care for the health of her guests, and ☞ food is all home cooked from all-natural ingredients, down to the jar of granola I helped myself to at breakfast.

A dinner of oven-baked chicken and scalloped potatoes is bound to have at least two vegetables, in addition to a delicious mixed-fruit salad. "I try to have a green and a yellow vegetable— it's good for people," says Myra.

"So many who come here are intelligent people. They're really thinking, and they tell me that, as they travel across the country, they get fed up with baked potato and tossed salad, and they're hungry for vegetables." Her three hearty meals a day are packed with good nutrition, and children of all ages find a wide variety to keep even finicky eaters happy.

☞ Meals are served family style, all you can eat. After spending all day in the great outdoors, I worked up quite an appetite and really dug in.

My room reminded me of the 1920s and 1930s—clean, comfortable, and not too fancy or fussy. Rag rugs are on the varnished floors, plants are everywhere, and the rooms are bright and sunny with the light from large, old-fashioned windows. Corner suites have sun porches, with marvelous views of the surrounding mountains.

Myra also provides sack lunches of home-baked bread to take walking, so you won't have to interrupt your nature-seeking. "Very seldom do people stay in," she says. "The big thing for people who come here is to be *out all day long.*"

How to get there: From Highways 90 or 180, when you get to Silver City, take 180 to the 4th traffic light. Take the right fork; that's Alabama. Turn north and go 2.8 miles, cross the first cattle guard, and go left on the dirt road .6 miles. Don't worry, there are signs to guide you.

Casa Europa
Taos, New Mexico
87571

Innkeepers: Marcia and Rudi Zwicker
Address/Telephone: 157 Upper Ranchitos Road; (505) 758–9798
Rooms: 6; all with private bath and air conditioning. Smoking only in common room.
Rates: $60 to $95, EPB and afternoon tea. Children $10 extra.
Open: All year.
Facilities and activities: Three private courtyards for play, a special clubhouse. Hiking, horseback riding, winter skiing. Nearby: Taos Indian Pueblo and museums; historic Taos Plaza with restaurants, shops, and art galleries.

Marcia and Rudi would like to list small son Maximilian as one of the innkeepers because he is such a fine small host when guests bring young children. "They're all welcome to play with his toys," Marcia told me, and Maximilian agreed with a wide grin. "Maxi has an open personality," she said. He's eager to share his special place where children can play. "Where Rudi comes from in Germany, everyone has a garden house. Rather than putting a garden house here, we have one on stilts—it's Maxi's private clubhouse."

Rudi and Marcia are the hospitable models their son patterns himself after. Both are used to the public and enjoy entertaining: They were proprietors of a fine restaurant in Boulder, Colorado, for many years before coming to Taos. But idleness is not for Rudi.

"I needed to do something with people again," he said.

"He needs to work about eighteen hours a day," Marcia added with a fond laugh.

"Well, we get our guests started, we introduce them, and then they are fine," Rudi said. I certainly was fine, my only problem being one of indecision at teatime; should I choose the chocolate mousse–filled meringue or the raspberry Bavarian? Or perhaps the Black Forest torte or one of the fresh fruit tarts? (I really wanted one of each, all made by chef Rudi, who was trained at the Grand Hotel in Nuremburg, Germany.)

Breakfast is another such feast prepared by Chef Rudi. For the grownups: fresh fruit salad, a mushroom and asparagus quiche, lean bacon edged in black pepper, home-fried potatoes, and fresh homemade Danish that absolutely melted in my mouth. Children dive into the blue-corn pancakes with bacon and eggs, "or they come into the kitchen to choose their own cereal. I've learned," Marcia said with a laugh. "Once I put fruit on cereal, and the child said 'yuck!', so I leave it alone!"

The house itself is a treasure, with fourteen skylights and a circular staircase to the gallery above the main salon. Appearing deceptively small from the outside, the large common rooms (but very uncommon!), both upstairs and down, lead to six exceptionally spacious and elegant guest rooms. Several rooms have built-in *bancos* that convert to a twin bed. Despite the elegance, it's also very comfortable, and, as Marcia observed, "Children nowadays appreciate the fine things, as well as their parents." The wood floors are graced with oriental rugs; the white-stucco walls are hung with original art by such New Mexican artists as Veloy Vigil and Danny Escalante, artists who can be seen in the museums and the galleries on the Plaza.

How to get there: Driving into Taos from the south on Highway 68, take Lower Ranchitos Road left at the blinking light intersection just north of McDonald's and south of Taos Plaza. Go 1½ miles southwest to the intersection of Upper Ranchitos Road, which will be on your right. (For a landmark, there's a Taos Photo Lab on the lefthand corner.)

El Monte Lodge
Taos, New Mexico
87571

Innkeepers: Pat and George Schumacher
Address/Telephone: Kit Carson Road; (505) 758–3171
Rooms: 13, including 4 2-bedroom suites; all with private bath, air conditioning, television. Some with kitchenette and fireplace, and others with refrigerator. Pets and smoking permitted.
Rates: $55 to $75, double occupancy, EP. Children, $10.
Open: All year.
Facilities and activities: Large picnic, barbecue, and play area for children. Laundry facilities. Within walking distance of historic Old Taos Plaza, Kit Carson Museum, horseback riding, and white-water tubing and rafting.

El Monte Lodge at first glance may look more like a motel than an inn, but don't let that fool you—the atmosphere is right. ☞ Mints will be placed on your pillow at night, and Pat and George are always ready for a chat in the small sitting area of the lobby. Fireplace, books, and green plants make it cozy; maps and brochures make it informative and educational. As for entertaining the kids, there are outdoorsy things nearby, such as horseback riding on the Lobo Ranch and white-water rafting and floating on the Rio Grande "although youngsters have to be at least eight before they can tube," Pat cautions.

"We should have started this when we were young," Pat says. "We both love people and we love it!" The coffeepot is always on, as well as a handy ice-making machine.

The lodge is more than fifty-five years old, George told me, according to a retired math teacher from Taos High School. "Last year I had a man call who said, 'I'm 93 years old, and in 1933 I stayed at the Monte.' "

Pat's pride is sharing letters and comments from guests, and I enjoyed reading them. Words like "It's *beautiful*, so clean and modern" or "A very special place, very homey with unusually thoughtful appointments" reaffirmed what I could see for myself.

Behind the main building, huge old cottonwoods shelter a well-kept barbecue and picnic area, and there's a fenced playground for the kids. Everything is spotless in the cabins, grouped in a half-circle facing the main building.

From the large apartment with fireplace to the smallest room with one double bed, desk, chair, and dressing room, all appointments are warm and comfortable. Kitchen units have drop-leaf tables, and the suite has a connecting bath and fireplace. Large, luxurious pale blue bath towels "are like those in the posh hotels," said one guest, while another told me how nice it was to find that the kitchen knives were sharp, "and the artwork on the walls isn't bolted down," her husband chimed in.

As one guest wrote, "Our room at El Monte has character and style, everything was spotlessly clean, innkeepers friendly and helpful."

But I thought this was the best accolade of all: "It seems . . . a perfect visit."

How to get there: From the traffic light at Taos Plaza, go east on Kit Carson Road for approximately ½ mile. The lodge will be on your left.

≥

E: *"Everybody leaves happy," comments assistant Benita Martinez, as she takes the key from two contented guests who say, "We'll be back." I ask her if she has been with the lodge long. "Only twenty-four years," is her beaming reply.*

Dixie Dude Ranch
Bandera, Texas
78003

Innkeeper: Clay Conoly
Address/Telephone: P.O. Box 548; (512) 796–4481
Rooms: 24 rooms and cottages; all with private bath and air conditioning.
Rates: $70 to $80, single; $60 to $70, double; group rate (minimum 10), $55; AP. Children under 6, $30; 6 to 12, $45.
Open: All year.
Facilities and activities: Horseback riding, hayrides, cookouts, swimming, poolside parties, barbecues, cowboy entertainment.

Clay Conoly's grandmother, Rose (Billie) Crowell, has had the Dixie Dude for so long, she doesn't need an address. The postman knows just where to find her. "This is not a resort ranch," she says. "This is an old-time Western Stock Ranch that has, through forty-nine years, become a guest ranch."

Now she's the "grande dame" of the ranch, according to Clay, who has taken over the management, and she still likes to call the Dixie Dude "your home on the range." You get a warm welcome, like you're part of the family.

Clay has instituted some lively goings-on at Dixie Dude, including delicious barbecue outdoors every Saturday night, a cowboy breakfast on the range twice a week, and pool parties featuring *fajitas* and "jukeboxes blasting away while everybody dances, even the kids," Clay says. Hayrides, bonfires, and marshmallow roasts keep both parents and offspring busy—there's even a ☞ *pinata* party if you tell Clay there's a birthday child on the premises.

Especially attractive to the youngsters is the ☞ cowboy trick-roping exhibition. Clay has a wrangler in to show off his expertise. You can imagine how that captures young imaginations—everybody wants to see if they can do the same.

"You can do just whatever you want to do at Dixie Dude," is the family motto, and one of the things I wanted to do was take the two daily trail rides. The rides, on good saddle horses and led by experienced cowboys, cover some truly scenic Hill Country; the ranch enjoys a beautiful view.

Back at the ranch, after a wonderful dinner of fried catfish, green garden beans with new potatoes, tossed salad, and corn bread, topped off with chocolate cake and ice cream, I was more than content to fall apart in front of the fireplace in the huge living room.

I let the other guests play the piano or the jukebox or sit around playing card games. I completely relaxed, like Lobo the dog, who was content to lie under the cedar-log bench on the front porch. Just as I was told to do, I was doing just whatever I wanted to!

After a while, I went out back and inspected the ranch's vegetable garden. Then, I went and inspected the tack room, as though I know all about horses. Well, I knew enough to be impressed; that's the cleanest tack room I've ever seen. Last but not least, I took a cool swim in the underwater-lighted swimming pool, and then I slept like a top, what with all the fresh air and exercise.

How to get there: Dixie Dude is south of town, on FM (Farm Road) 1077 west of Highway 173 to Hondo. Drive approximately 9 miles and the ranch entrance will be to your right. There are signs to guide you.

Mayan Dude Ranch
Bandera, Texas
78003

Innkeepers: Judy and Don Hicks
Address/Telephone: Box 577; (512) 796–3312
Rooms: 60; all with private bath and air conditioning.
Rates: $65 to $75, depending on season; $65 per day for a week's stay, AP. Children 12 and under, $35; 13 to 17, $45. No one-day stays.
Open: Open all year.
Facilities and activities: TV room, cocktail lounge. Daily activity schedule for adults and children; special celebrations like Mexican Fiesta or Irish Night. Family activities such as Lore & the Legends; Buckaroos, Dogies, Mavericks, and Cowpokes program for youngsters. Horseback riding, hayrides, cookouts, swimming in pool and Medina River, tubing in river, weight room, tennis.

Except that it's for real, Bandera's Mayan Ranch could fill in for anybody's fantasy of a true Western dude ranch. Rock cottages, furnished with Western furniture right off the ranch, nestle under old cedar trees. Down by the corral, wranglers (one of them a Hicks son, Randy) saddle up the horses for trail rides twice a day. The cool, clean Medina River winds along one boundary of the ranch, begging for you to lie back on an inner tube and just float along.

Bandera, Texas

Guests, says Judy, just can't believe the quiet. "They get on the tubes and just float down the river." If you keep on going, maybe you won't have to go back to the same old grind!

Children, though, don't want to be quiet, and the Buckaroos, for instance, might meet early in the TV room for Italian coloring with Kelly; next, they'll have horse lessons with Tommy. The Dogies might play Donkey Kong in the Trading Post until they meet the Buckaroos for a Mayan Round-Up, a game played with beans. If the teenage Mavericks don't want to eat in the dining room one evening, after their trail ride they can join the Dogies and Buckaroos for dinner and then join the hayride down to the tennis courts for dodgeball and other games. Kids are also welcome at early evening programs such as Lore & The Legends, a special kind of country-western music.

The Mayan is run by an entire herd of Hicks—Judy and Don have thirteen children, several of whom have children themselves. The Hicks have been running the Mayan for more than thirty-five years, and they're experts at making you feel at home, because they invite everyone to "join the family."

I love the cowboy breakfast (scrambled eggs, bacon, sausage, grits with butter, cottage-fried potatoes, biscuits and cream gravy, jellies, coffee) served on a bluff above the river—but you have to ride to it first. I signed up for a horse, but another option is the wagon, which goes faster—my horse liked to lag behind. I guess she knew she wasn't going to get any of the delicious food that was busy sizzling on the fire for us.

Great fun was the softball game before dinner, between the "Cowboys" and "Indians." We were Indians, and our team won! Win or lose, all the players won a hearty appetite for the barbecue at the river and the Western sing-along. (But you still get to eat even if you prefer just to watch the game.)

From the large glass-windowed dining room, the view is of miles and miles of Hill Country. Watching the sunset from the deck outside the dining room and bar is a renewing experience. So is just sitting there, enjoying the cool breezes blowing over the trees. One of the best things I got at the Mayan was "lots and lots of loafing."

How to get there: From Highway 16 turn north onto Main Street, west onto Pecan, and then follow the Mayan signs to the ranch, which is 1½ miles northwest of Bandera.

Twin Elm Guest Ranch
Bandera, Texas
78003

Innkeepers: Mary and Frank Anderwald
Address/Telephone: P.O. Box 117; (512) 796–3628
Rooms: 21, plus 2 2-bedroom suites; 19 with private bath, all with air conditioning.
Rates: $65, single; $55, double occupancy; AP. Children, $35 to $45 depending upon age. Usual minimum stay two or three days, depending upon season. Check-in 4:00 P.M.
Open: March 1 to Labor Day.
Facilities and activities: Recreation porch with television, Ping-Pong, and pool. Horseback riding, hayrides, swimming, tubing, fishing. Nearby: New Sea World in San Antonio.

Twin Elm, a genuine Western guest ranch, is named for the twin elm trees entwined in front of the lodge. ☛ An old chuck wagon is in front, too, and it gives a great air of the Old West to the premises. More to the point, several times a week meals are served from it, just like the old days on the range.

Twin Elm is a family place, and there's ☛ lots of good emphasis on seeing that the kids have a good time. "We have campfires around the pool," says Mary, "and have the kids toast marshmallows. It's a nice gathering place. That is, if it's not too hot," she adds with a laugh.

Bandera, Texas

It's entirely possible that it won't be, not even in midsummer— ☞ Twin Elm is located on one of the highest peaks in the Bandera Hills, and I really enjoyed the breeze. The ranch overlooks the beautiful Medina River, and that's a refreshing sight, too.

After a trail ride through the beautiful scenery, both the river and the pool were great places to be, whether splashing in the pool or fishing in the river. The river yields bass and catfish, and, says Mary, "the kids love it."

Not only the kids loved being in the great outdoors. I thought it was pretty exciting seeing the deer wandering around making out like they lived there, too. And the rabbits, out there in the woods, gave the children at the ranch quite a chase. As Mary says, they have a good time out there trying to catch those little whitetails.

All this nature lovin' works up a good appetite, and meals were hearty enough for any ranch hand. We had good things like scrambled eggs with grits and cream gravy for breakfast, hamburger on the grill with beans and chips for lunch, and good old Texas chicken-fried steak for dinner.

Rooms, small but comfortable, have Western names like "Gunslinger" and the "Outlaws' Room." There's a TV on the screened-in recreation porch, as well as both Ping-Pong and pool tables. There's a wooden pew from an old church to sit on and watch the game players, too.

How to get there: Twin Elm Guest Ranch is on FM (Farm Road) 470, which begins off Highway 16 west of Bandera. The ranch will be on your right just a short distance after you turn off onto 470.

E: *"I 'country-cook',"* Mary says, *and her barbecued brisket and chicken, hot biscuits, homemade pies and cobblers bear witness to her mastery of that hearty cuisine.*

Long Point Inn
Burton, Texas
77835

Innkeepers: Jeannine and Bill Neinast
Address/Telephone: Route 1, Box 86-A; (409) 289–3171
Rooms: 3; 1 with private bath, one shares bath with innkeepers, 1 a suite with sunken tub, all with air conditioning. No smoking in bedrooms.
Rates: $60, double occupancy, EPB. Children over 6, $20. No credit cards.
Open: All year.
Facilities and activities: Dinner by reservation. Fishing in five ponds stocked with catfish and bass, feeding the cattle on 175 acres of ranchland, swimming in swimming hole beneath a waterfall, hiking. Nearby: Miniature Horse Farm, Bluebell Creamery (with tours and free ice cream cones), Star of the Republic Museum at Washington-on-the-Brazos State Park.

"We're so pleased. We never expected to be so busy and to have so many happy guests," says Innkeeper Jeannine. The Neinasts opened their lovely ☛ chalet-style home to guests because they wanted to share the wonderful lifestyle they have created for themselves out on the land. They especially welcome families with children. "After all," Bill says with a laugh, "we have five grandchildren."

"Come and feed the cows, fish the ponds, traipse the woods,

listen to the quiet," they say enticingly. This is hard to resist, especially as you return from the cows, the ponds, and the woods to the lap of luxury in the form of a large story-and-a-half house that is completely and wholeheartedly turned over to guests. There's a piano in the parlor—may guests play it? But of course.

"In fact, we would love it if they would come and play. But so far nobody has," mourns Jeannine.

She compensates by lavishing on her guests such marvelous breakfasts as eggs Newport (with sour cream and bacon) or a casserole of cottage cheese, spiced ham, Monterey Jack cheese, mushrooms, and chili peppers, all with biscuits and homemade wild-plum jam. The fruit compote is always a hit with children, "and, of course, we have cereal for the youngsters who want it," Bill says.

Exciting for city kids is a hike on the land, hoping to spot the deer, raccoons, opossums, foxes, and armadillos that live at Long Point Inn, as well as rabbits, both jack and cottontail. Birds, too, are there aplenty: bluebirds and jays, hawks and crows, robins and hummingbirds. "Kids especially like it when I take them down to feed the cattle," Bill says. "They're so gentle, they come and stick their heads in the truck for ranch cubes—that's like candy to them, and they'll take them from your hand." (They don't bite, he adds reassuringly. "They don't have the right teeth for it even if they wanted to, which they don't.")

Other country doings include swimming in an old-fashioned swimming hole underneath a waterfall on the farm, and fishing with a string and a pole (or bring your own more sophisticated equipment) in the five farm ponds. Outings include a trip to see the miniature horses nearby. "For little folks, that's often the high point of their trip, especially if they get to see a little foal."

Pie, cookies, and coffee are served in the evening. The Neinasts believe in Texas hospitality with a capital H, and Long Point Inn is an ideal hideaway from the hectic pace of city living, and for youngsters, a wonderful introduction to the joys of the countryside.

How to get there: From US Highway 290, take FM (Farm Road) 2679 to FM 390. Turn right, and Long Point Inn will be on your left on a hill not far from the intersection.

Indian Lodge
Fort Davis, Texas 78734

Innkeeper: Angela Ernhart
Address/Telephone: P.O. Box 786; (915) 426-3254
Rooms: 39; all with private bath and air conditioning.
Rates: $42 to $45, double occupancy, EP. Children under 6, free; 6 to 12, $2.
Open: All year except Christmas Day.
Facilities and activities: Breakfast, lunch, dinner. Heated swimming pool. Board games. Fort Davis National Historic Site with museum, barracks, and "soldiers" in uniform; McDonald Observatory; nature and hiking trails in Davis Mountains State Park; horseback riding at nearby Prude Ranch.

Indian Lodge is unique in several ways, all delightful. To begin with, it's set in a state park in the midst of the beautiful Davis Mountains and consequently is managed by the Texas Parks and Wildlife Department. Secondly, it was built by the C.C.C., the Civilian Conservation Corps, in the 1930s. Finally, it was built Indian-pueblo style, and it was built to last.

The lodge's ☞ adobe walls are more than 18 inches thick. Still in use are many of the massive cedar beds, chests, dressers, and chairs the C.C.C. crew built. In 1967 a complete renovation added twenty-four rooms, a heated swimming pool, and the restaurant.

The restaurant serves a wide variety of food—seafood, steak, Mexican food, hamburgers, sandwiches—which is a good thing: The lodge is in an isolated, if beautiful, spot. "We fix box lunches for our guests who want to be out in the park all day," says Angela. Which is what most people want to do.

This part of trans-Pecos country (west of the Pecos River) is greener than I expected. It seems that the mountains surrounding the lodge catch moisture-filled winds, and consequently more rain falls. Added bonuses are the cool nights even in the middle of summer.

"Indian Lodge is so popular, you'll need to make reservations well in advance," says Angela. "Not only is the lodge a fine place in which to stay, but the surroundings are heaven for nature and wildlife buffs as well as for bonafide geologists, botanists, and other nature experts." ☞ All the rooms face the east, too, so everybody gets a gorgeous view of sunrise over the mountains.

The lodge lobby is huge, with massive cedar furniture around fireplaces at each end of the room. I joined most of the guests, however, outside on the verandas; we watched the great view of the landscape, with its prickly pear, yucca, and other desert plants marching up to the mountains.

Although delighted guests agree that the lodge is a perfect place to rest, relax, go hiking, and then "sleep a lot," be sure to take in the many sights offered in the surrounding areas. McDonald Observatory, operated by the University of Texas, offers public information lectures and displays. (Visitors' viewing through the telescope, however, is limited to the last Wednesday night of each month.)

Fort Davis National Site has a sound re-creation of an 1870s military-retreat parade, with a present-day volunteer in period costume at attention. He sits silently on his horse, while the recording of bugles sounding the retreat mingles with the sounds of shouted orders and the jingle of horses' harnesses. It's vivid and haunting.

How to get there: The lodge is 4 miles northwest of Fort Davis, via Highway 118, in the Davis Mountains. Take 118 west 3 miles to the Park Road–3 entrance and follow the park road to the lodge.

River View Farm
Fredericksburg, Texas
78624

Innkeeper: Helen K. Taylor
Address/Telephone: Highway 16 South; (512) 997–8555
Rooms: 2 suites upstairs accommodating up to 8, shared bath; 1 suite downstairs accommodating 4, private bath; all with air conditioning. Pets at discretion of innkeeper.
Rates: $59 to $65, double occupancy, EPB. Children, $5 to $20, depending on age and room.
Open: All year.
Facilities and activities: Farm acres to wander over, river to fish in, cattle to visit, vegetable garden, books, games. Nearby: Lady Bird Johnson Municipal Park with swimming pool, tennis, 9-hole golf course (1 mile); Fredericksburg with restaurants and Admiral Nimitz World War II Museum and German Heritage museums; Kerrville and the Cowboy Museum (18 miles).

Breezy is the word for River View Farm. It's set on a hill in the Hill Country and has a breezeway that catches a round-the-clock cool wind. I could just sit here for hours, cooling off and taking in the sweep of the green hills and ☛ listening to the lowing of the longhorns and the buffalo that Helen's neighbors raise.

Helen herself raises native Texas herbs, and what a refreshing

Fredericksburg, Texas

treat it is to have her show you her garden. "You just ought to see!" She also has a vegetable garden close to the house, and young guests enjoy picking the "veggies," especially when they can take them home.

Helen's guests practically have the run of the house. The kitchen, the large and comfortably furnished living room with its large stone fireplace, the glass-enclosed sun porch, and the breakfast room with its china cabinet full of heirloom china, framed German mottos, and bird collection (mostly hummingbirds, which are Helen's favorite), all conspire to make guests feel truly at home.

The front porch and the large upstairs area, in particular, are great places for kids to read and play games. "But we're never locked in to the weather here," Helen reminds me. "Not much rain, so everybody's usually out and doing, going to town or to the park."

The downstairs bedroom has a beautiful quilt draped over a handmade cedar chest. The furniture is 1920s Queen Anne reproduction: dressing table, dresser, bureau, bed, and chair. The bathroom tub has a Jacuzzi, a nice luxury to find out in ranch country.

☞ Helen's breakfast is hearty enough for a rancher, too. Fresh, local German sausage, scrambled eggs with jalapeños (but not too hot, says Helen), cheese, biscuits, fresh peach cobbler, and jellies and jams, including Helen's specialty, blackberry jam.

It's all topped off by the centerpiece, fresh fruit in season, which everybody proceeds to eat. "The kids run off to play, but the grownups always linger," says Helen, "having more coffee and munching on the centerpiece." I can taste why: The county is known for blackberries, nectarines, peaches, strawberries, mangoes, and melons—watermelon, honeydew, and Persian.

How to get there: The farm is 4 miles south of Fredericksburg on Highway 16, 1 mile south of Lady Bird Johnson Park. To the left you'll see a white fence and a cattle guard. Drive over it and there you are.

✽

E: *If guests aren't munching fruit or sitting on the breezeway, they'll be on the porches, rocking or swinging on the dogwood glider and waiting for the cows to come home.*

Bullis House Inn
San Antonio, Texas
78208

Innkeepers: Anna and Steve Cross
Address/Telephone: 621 Pierce Street; (512) 223–9426
Rooms: 8; 1 with private bath, others share 2 baths, and all with air conditioning and television.
Rates: $30 to $49, single; $36 to $55, double, continental breakfast. Children under 18, $5. EP rates also available.
Open: All year.
Facilities and activities: Affiliated with American Youth Hostels, with hostel on premises. Swimming pool, badminton, volleyball, Ping-Pong, board games. Nearby: the Alamo, Paseo del Rio (River Walk), La Villita, Institute of Texan Cultures, Hertzberg Circus Museum, Brackenridge Park and Zoo, Spanish Missions, many fiestas.

Bullis House Inn and San Antonio International Hostel make for an unusual experience because the combination offers the best of two worlds. While staying in the historic home of Civil War General John Bullis, you get to mix with travelers from all over the world. ☛ More than 90 percent of the guests staying at the hostel at the rear of the inn are international visitors. The inn's four parlors are open to all guests, and in interacting with hostel guests from France, England, Australia, Germany, and Japan, I felt as if I was taking an international voyage.

San Antonio, Texas

The innkeepers say they believe that a certain sort of person stays at an inn—one who is more warm and more open—and that the lost art of conversation revives at an inn. "Guests can read or watch TV in the parlors, but since the inn guests have a TV in their rooms, mostly they come down to visit with the international hostel guests," said Nathan, one of three managers who help out when the Crosses are absent. "And the kids can keep busy with our new swimming pool, or play volleyball, Ping-Pong, badminton, board games. . . . there's a lot for them to do here, plus we're within five minutes of downtown with the River Walk and the Alamo."

Bullis House, a large white Neo-Classical mansion, was built by the general when he came to town from New York in 1865. But he didn't settle down. He fought hostile Indians in Texas and saw action in the Spanish–American War. The colorful general, called "Thunderbolt" by the Indians and "Friend of the Frontier" by the settlers, earned formal thanks from the Texas Legislature.

Large white columns support the front portico. Inside, parquet floors, marble fireplaces, and chandeliers attest to early Texas elegance. Guest rooms are large, with high ceilings, and most have fireplaces ☞ (there are ten altogether!). I particularly loved the French doors in the rooms opening off the upstairs porch. Especially helpful for families is the trundle bed in each guest room, making each room able to accommodate four persons, while the large "family room" can sleep six.

Breakfast is cold cereal; hot apple, cinnamon, or orange muffins; orange juice; and coffee, tea, or hot chocolate. San Antonio abounds in fine restaurants, and the Crosses have many recommendations. Mi Tierra, in the Mercado (market), is a special regional favorite. San Antonio, a warm and happy combination of Anglo and Hispanic cultures, always has some kind of parade or festival going on—I've never been in a city that parties so much; there are no strangers here!

How to get there: Take the New Braunfels–Ft. Sam Houston exit off I–35 or the Grayson Street exit off Highway 281. The inn is on the corner of Grayson and Pierce, adjacent to Fort Sam Houston.

Aquarena Springs Inn
San Marcos, Texas
78666

Innkeeper: Paul Trottman
Address/Telephone: 1 Aquarena Springs Drive; (512) 396–8901
Rooms: 24; all with private bath and air conditioning.
Rates: $50 to $65, double occupancy, continental breakfast. Children over 4, $8.
Open: All year.
Facilities and activities: On a family amusement park at the site of prehistoric Indian ruins, with Olympic-size swimming pool. Lake with glass-bottom boats, sky ride to educational aviary and cliffside gardens, Texana Village, submarine theater, golf. Newly remodeled Spring Lake Restaurant has children's menu.

Aquarena Springs Inn is built on the site of the oldest permanent Indian encampment in North America. I'll bet that's a surprise; it sure was for me! ☛ Archaeologists have found the remains of Clovis Man, the hunter-gatherer who lived on the San Marcos River over 12,000 years ago.

Another surprise— ☛ you can see where they lived if you peer down from your glass-bottom boat. The site is covered by Spring Lake, and I also saw some of the 100 varieties of aquatic life swimming or growing down below.

San Marcos, Texas

Over 150 million gallons of Texas's purest water filter through honeycomb limestone to make Spring Lake, and on its shores is perched the prettiest white-and-aqua Mediterranean villa, Aquarena Springs Inn. It's been here since 1927, and nineteen of its rooms overlook the lake. Ducks and swans swim along, waiting to be fed bread crumbs—generations of inn guests have spoiled them rotten.

The back hall of the inn has huge glass windows so you can see the flora growing up the steep cliff immediately behind the inn. I also got a thrill from riding the Swiss Sky Ride and catching the Texas Hill Country view from the 300-foot-high Sky Spiral. Children will love watching Bertha the Bicycling Parrot perform at Texana Village and Ralph the Diving Pig do his famous Swine Dive at the submarine theater.

"It can be quiet here even in a crowd," said longtime innkeeper Paul Trottman, who retired to rest and write his memoirs but couldn't resist coming back on the job. "The only noise we hear are ducks and trains—everybody mentions it. Even on the busiest days, it never seems crowded."

That's because there's plenty of room for everyone to spread out in this beautiful green parkland full of both fun and relaxing things to do. I munched on a plate of king-size nachos outdoors by the river at Peppers at the Falls and took deep breaths of the fresh air alongside the crystal-clear water. Then, at the restaurant, I feasted on huge fried shrimp and a plateful of wonderful selections from the salad bar. Later, I sat on the inn veranda overlooking the lake and watched little children feeding the ducks. All I could hear was the laughter of the children and the quacking of ducks.

How to get there: From I–35 take exit 206 and go ½ mile west to Aquarena Springs Drive. There are signs—you can't miss it.

ROCKY MOUNTAIN REGION

by
Doris Kennedy

In the second edition of *Recommended Country Inns—Rocky Mountain Region,* Doris Kennedy profiles 155 of the best and most interesting inns in six western states: Colorado, Idaho, Montana, Nevada, Utah, and Wyoming. In this region, inns include one-time boardinghouses in old silver-mining towns, rustic log cabins, elegant historical hotels, a Bavarian mountain guest house overlooking the Aspen ski resort, a stagecoach inn in a Montana boomtown of long ago, high-mountain inns where the fishing is good, and cozy lodges with mountain or desert vistas.

Doris is a full-time travel journalist whose work appears in the travel sections of major newspapers. A member of the prestigious Society of American Travel Writers, she frequently journeys to Europe and travels extensively throughout Canada and the United States with her husband, professional photographer Gary Kennedy. When not traveling, writing, or shooting, they like to hike the Rockies, explore old mining towns, make gigantic pots of homemade soup, and spoil their cats.

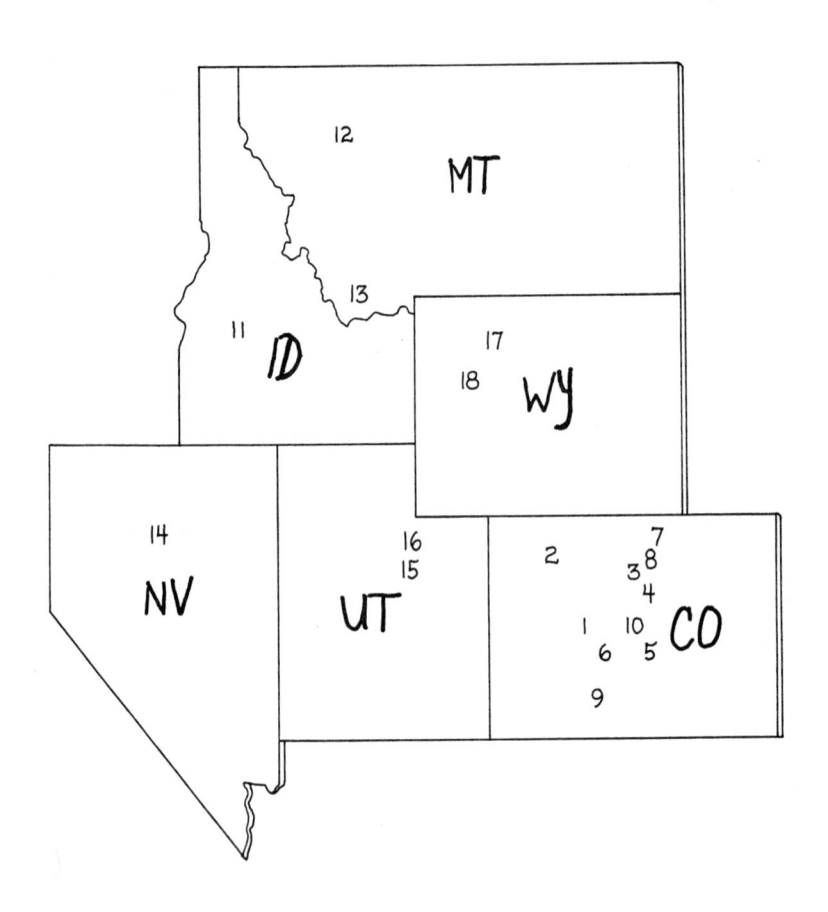

Rocky Mountain Region

Numbers on map refer to towns numbered below.

COLORADO
1. Aspen, Little Red Ski Haus 204
2. Clark, The Home Ranch 206
3. Estes Park, The Aspen Lodge at Estes Park 208
4. Grant, Tumbling River Ranch 210
5. Green Mountain Falls, Outlook Lodge 212
6. Gunnison, Waunita Hot Springs Ranch 214
7. Loveland, Sylvan Dale Ranch 216
8. Lyons, Peaceful Valley Lodge and Guest Ranch 218
9. Pagosa Springs, Davidson's Country Inn 220
10. Victor, The Portland Inn 222

IDAHO
11. Idaho City, Idaho City Hotel 224

MONTANA
12. Bigfork, Averill's Flathead Lake Lodge and Dude Ranch 226
13. Nevada City, Nevada City Hotel 228

NEVADA
14. Old Pioneer Garden, Unionville 230

UTAH
15. Midway, The Homestead 232
16. Park City, The Old Miners' Lodge 234

WYOMING
17. Cody, Rimrock Dude Ranch 236
18. DuBois, Lazy L & B Ranch 238

Little Red Ski Haus
Aspen, Colorado
81611

Innkeeper: Marjorie Riley
Address/Telephone: 118 East Cooper; (303) 925-3333
Rooms: 21; 4 with private bath, 17 share 8 baths. Smoking in parlors only.
Rates: Winter: $58 to $82, single or double; 4 to a room, $25 each; EPB. Summer: $48 to $68, single or double; 4 to a room, $20 each; continental breakfast included. No credit cards.
Open: Mid-June to mid-April.
Facilities and activities: Many restaurants within walking distance. During winter months, once-a-week, hot-spiced-wine, get-acquainted parties. Ski movies. Coffee, tea, and cocoa always available. Elevation 7,908 feet. Nearby: shopping, art galleries, summer music festivals, hiking, fishing, river rafting, downhill and cross-country skiing, ice skating.

If your family's interests lean toward skiing or music, it's worth noting that the Little Red Ski Haus puts you smack-dab in the middle of some of the finest winter skiing and world-class, summertime music festivals to be found anywhere.

This inn is so ☛ popular with skiers in winter and musicians during the summer music festivals, there are times when the sitting room is wall-to-wall people. Noisy and a bit hectic? Yes. Fun and

Aspen, Colorado

exciting? Absolutely! The decor is an eclectic mix of antiques, primitives, and memorabilia, with velvet settees likely to be sharing space with a homemade table suspended from the ceiling by heavy chains. Or a room with a delicate brass bed and dainty rocker might be neighbor to one with shake walls and handmade bunks.

You get the feeling that, structurally, this inn just sort of happened: a room added here, a hallway there. At the front of the house a narrow, winding stairway leads to three little rooms, all with private baths. The guest rooms in the back part of the house are less fancy and share baths. Ask about the bunk-bed rooms. They are children's favorites.

☞ Marge is as diversified as her inn. A schoolteacher for many years, she and her twin sister, Norma Dolle, who lives next door and operates a small bed and breakfast, were also professional singers and dancers. In the days of Shirley Temple, the bouncy curlyheads ☞ had a contract with MGM, sang on the Tom McNeil Breakfast Club radio show, and later became one of the famous sets of Toni Twins, of home-permanent fame. They are so identical that, when they were babies, their mother sometimes fed the same twin twice; and, when in college, they would switch dates while jitterbugging on the dance floor and get away with it!

Marge skis three times a week with her guests, helps them with their plans, and serves a full breakfast in winter, sometimes to as many as fifty. In summer, the morning meal is continental-plus. There are more than seventy restaurants within a few blocks, and Marge will help you find the sort you are hungering for. For inexpensive barbecued ribs, an active, energy-packed bar, and a chance to meet the locals, I recommend Little Annie's Eating House; for fine dining in a restored Victorian homestead, there's Poppie's; and for innovative and traditional French cuisine, it's Charlemagne's.

How to get there: From Main Street, turn south onto Aspen and right onto Cooper. Inn is on the right.

The Home Ranch
Clark, Colorado
80428

Innkeeper: Ken Jones
Address/Telephone: 54880 County Road 129 (mailing address: P.O. Box 822); (303) 879–1780
Rooms: 7 cabins; all with private bath and hot tub.
Rates: $275 to $316, double, per day; $1,890 to $2,172, double, per week; AP. Children age 5 and under, free.
Open: June 1 to October 1 and mid-December to April 1.
Facilities and activities: No smoking is permitted in the dining room. Children's program, baby-sitting, laundry service, children's playroom, swing, slide, ski equipment for kids. Heated outdoor pool, sauna, hiking, fishing, cross-country skiing, sleigh rides—all on ranch property and on adjacent National Forest land. Guides and instructors available for all activities. Elevation 7,200 feet. Nearby: river rafting, lake fishing, ice fishing, downhill skiing.

Ken humbly refers to his accommodations as "cabins," giving an entirely new connotation to the word.

If beautiful little log dwellings, set among groves of aspen trees and enhanced with designer furniture; down comforters; hand-woven, wool-blend bedspreads; hardwood floors; authentic Navajo rugs; small wood-burning stoves; and ☛ private Jacuzzi hot tubs on individual decks qualify as "cabins," then I am compelled to add "luxurious" and "splendid," because they are that and more. Soft terry robes hang in the closets; the baths have the thickest towels I've ever seen; and ceramic baskets hold Scottish Pine toiletries. Coffee, tea, imported cheeses, honey, crackers, and a jar of homemade cookies (refilled every day) are also provided.

The main lodge is a beauty, too, with its antique grand piano, a 32-foot-high stone fireplace, brown leather chairs and couches, and more Navajo rugs. Just off the sitting room, one finds a small glassed-in sun porch with inviting window seats, a loft library, and a sunny, sweet-smelling greenhouse.

Ken plays the guitar and bass fiddle, and he takes music and performing abilities into account when hiring staff. Impromptu music is not uncommon during the evenings.

Ken describes his dining as "family gourmet," which translates to nonstuffy but ☞ fantastically prepared cuisine like peach-filled German pancakes, a nine-vegetable minestrone soup, shrimp macadamia on wild rice, and raspberry Bavarian pie with chopped almond–pastry crust. The one responsible for all these gastronomic delights is Jodi Calhoun, who has been ranch chef for five years.

In the recreation building, I found an intriguing toy box, a dollhouse, lots of books, and a Ping-Pong table. There are special horses for youngsters to ride, and, for those who would rather pretend, there's a brightly painted, antique carousel steed that has been made into a rocking horse strong enough for the biggest kids among us.

How to get there: From Highway 40, northwest of Steamboat Springs, turn north (toward Clark) onto County Road 129. Ranch is on the right.

✱

D: *The Home Ranch has the distinction of being* ☞ *listed in the prestigious, French-based* Relais and Châteaux, *a directory of 372 outstanding lodgings and restaurants including castles, manor houses, and grand estates from 37 nations.*

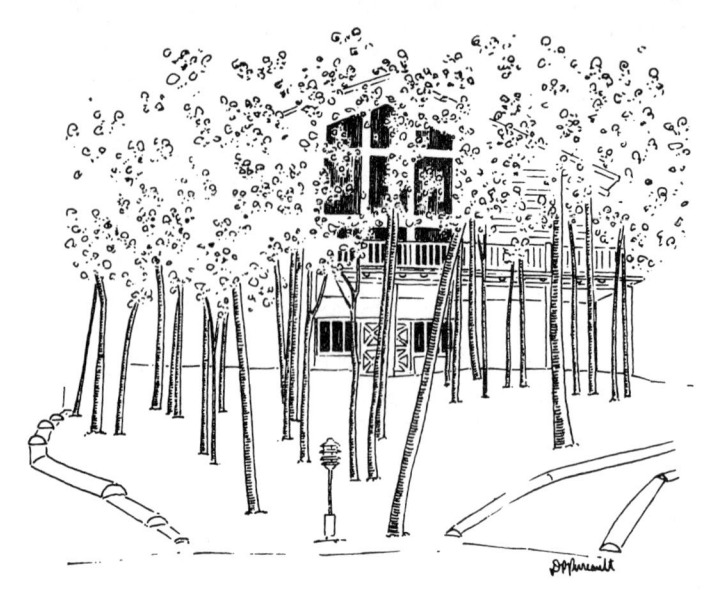

The Aspen Lodge at Estes Park
Estes Park, Colorado
80517

Innkeeper: Boyd LaMarsh
Address/Telephone: Highway 7, Long's Peak Route; (303) 586–8133, (800) 332–6867 outside Colorado
Rooms: 36 in lodge, 21 luxury cottages; all with private bath. Wheelchair accessible; 2 rooms fully equipped for handicapped.
Rates: $75 to $110, per person, AP. Children 2 and under, free; 3 to 10, 50 percent of adult rate. EPB and EP rates also available.
Open: All year.
Facilities and activities: Dining room, lounge. Sunday brunch. Conference facilities. Children's progrmas, full-time counselors, day care. Heated outdoor pool, exercise equipment, hot tub, racquetball, tennis, hayrides, sleigh rides to working cattle ranch, horseback riding, hiking, cross-country skiing, snowmobiling, ice skating, jeep tours. Elevation 9,100 feet. Nearby: resort town of Estes Park offering many family activities; white-water rafting, golf, downhill skiing.

What began as a fur trapper's cabin in 1910 has been skillfully developed into a luxury dude ranch with ☛ the warmth of a small inn. Quite an achievement! With Boyd's down-home friendliness and genuine Western hospitality, guests are encouraged to "prop up their feet in front of the fireplace and make themselves at home." The entire staff calls you by name, and they behave as though they are there only for you.

Made of pine, the lodge is ☛ the largest log structure in Colorado. Original western art is featured throughout the building; and a 24-foot moss rock fireplace graces the main room, where cushioned, handmade aspen-wood couches almost insist that you sit a while. If a log building can be called exquisite, this one qualifies!

The grounds are spacious, so children have lots of room to run, play, and get the kinks out. If they need a little quiet time, TVs are located in public alcoves.

The guest rooms are color coordinated beautifully; the beds have quilted coverlets and ruffled skirts; and each room has one wall made of logs, their crossed ends protruding from the corners. Brass lamps on writing desks, fan ceiling lights, and panoramic views of craggy mountain peaks all add to this fine mix of rustic elegance.

A special moment for me happened as I walked from the lodge to the dining room along a stone pathway and through a glen of whispering aspen trees: I saw ☛ snowcapped 14,000-foot Longs Peak awash with moonlight. Breathtaking!

The food here is excellent. The barbecued ribs are delightfully flavored, and the meat virtually falls from the bones. I hope you get a chance to try the house dessert, a layered masterpiece of crushed walnuts, cream cheese, silky chocolate pudding, whipped cream, and more walnuts. Isn't that something! And if you catch a trout in the stocked private lake, the chef will cook it to perfection for you.

How to get there: From I-25, take Highway 34 west to the town of Estes Park. Turn left at first stoplight onto St. Vrain Avenue. Go 8 blocks, turn onto Highway 7. Continue for 7 miles. The lodge is on the left.

❈

D: *The nearby resort of Ski Estes Park has a ski school during the winter. The town of Estes Park offers all sorts of summertime family activities, including a mini-train, go-carts, bumper boats, miniature golf, and an aerial tramway to picnic areas. The YMCA has an indoor roller skating rink that is open year round.*

Tumbling River Ranch
Grant, Colorado
80448

Innkeepers: Jim and Mary Dale Gordon
Address/Telephone: P.O. Box 30; (303) 838–5981
Rooms: 12 in 2 lodges, plus 13 cabins; all with private bath and fireplace, 2 with hot tub.
Rates: Adults, $900 per person per week; children under 6, $600; ages 6 to 11, $700; AP. No credit cards.
Open: May 1 to October 1.
Facilities and activities: Children's counselors, complete program for children age 3 and older (optional). Daily maid service, sauna, game room. Heated outdoor pool, square dancing, horseback riding, rodeo activities, 4WD trips. Elevation 9,200 feet. Nearby: Pike National Forest, wildlife, mining towns, hiking, fishing, white-water rafting.

If you like the jeans, sweatshirts, barns, and animals part of dude ranching, but you also appreciate fancy guest rooms and extraordinary dining, you're going to like it here.

Tumbling River Ranch has several cottages and two lodges, the most unusual being The Pueblo, built for the daughter of Adolph Coors of Colorado beer fame and used for many years as her mountain home. It is classically Spanish-Indian in design; Indians from Taos, New Mexico, participated in the building's

Grant, Colorado

construction and the decorative carving of the wooden beams. Indian rugs, adobe walls, beehive fireplaces, small alcoves for books and artifacts, and strings of hanging, dried red peppers add to the authenticity of this inn's Southwestern ambience. A large sitting room with massive fireplace, a game room, a lounge, an attractive dining area, and seven lovely guest rooms, each with its own fireplace and bath, make this, without a doubt, my choice of lodging.

The second lodge, built in the 1920s for a former Denver mayor, also exhibits an abundance of warmth and charm. It has five guest rooms, each with fireplace and bath, and a dining room and lounge from which one can sometimes ☛ spot bighorn sheep grazing on the hillside.

Mary Dale is in charge of the kitchen, and food preparation is taken seriously. All is made from scratch, and Jim proudly says that the mashed potatoes even have a few lumps, attesting to the fact that they are the real thing, not box variety. (They are also made with *real* butter and *real* cream!) There are lots of cookouts, and a favorite seems to be Jim's Brunch, celebrated each Tuesday. Imagine for a moment an open fire, ☛ Jim's *3½-foot* frying pan with 150 eggs scrambling all at once, potatoes browning, bacon crisping, cowboy coffee perfuming the air. . . . Incidentally, do you know the recipe for cowboy coffee? The author is anonymous, probably to keep from being shot!

> *Cowboy Coffee*
> Dump two pounds coffee in pot.
> Add jist 'nough water to wet it down good.
> Boil fer two hours.
> Next, throw in a hoss shoe.
> If the shoe sinks,
> the coffee ain't done.

How to get there: From Denver, take Highway 285 southwest to Grant. Turn north onto Guanella Pass Road. Ranch is on the left.

※

D: *Ducks, geese, burros, dogs, cats, and a pet goat named Rocky do their very best to keep the children amused.*

Outlook Lodge
Green Mountain Falls, Colorado 80819

Innkeepers: Rodney and Sherri Ramsey
Address/Telephone: 6975 Howard Avenue (mailing address: P.O. Box 5); (719) 684–2303
Rooms: 9, including 2 suites; 6 with private bath, 3 share 1 bath.
Rates: $35 to $40, single; $37 to $45, double; $65, family suite for 4; generous continental breakfast. Children in rooms, $4.
Open: All year.
Facilities and activities: Yard, patio, use of barbecue and refrigerator. Television in parlor. Elevation 7,800 feet. Nearby: restaurants, swimming pool, bingo, trout-stocked lake, Pikes Peak, cog railway, U.S. Air Force Academy, North Pole (amusement center for young children), museums, hiking, stream fishing, tennis, horseback riding.

Perched high on a hillside, almost in the shadow of 14,000-foot Pikes Peak, the Outlook Lodge was built in 1889 as a parsonage for visiting ministers and their families. In the 1920s, it was sold and reopened as an inn.

A hand-carved, golden oak staircase, creaking from the tread of many footsteps, leads from the Victorian parlor to the upstairs guest rooms. ☛ Many of the original furnishings remain, and the rooms, filled with time-worn antique pieces, appear much as you'd expect they did at the turn of the century, except for the addition of new wall and floor coverings.

The lemon yellow claw-footed tub in one of the shared bathrooms was the first such luxury item in Green Mountain Falls; during the 1920s, the enterprising owner of the inn rented it out to the townspeople for twenty-five cents a bath, including hot water, soap, and towel. An old-time resident still remembers seeing folks patiently waiting in line with their towels draped over their arms.

The front veranda looks out through tall pines and blue spruce to the town below. Down the hill to the right, next door to the inn, is "The Little Brown Church in the Vale," said to be the inspiration for the hymn of the same name.

For breakfast, Sherri serves fresh fruit, fruit juice, coffee, tea, or milk, and one of several of her tasty homemade breads, including cinnamon rolls, monkey bread, apple or carrot muffins, or, perhaps, a moist, flavorful pumpkin bread.

Guests have full use of the parlor and dining room. ☞ You are welcome to prepare a family barbecue on the patio grill. There's even an extra refrigerator for picnic supplies, baby bottles, and snacks.

Several restaurants are within walking distance. I recommend the Li'l Pantry for homemade soups, breads, and pies and the Pub & Grub, built of logs with stone fireplaces, for complcte meals. Both are very casual, so there's no need to dress up for dinner.

If you have young children, they are sure to love the nearby North Pole/Santa's Workshop, open from May through Christmas Eve. Besides a castle, miniature train, and other rides, this small playland has a real live Santa who, along with his helpers and a pet reindeer, is happy to pose for photographs with your youngsters. What could be better for next year's photo Christmas card?

How to get there: Take Highway 24 west from Colorado Springs to Green Mountain Falls turnoff. Inn is on the left.

Waunita Hot Springs Ranch
Gunnison, Colorado 81230

Innkeepers: Rod and Junelle Pringle
Address/Telephone: 8007 County Road 887; (303) 641-1266
Rooms: 22; all with private bath.
Rates: $595 per person, per week, double occupancy; $650 per person, per week, single occupancy; $325 to $555 per week, per child; AP. No credit cards.
Open: May 20 to September 30 (complete dude-ranch program), October 15 to November 15, December 15 to April 15.
Facilities and activities: No alcohol allowed on premises. Children's activities, part-time child care, teen rides, farm animals. Game room with Ping-Pong, pool table, and air hockey. TV room. Hot springs–fed swimming pool. River float trips. Elevation 8,900 feet. Nearby: fishing, 4 x 4 trips, downhill and cross-country skiing, Black Canyon of the Gunnison National Monument, Great Sand Dunes.

Kids love it here so much that, according to Rod and Junelle, "When it's time to leave for home, parents invariably have to pull their children off the front porch rail!"

And it's easy to understand why there aren't any complaints

at dinnertime. How about pan-fried trout, cowboy beans, and apple fritters cooked over an open fire? Or corn chowder, grilled steak, angel biscuits (that's right, they're perfect in every way), and fresh strawberry pie? That's the kind of fare you will find at this ranch. Junelle is thinking of publishing a cookbook, and she should.

The guest rooms are large, pine-paneled, and located in both the main ranch building and an attractive annex with full-length veranda and porch swings. You probably won't want to spend much time in your room, though, because there is so much to do here: hayrides, breakfast and dinner rides, square dancing, fishing in the Pringles' private lake stocked with rainbow trout, and side trips to the Great Sand Dunes, the Black Canyon of the Gunnison, and to the ski village of Crested Butte. And then there's the outdoor pool, a ☛ gigantic (30' x 90') hot springs–fed, mineral-water oasis. Even bathing is special here because your bath water is supplied by the mineral hot springs, too.

As you cross the little bridge heading toward the barn and corral, pause to see the ducks swimming in the creek, and the turkey pen just beyond. Look closely. There are apt to be lambs, baby goats, piglets, and perhaps a colt or two nearby. Youngsters are allowed to help feed the small animals and gather eggs. Inside the barn, a ☛ miniature fringed surrey waits to be pulled by two Shetland ponies. Can you imagine a better opportunity to get truly special photos of children?

Upstairs in the loft, there is square dancing on Tuesday nights; on Friday evenings, ☛ live, Western music is provided by the Pringle sons and their wives. And, believe me, they can really get the place rockin'.

This is a family-run ranch, with all members having a hand in the operation. Whether it's riding, cooking, cleaning, or caring, one of the Pringles will be there. And from Rod and Junelle on down to their grandchildren, who share the toy box with small guests, the hospitality is unsurpassed.

How to get there: 18 miles east of Gunnison, on Highway 50, turn north at the Waunita Hot Springs sign. Continue on for 8 miles to the ranch.

❈

D: *An activity that is always a hit with guests is the midweek float trip down the Gunnison River. A wonderful experience.*

Sylvan Dale Ranch
Loveland, Colorado
80537

Innkeepers: The Jessup family: Maurice, Tillie, and Susan
Address/Telephone: 2939 North County Road 31 D; (303) 667–3915
Rooms: 27; 14 in Wagon Wheel Barn, 1 suite in lodge, 12 cottages; all with private bath. Wheelchair access.
Rates: $51 to $75 for two, $12.50 for children under 12, for Bunk and Breakfast (EPB). $258 to $315 per adult, AP, 3-day package including all activities (separate charge for horseback riding). $495 to $615 per adult, AP, 6-day package including all activities (separate charge for horseback riding). Children's weekly rates available. "No tipping" policy. No credit cards.
Open: All year.
Facilities and activities: Extensive children's program, heated outdoor pool, tennis courts, horseback riding, trout fishing in river and stocked pond, hiking, evening entertainment, farm animals and activities, square dancing. Elevation 7,500 feet. Nearby: white-water rafting, golf, lake fishing, boating, Rocky Mountain National Park.

The children's program at Sylvan Dale Ranch is particularly noteworthy. No sitting in circles, cutting and pasting. No siree, "pahdner." Depending on ages, ☛ the little buckaroos are allowed to help groom the horses and soap the saddles, take off on accompanied nature hikes and scavenger hunts, float on inner

Loveland, Colorado

tubes on the pasture ponds, fish, pan for gold, or take a farm tour. Next time, I'm going disguised as a kid!

Maurice and Tillie have operated their working guest ranch for more than forty years. Maurice conducts the farm tours, Tillie does all the baking, and daughter Susan is general manager and hostess. These are good people, dedicated to the pleasure of their guests.

You can ☞ watch cattle being branded or play a set of tennis; help clean the barn or swim in the heated outdoor pool; take a tour of the haying operation or fish the river and stocked lake. Or how about a hayride, overnight pack trip, an authentic Fourth of July cattle drive, square dancing, or an ice cream social?

Keep in mind that while all these activities are available, there is no pressure to participate. For one entire day, I chose ☞ the luxury of doing absolutely nothing. I sat for a long time beside the sparkling clear river that ripples through the property and watched this year's crop of frisky colts frolicking in the meadow across the way while shadows lengthened on the red, rocky cliffs in the distance. I was certain I'd never want to move . . . until I heard the dinner bell!

Picnic tables piled high with barbecued chicken, corn on the cob, baked beans, and homemade bread brought on colossal appetites, lively conversation, and nary a frown to be seen. Farm-style breakfasts, including Tillie's outstanding cinnamon rolls, are served in the old-fashioned dining room or out on the porch by the river.

I stayed upstairs in the main lodge in a lovely corner suite where the windows opened wide and ☞ the river below sang me to sleep. Other accommodations are in country-style cabins and in the Wagon Wheel Barn, a for-real barn nicely renovated for people occupancy. Three of the cabins are new additions. Each has its own fireplace and is named for a Colorado heroine: Baby Doe, Molly Brown, and Annie Oakley.

How to get there: From I–25, take exit 257-B west onto Highway 34 and proceed 9 miles. Ranch is on the right.

Peaceful Valley Lodge and Guest Ranch
Lyons, Colorado 80540

Innkeepers: Karl and Mabel Boehm
Address/Telephone: South Star Route; (mailing address: P.O. Box 2811); (303) 747–2881
Rooms: 50; all with private bath. Wheelchair access.
Rates: Winter: $51.50 to $72.50, single, EPB; $58 to $79, double, EPB; $60 to $94, per person, AP. Summer: $51.50 to $72.50, single, EPB; $58 to $79, double, EPB; $86 to $120, per person, AP, includes all activities; $534 to $826, per person per week, AP, includes all activities. Six-day week and children's rates also available.
Open: All year.
Facilities and activities: Complete children's program: pony, wagon, and pony cart rides and petting farm for very young children; baby-sitting available; special activities for older children and teens. Lounge. Swimming pool, tennis court, riding arena, horseback riding, square dancing, jeep tours, trail rides, hiking, fishing, climbing, cross-country skiing. Sunday services in alpine chapel. Elevation 8,474 feet. Nearby: Shopping in small mountain towns.

Austria without jet lag—that's Peaceful Valley Lodge. ☛ Red hearts and edelweiss, Tyrolean music and dirndls, window boxes

Lyons, Colorado

full of geraniums, and, high on a hill, an awe-inspiring, alpine-style chapel complete with "onion" steeple. I was sure, any minute, Julie Andrews and her brood would come swinging across the meadow singing "The hills are alive . . ."!

This is ☞ probably the most extensively equipped inn I've ever been to. That's not to say that it is excessively large or impersonal. It isn't. It's homey, quaint, and authentically European, and yet it offers everything imaginable: swimming, tennis, indoor riding arena, lessons in horsemanship, square dancing, jeep tours to ghost towns and abandoned mining camps, coffee shop, two dining rooms, a Western shop, gift shop, sport shop, and family room and lounge. Nearly all the guest rooms have recently been remodeled. Thus, what were already very attractive accommodations are now absolutely beautiful.

Mabel comes from Kentucky, has a degree in sociology, and is a marvelous cook. Karl is from the Austrian Tyrol community of Tarrenz and has a master's degree in foreign affairs. They have owned their inn for more than thirty-three years.

In addition to family-style meals of meat, mashed potatoes and gravy, fresh vegetables, and homemade desserts, Chef Oskar Berger, from Krems, Austria, creates ☞ some of the best European-inspired cuisine to be found. Apple pancakes with apple syrup; *bircher muesli*, a Swiss oatmeal made with fresh fruit and fruit juice; and *rouladen*, thin slices of beef rolled around carrots and dill pickle and served with gravy are only a few of the specialties you will find here.

How to get there: From I-25, north of Denver, take exit 243 west onto Highway 66 and proceed to Lyons. From Lyons, take Highway 7 southwest to the lodge.

Davidson's Country Inn
Pagosa Springs, Colorado 81147

Innkeepers: Evelyn and Gilbert Davidson
Address/Telephone: P.O. Box 87; (303) 264–5863
Rooms: 9; 1 with private bath, 8 share 4 baths. Well-behaved pets considered. Smoking outside only.
Rates: $32, single; $43.50, double; $55, 2-room suite; EPB. Group rates available. Children under 4, free; 4 and over $6.
Open: All year.
Facilities and activities: Picnic lunches available with advance notice. Alcohol not permitted. Sun deck, solarium with television, library, game room, horseshoes, outdoor barbecue and picnic area. Children's indoor play corner, back-porch toy box, and sandbox. Gift shop with handmade country items. Elevation 7,079 feet. Nearby: restaurants, hot springs, hot tubs, hiking, fishing, hayrides, downhill and cross-country skiing, snowmobiling, sleigh rides.

What a find for families with young children! Davidson's Inn has ☞ a children's corner that is guaranteed to delight small tykes. The doll bed filled with "babies," the school desk, play church, dollhouse, books, and child-size cupboard, sink, and stove are sure to keep the little ones busy.

When you come to stay at the Davidsons', be sure to make

Pagosa Springs, Colorado

friends with every guest so you can take a peek into all their rooms. I wandered up and down the hallways on all three floors and couldn't decide on a favorite. High on my list, though, is the dainty Hummingbird with its ☞ quilt wall-hanging, brass bed, two old kerosene lamps, and antique dresser. For contrast, there's the third-floor Mountain Man Country, which feels like a frontier cabin, with wooden-spoked wagonwheels hanging from the ceiling and snowshoes tacked to the walls. This hideaway is the only room with a water bed, and I'm not sure what a mountain man would think of that; but being an adventurous sort, he'd probably love it.

The Davidson's family suite is perfect for those traveling with children. The inn also has some very large rooms with queen-size and twin beds and enough additional space to add a rollaway.

Each room is ☞ tastefully decorated with family heirlooms, valuable antiques, carefully chosen country touches, and fine pieces of handmade furniture. This would be a good place to pick up some excellent home-decorating ideas.

All the quilts were made by Evelyn's mother and 90-year-old grandmother. And there's a stuffed-goose doorstop and a calico pig that I would like to have in my own menagerie. One thing is for sure; when I go back, I'm going to allow time to look up the gentleman who made the wooden rockers and see if I can order one. They are really special.

Since the last time I was here, the Davidsons have added a game room with a pool table, bumper pool, and Ping-Pong.

Evelyn serves a full country breakfast including a hot dish, her special apple kringle, fresh fruit, cereals, juice, coffee, homemade jellies, and farm-fresh honey. Stay a second day, and you may get to try her strawberry muffins. Coffee, iced tea, and hot chocolate are always available.

Evelyn will pack box lunches for picnickers, hikers, and fishermen; or she recommends The Pie Shoppe for sandwiches, homemade breads, and pies and the Old Miner's Steak House for good, hearty dinners.

How to get there: Inn is on south side of Highway 160, 2 miles east of Pagosa Springs.

The Portland Inn
Victor, Colorado
80860

Innkeepers: Guido and Sandy Honeycutt
Address/Telephone: 412 West Portland Avenue (mailing address: P.O. Box 32); (719) 689–2102
Rooms: 4 share 1½ baths. Smoking permitted only if other guests don't mind.
Rates: $30, single; $38, double; continental-plus breakfast. Children under 5, free; 5 and over, $8.
Open: All year.
Facilities and activities: Kitchen facilities. Hot tub. Two large decks. Complimentary evening tea and sherry with cookies or cake. Play area, sandbox, and swing set for children. Elevation 10,000 feet. Nearby: Florissant Fossil Beds National Monument, Mueller State Park, Victor/Lowell Thomas Museum and other museums, gold mine tours, walking tour, excursion steam train, restaurants, shopping, hiking, fishing, ice skating, downhill and cross-country skiing.

Peace and quiet and bed and breakfast go hand in hand in this small, unassuming community. The handsomely restored, circa-1898 Portland Inn, located on a tranquil side street only a few blocks from the town's main thoroughfare, provides a great place to relax and unwind.

Sandy and Guido have worked hard to restore dignity to their inn, and they have obviously succeeded. The guest rooms are lovely, furnished with antique beds and dressers and decorated with dainty wallpaper, lace, and ruffles. A stay here gives one the chance to ☞ experience life at the turn of the century while soaking up the history of the area. It's easy to imagine your way back to the early 1900s as you chat over tea in the parlor, ☞ peek out through lace curtains to rolling hills capped with now-abandoned mining headframes and ore dumps, or sit on one of the two decks and hear nothing but the distant bark of a far-away dog.

Victor, however, did not always possess the calm it does today. During the gold rush of the late 1800s, it was a bustling, sometimes riotous mining town and, from 1891 to 1951, over $432 million worth of gold was mined here.

Guests at The Portland Inn have the use of a small, sunny kitchen, perfect for preparing family picnics or keeping snacks for kids' between-meal hungries; a pretty parlor; and an outdoor hot tub. A generous breakfast of Sandy's homemade breads, seasonal fresh fruit, hot and cold cereal, juice, and coffee is served in the parlor or on the deck.

For dinner, I walked to Sugar Plums, and I recommend that you try it, too. They prepare just about everything from scratch including homemade soup and wonderful, wonderful pies. I had peanut butter pie, and it was excellent.

"We like children," say Sandy and Guido, and their two small daughters, Heidi and Kelsi, will make good playmates for your little ones.

How to get there: From I–25 at Colorado Springs, take Highway 24 west to town of Divide. Turn south onto Highway 67 and proceed to Cripple Creek. Continue on Highway 67 for 6 miles to Victor.

Idaho City Hotel
Idaho City, Idaho
83631

Innkeepers: Don and Pat Campbell
Address/Telephone: P.O. Box 70; (208) 392-4290
Rooms: 5; all with private bath. Pets permitted.
Rates: $30, single; $32.50, double; $42.50 suite for 4; EP. $40.50 for lodging, breakfast, and activity package for two.
Open: All year.
Facilities and activities: Complimentary coffee. Restaurants 1 block away. Located in center of 1860s mining town designated as a National Historic Site. Gift shop. Elevation 4,000 feet. Nearby: Historic buildings, shopping. Boise National Forest, Sawtooth National Recreation Area, ghost towns, hot springs, hiking, great fishing, snow tubing, cross-country skiing, snowmobiling.

This is a great place for kids—not so fancy that you have to be overly concerned about their touching something they shouldn't.

And, if you want to escape into the past, you can't do much better than to spend a few days or a week here.

I expected any minute to see the likes of John Wayne jump from the upstairs veranda, land on the back of his faithful steed, and ride off into the sunset. That's how authentically Old West this little hotel is.

Idaho City, Idaho

Built in the 1920s, it is really the "new kid on the block" compared with its circa-1860 neighbors. The guest rooms are furnished with white iron beds and antique oak dressers. Room 4 is especially nice, with its ornate bed, ruffled curtains, satin bedspread, and super-large, oak-fixtured bathroom. Mickey the shaggy dog is usually flopped on the front porch; tame ducks frequent the creek out back; and there are five cats that, if invited, will sleep with you.

Don and Pat offer ☞ a package deal that just could be the value of a lifetime. It includes overnight lodging for two, two breakfasts at Calamity Jayne's cafe, passes to the geothermally heated warm-springs pools, two admissions to the local museum, 10 percent off at the hotel's gift shop, and 2-for-1 drinks at Idaho City saloons. The cost? $40.50 for two!

A rip-snorting gold camp during the 1860s and, for a short time, the largest city in the Pacific Northwest, with more than 6,000 residents, 5,691 of them men, Idaho City is still the county seat of Boise County and remains a nonglitzy, educational, historic site. A self-guided walking tour encompasses eighteen buildings, sixteen of which were built before the turn of the century. These include a hand-hewn 1864 jail, a former schoolhouse, the newspaper office, and Idaho's oldest existing mercantile store.

Gift shops, an ice cream parlor, and several restaurants and saloons line the boardwalks and dirt streets. I recommend the Golden Nugget for hefty steaks, hamburgers, and homemade pies.

How to get there: From I–84 at Boise, go north on Highway 21 for 38 miles to Idaho City. From Main Street, turn left onto Walulla and drive one block. Hotel is on the corner of Walulla and Montgomery streets.

✻

D: *Bring good walking shoes or hiking boots. And, if your children are small, bring extra play clothes. Your family will want to spend a lot of time outdoors in this beautiful part of Idaho.*

Averill's Flathead Lake Lodge and Dude Ranch
Bigfork, Montana
59911

Innkeepers: Doug and Maureen Averill
Address/Telephone: P.O. Box 248; (406) 837–4391
Rooms: 19 in lodge, plus 16 cottages; all with private bath. Wheelchair access.
Rates: $989 per adult, single or double occupancy, for one week (minimum) stay; AP and all activities. Special rates for teens and children. No credit cards.
Open: May through September.
Facilities and activities: Saddle Sore Saloon for setups. BYOB. Outdoor swimming pool, game room, laundry facilities. Children's arts and crafts classes. Horseback riding, breakfast rides, steak-fry rides, hayrides, tennis, hiking, fishing, swimming, boating, windsurfing, waterskiing, sailing. Nearby: Glacier National Park, Swan River, whitewater rafting, kayaking.

You don't normally expect a dude ranch to offer many water activities, but at this ranch, the lake provides as much pleasure as the trails and wilderness do.

The family-operated ranch covers 2,000 acres of sprawling

Bigfork, Montana

lawns, tree-studded hillside, and remote mountain terrain and borders on the largest natural lake west of the Great Lakes.

The attractive lodge rooms have log-beamed ceilings and paneled walls, queen- and king-size beds, ruffled curtains, and writing desks. Some rooms have lofts and claw-footed bathtubs. Two- and three-bedroom cottages are also available.

Dining is family style in the large dining room. Long tables are spread with meat-and-potato-type meals that include soups made daily from fresh-from-the-garden vegetables, cheese breads and cinnamon breads, homemade baked beans, ten-ounce steaks, barbecued ribs, and special brownies made from an old family recipe. Kids can help with cookie baking and, if they get the in-between-meals hungries, they are welcome to stop by the kitchen for a snack.

After breakfast, lunch, and dinner at this "chuckwagon," you'll be ready for some outdoor activities, and there is no end to things to do. You can participate in ranch chores, learn to rope, take rodeo instruction, help train the new crop of colts, or hit the trail for a long, leisurely ride.

Just about every water sport imaginable is available here, too, including fishing, swimming, sailing, water-skiing, and 👉 cruising on the ranch's motorlaunch or 51-foot sailboat.

This ranch is known nationwide, and 60 to 70 percent of its guests are returnees, so it's best to get your reservation in early. 👉 *Better Homes and Gardens* magazine twice named the ranch as the "Outstanding Family Vacation Spot" in the west; *Sunset* magazine featured it in its "Unique Vacations"; *Arco* magazine claims it to be one of the ten best ranches in America; and *Mobil Travel Guide* gave it a four-star rating. Not bad, I'd say.

How to get there: From Highway 35 in northwestern Montana, 1 mile south of Bigfork, turn west onto Flathead Lodge Road. Turn right at the stagecoach that sits beside the road. Inn is at the end of the trail.

❇

D: *In addition to the horses, cows, chickens, steers, goats, cats, and dogs that live on the ranch, deer, bear, and bald eagles are often seen in the pastures or on the mountainside. The National Bison Range, harboring buffalo and elk, is only an hour away.*

Nevada City Hotel
Nevada City, Montana
59755

Innkeeper: Bruce D. McCallum
Address/Telephone: P.O. Box 338, Virginia City, MT 59755; (406) 843–5377
Rooms: 31 rooms and cabins; all with private bath. Wheelchair accessible. Pets allowed.
Rates: $34, regular rooms and cabins, single or double; $42, large Victorian rooms, single or double; EP. Children under 12, free; age 12 and over, $3 to $4.50.
Open: Memorial Day through mid-September.
Facilities and activities: Restaurant next door. Hotel is part of preserved 1860s mining camp. Elevation 5,440 feet. Nearby: railroad museum, working narrow-gauge railroad, melodrama theater.

From my room, I could hear ☞ old-time tunes coming from the mechanical music machines in the Nevada City Music Hall next door. In this nineteenth-century version of a video-games parlor, kids can play "The Loudest Organ in Montana" for a quarter, "The Smallest Wurlitzer Band Organ" for a dime, and find out who they are likely to marry for a nickel. They also can peer through several flip-flop stereoscopic viewers and listen to the "Famous and Obnoxious Horn Machine," said to have driven

Nevada City, Montana

twenty-eight changemakers, seventy-two bartenders, and nearly a million tourists to the brink of insanity.

My room, Number 7, and the one across the hall, number 8, are completely furnished with gorgeous antiques. Each has two double beds with 8-foot headboards; marble-topped dressers; velvet-upholstered, high-back chairs; and gigantic armoires. The walls and ceilings are made of split logs painted white; the floors are carpeted in what appears to be wall-to-wall braided rug. Between these two rooms, and shared with all guests, is a Victorian parlor with plush chairs and an old Beatty's Beethoven organ. The other accommodations are not done in antiques, but they are country comfortable.

The upstairs veranda, facing the main street, looks across to ☞ an old railroad museum with vintage train cars that one can leisurely stroll through.

This hotel is unique in that it is part of a restored open-air museum. A step out the back door, past the two-story outhouse (said to be the most-photographed building in Montana!), brings you to dirt streets and authentic shops and homes from another era. A walk through the wagon barn, with dusty sun rays lighting the way, reveals ☞ old buggies, stagecoaches, and a seemingly endless assortment of wagon wheels.

I tiptoed through one old Victorian house and sat on the front porch of another, listened to the screen door softly creaking in the breeze, and imagined petticoated little girls giggling on their way to the schoolhouse just two doors away. Behind them, I was sure I saw several rosy-faced boys, dragging their feet to delay submitting to another day of dreaded 3 Rs. Oh my, was that really a frog peeping out from a coat pocket?

Dinner that night was in the patio garden of the Star Bakery, just up the street. I had the char-broiled pork chop, and my guest had linguine and clams. Good-sized portions, nicely prepared and seasoned. The hamburgers were huge and looked great.

How to get there: From I–90, take Highway 287 south to Ennis, then west to Nevada City. Inn is on right.

❀

D: *Be sure to allow time to take the kids on the narrow-gauge passenger train that chugs along the 1½ miles between Nevada City and Virginia City during the summer.*

Old Pioneer Garden
Unionville, Nevada
89418

Innkeepers: Lew and Mitzi Jones
Address/Telephone: #79; (702) 538–7585
Rooms: 9, 4 with private bath; 1 2-bedroom cabin with kitchen. Pets permitted. No smoking inside inn.
Rates: $35, single; $45, double; EPB. Children under 2, free; over 2, $10. Cabin, $80 for 3 people or $90 for 4. No credit cards.
Open: All year.
Facilities and activities: Breakfast, lunch, dinner. Nearby: Rye Patch State Park and Reservoir, hot springs, hiking, fishing, boating, horse and mountain-bike trails. No television reception but VCR and extensive library of older movies available. Farm animals, creek.

A visit to the Old Pioneer Garden is a wonderful experience for children. Lew will teach them to milk a goat, throw hay to the animals, gather the eggs, and feed the ducks, geese, and guineas.

☛ This inn has it all—a fine assortment of friendly farm animals; very special innkeepers; country-cottage accommodations; farm-style meals; clean air; an extensive orchard, grape arbor, and vegetable patch; and a gazebo beside a rippling creek.

When I arrived, Lew had a warm fire going in my room. After settling in, I walked to dinner at the 1865 Talcott House under

Unionville, Nevada

stars so bright they seemed to touch the ground. Mitzi had vegetable-beef stew, salad, and apricot-pudding cake waiting in the kitchen. Next morning's generous breakfast included apple-filled pancakes made with hand-ground cornmeal. Delicious! ☞ Meal conversation is so easy here that, long after you've oversatisfied your appetite, you find you're still at the table chatting as though you've all been friends forever.

The next morning, snuggled under an antique, handmade quilt, I wondered about Thomas J. Hadley, the blacksmith whose home this cottage had been back in the 1860s and who, besides shoeing the horses and repairing farm and mining equipment, had raised the vegetables and fruit for the community in his pioneer garden.

Unionville was a booming mining camp back then. Today it has a population of twenty-two.

Lew and Mitzi live in the Talcott House, which has four guest rooms. The Ross House is a rustic, two-bedroom, former-wagonmaster's cabin, while the Hadley House, where I stayed, has more guest rooms, a library, a farm kitchen where breakfast is served at an 8-foot-long table, and a large sitting room.

Lew and Mitzi have done a commendable job of extending and refurbishing this last building, making it into one of the most inviting and attractive country inns I have visited. ☞ The emphasis is truly on "country" with all the right touches including a beautiful armoire handmade by Lew, who used screws and pegs but no nails. The upstairs ceilings slope over dormer windows; ceiling-to-floor bookshelves line the walls; and heavy, perfect-condition, overstuffed furniture from the 1930s waits to envelop you with cozy security.

I can't wait to turn off the gravel road again and walk under the weathered "Old Pioneer Garden" sign and up the lane to a chorus of baa's from woolly white sheep and inquisitive brown goats. This is country at its best.

How to get there: From I–80 at Mill City (139 miles east of Reno), take exit 149 south onto Highway 400 and proceed 16 miles to Unionville turnoff. Inn is only a short distance up the road, on the left.

The Homestead
Midway, Utah
84032

Innkeepers: Jerry and Carole Sanders

Address/Telephone: 700 North Homestead Drive; (801) 645–1102 inside Utah or (800) 327–7220 outside Utah

Rooms: 43 including 7 guest houses; all with private bath and air conditioning.

Rates: $59 to $165, single and double; $79, Bunkhouse for 4; EP. Children under 2, free; 2 and over, $7.50. Ski and guest ranch packages available.

Open: All year.

Facilities and activities: Breakfast, lunch, dinner, Sunday brunch. Bar service in dining room. Children's programs during summer. Babysitting available with advance notice. Indoor swimming pool, outdoor swimming pool and hot tub, mineral bath, tennis, golf, horseback riding, hayrides, volleyball, horseshoes, sleigh rides, cross-country skiing, snowmobiling. Nearby: trout fishing and water sports at Deer Creek Lake, downhill skiing at Park City and Robert Redford Sundance ski areas.

In 1886, Swiss-born Simon Schneitter may have cursed the mineral hot springs that made farming his land next to impossible. But as friends and neighbors arrived to bathe in the health-giving waters, he, a resourceful man, soon realized the potential of the

Midway, Utah

warm water that bubbled from his "hot pots." He constructed a pool and bath houses, added a few guest rooms, and, when his wife, Fanny, began serving up country-fried chicken, built on a dining room. Simon decided that the resort business was much more lucrative than trying to grow alfalfa.

The Homestead is set on forty-three acres and comprises the main lodge plus seven distinctly different guest houses, including the Victorian Virginia House, the sprawling Ranch House, the rustic Barn, and the Milk House. My favorite is the Milk House with its provincial-print wallpaper and white woodwork. It's cool and clean, with a country feeling, just as a milk house should be. At one time, it was a cold storage for milk, and, during Prohibition, it housed liquor for a thriving gambling business. When making reservations, ask about the Bunkhouse. It has two queen-size beds and a separate bunk room for the kids.

This inn can be just about anything you want it to be: casual, elegant, social, or private. Children can do their own thing while you do yours, or, if you choose, you can participate in numerous activities together as a family.

You can ride horseback through beautiful Heber Canyon, swim in either the indoor or outdoor pools, soak in a spring-fed mineral bath, or doze on a lawn chair under whispering pine and fluttering aspen. Small children enjoy playing outdoors on beautifully landscaped lawns with favorite toys brought from home, and teens find more than enough to do, organized or individual, to keep them busy.

The dining room is large, with an expanse of windows providing a view of rolling range lands. I can vouch for the chicken cordon bleu, stuffed to bursting with melted cheese and ham. But the clincher was the mousse cake, a French–Genoese delight made with butter, cream, and white chocolate and adorned with dark-chocolate mousse. The only item that can compete with this is The Homestead's praline cheesecake. You must try both, preferably at different meals.

How to get there: 11 miles south of Park City on Highway 40, turn west at Midway/Homestead exit. The way is well marked with signs.

The Old Miners' Lodge
Park City, Utah
84060

Innkeepers: Susan Wynne, Hugh Daniels, and Jeff Sadowsky
Address/Telephone: 615 Woodside Avenue (mailing address: P.O. Box 2639); (801) 645–8068
Rooms: 7; 4 with private bath, 3 share 2 baths. Smoking in living room only.
Rates: $40 to $80, from April 15 to November 15; $70 to $135, November 16 to April 14; $90 to $155, December 20 to January 3; EPB. Depending on season, children 12 and uner, $5; 13 and over, $15.
Open: All year.
Facilities and activities: Dinner for groups upon request. Complimentary wine. Kitchen and laundry privileges. Toys and games for children. Elevation 7,000 feet. Nearby: Park City Ski Area, Park West Ski Area, Deer Valley Ski Resort, championship golf courses, indoor and outdoor tennis, hiking, fishing, alpine slide, gondola rides, swimming, horseback riding, hot-air-balloon rides, downhill and cross-country skiing, helicopter skiing, snowmobiling.

Built in 1893 as a boardinghouse for miners, this Western Victorian has been standing above this old mining town for generations.

Whereas the miners probably stayed in dorm-style rooms with a minimum of comforts, today's guests enjoy down quilts, feather pillows, electric mattress covers, turn-down service, and complimentary wine, cider, cheese, and popcorn in the evenings. Such amenities would have been wishful thinking only on the part of even the most imaginative of miners.

During winter, you can ☞ ski out the back door or ☞ sit in the hot tub and watch fellow skiers glide by on the ski lift within a few feet of your steamy domain. In summer, the hot tub is just as special after a long hike.

The guest rooms are named after colorful characters from the town's past. The Jedidiah Grant has a king-size bed, enclosed sun porch, ruffled curtains, claw-footed tub, and corner sink. It shares the best view in the house with the Flip Wing Suite. Both look down into the valley and up to Old Town.

The most interesting guest room is the Black Jack Murphy. ☞ One enters via a narrow, timbered passageway constructed to resemble a mine shaft. The room itself, reminiscent of a miner's cabin, has log walls, bare light bulb hanging from the ceiling, and curtained closet; but I noticed that even bad Jack had a mint on his pillow and a terry-cloth robe for walking to the hot tub. Black Jack Murphy's claim to fame (or infamy) comes from his being the only person in Park City's history to have been lynched. He is said to have jumped a claim and murdered the owner. As the sheriff took him to jail, he was seized by a mob of outraged miners and hanged.

Breakfast is miner size and might be German pancakes with bacon, egg burritos, or whole wheat waffles from an old-time recipe. Hugh, the main chef, will prepare a seven-course dinner for groups of six to eight people with prior arrangement. Or it's only a couple blocks down the hill to numerous restaurants.

How to get there: Highway 224 south turns into Park Avenue at Park City. Turn right onto 8th Street and proceed 1 block to Woodside Avenue. Turn left onto Woodside. The inn is on the right.

D: *This is sort of a sit-on-the-floor, wear-your-robe-to-breakfast kind of place. Children will like its informality as well as the toys, stuffed animals, and games waiting for them.*

Rimrock Dude Ranch
Cody, Wyoming
82414

Innkeepers: Glenn and Alice Fales
Address/Telephone: 2728 North Fork Road; (307) 587–3970
Rooms: 9 cabins; all with private bath.
Rates: $95, single; $74 per person, double. Reduced rates for additional guests sharing same cabin. Rates are for 7-day minimum stay, AP, and include horse and all ranch activities. No credit cards.
Open: June 1 through August 31.
Facilities and activities: BYOB bar with locked cubbyhole for your bottle; ranch furnishes ice and mixes. Children's program, recreation room. Riding instruction, breakfast rides, wine-and-cheese rides, float trips, western dancing, rodeo tickets, tour of Yellowstone Park, stocked trout pond. Elevation 6,500 feet. Nearby: Big Horn Sheep Preserve, Buffalo Bill Historical Center, Yellowstone Park, hot springs, hiking, great fishing, golf, tennis.

Some families have been returning to Rimrock for as many as twenty-two years, and young adults who began coming here as children are now bringing their own youngsters. According to Alice, "All activities are geared around children, and we let the adults join in." Now, that should make it a perfect place for all us "grown-up kids," right?

Cody, Wyoming

I've had an occasional innkeeper tell me that former guests sometimes send letters or small gifts of appreciation and invitations to come visit *them*. Well, Alice and Glenn have received all three, but they can go one more. Their ranch dog, Badger, who has learned his share of social skills, was recently the recipient of a box of new toys, sent by one of many human pals he has made over the years. It looks to me as though ☞ folks depart the Rimrock feeling more like they are *leaving* home rather than *returning* home.

And it's no wonder. Alice is ☞ one of the warmest innkeepers I've met, the sort who makes you feel like family. And Glenn, former rodeo contestant, range cowboy, and horse trader, will do anything possible to make your stay exactly as you hoped it would be.

Rocky steps and dirt paths lead through natural grass to log cabins, perfectly placed along a bubbling brook that flows through the property. Furnished in western fashion with log walls and braided rugs, some cabins have stone fireplaces and sitting rooms, and all have baths, heat control, and maid service. Sitting on ☞ your own private porch among shade trees and bright flowers, while listening to the water tumble past your front door, is one of the most peaceful experiences possible.

The meals here are outstanding. Guests and ranch hands eat together, and this results in a hearty helping of laughter and camaraderie served up with ranch cooking at its best. Once a week there is a full Thanksgiving-type dinner with roast turkey and all the trimmings. Other days it's prime rib, steak cookouts, and fried chicken, the likes of which would make the Colonel take to grilling hot dogs.

How to get there: Ranch is located on Highway 14–16–20, 26 miles west of Cody and halfway between Cody and Yellowstone National Park. Watch for sign, turn south on gravel road, and proceed for 1 mile.

Lazy L & B Ranch
DuBois, Wyoming
82513

Innkeepers: Bernard and Leota Didier
Address/Telephone: East Fork Road; (307) 455-2839
Rooms: 16 cabins; all with private bath. Pets considered.
Rates: $595 single occupancy, per week; $575 per person, double occupancy, per week; $475 per child under 12, per week; AP, horses and all activities included. No credit cards.
Open: June 1 through September 10.
Facilities and activities: Nightly "Happy Hour" in Ranch House; setups; BYOB. No television reception but large selection of video tapes. Supervised and planned activites for children, 4 stocked trout ponds, square dancing, hayrides, breakfast rides, steak fries, unlimited trail and wilderness riding, heated outdoor swimming pool. Elevation 7,000 feet. Nearby: fishing, hiking, visits to cowboy town of DuBois and to ghost town.

Settled in the late 1800s by Scottish sheepherders, Scots Valley is a lush, green carpet of land flanked by flaming red rock, sagebrush-dotted hills, and three mountain ranges.

Tucked away in the midst of all this splendor is the 1,800-acre Lazy L & B Ranch. The accommodations are rustic but comfortable log cabins. The dining room and library are located in the original farmhouse.

DuBois, Wyoming

The daily trail rides are special because of the ☛ primitive, unspoiled area they traverse. A short venture through the valley took us to the old Duncan homestead, now owned by Bernard's brother and sister-in-law. A tiny regional post office, operational until only a few years ago, sits on the front porch. Only about 4 by 5 feet, it still has the original cubbyholes used for the ranchers' mail.

Another trail takes riders to the scenic East Fork Gorge, where one views a spectacular panorama of mountains, valley, badlands, and prairie.

My favorite outing was to ☛ an abandoned Scottish homestead. The log house stands alone on the prairie, its sod-roofed outbuildings, corral, and root cellar still intact. I pondered the fate of the people who had brought their hopes here, labored here, and, perhaps, died here. Did their dreams come true? I wonder.

Guests enjoy lunch served from the chuck wagon under the tall cottonwood trees down by the river and breakfast and dinner in the ranch dining room. No one is allowed to leave hungry. I was treated to a garden salad so fresh it actually had been part of the garden an hour before. Your entree might be steak, chops, or trout; but whatever the cook's choice happens to be, it is always hearty, tasty, and filling.

The children are served first and then entertained by the wranglers while the adults dine. A nice feature, I think.

Breads are homemade, a specialty being "bucket bread." This is a whole wheat bread baked in cans and often served on trail cookouts because it doesn't smash when it is carried in the cans.

If you are looking for an authentic Old West experience, you are sure to like this place.

How to get there: 11 miles east of DuBois on Highway 26–287, watch for sign, "Elk Winter Feeding Refuge." Take gravel road north for 12 miles. Ranch is on right.

D: *The weekly hayride in an old ranch wagon to a haunted house out on the prairie is sure to thrill youngsters and adults.*

WEST COAST

by
Julianne Belote

Julianne Belote claims she writes about country inns because it gets her out of the house and because she loves breakfasts that someone else fixes. A love affair with the West Coast and a husband's penchant for back roads began her discovery of inns more than twenty years ago, when there were few such havens. Now she drives to hundreds from the Mexican border to the San Juan Islands.

Julianne says about inns, "On the West Coast, at least, no one is certain what you mean when you talk about an inn. Inns snuggle uncertainly in a lodging land bordered by small hotels, motels, cabins, resorts, and homestays. We have only a few that serve meals beyond breakfast, and the emergence of urban inns rules out the strictly 'country' definition." Nevertheless, Julianne recommends 199 inns in the second edition of *Recommended Country Inns—the West Coast* "that offer a level of individual decor not found at motels, an ambience cozier and more intimate than that found at a resort, innkeepers who treat you like their very special house guest, and homemade meals or knowledgeable pointers to the best food nearby."

Julianne has written three other books, including one about Colonial housewives, and she frequently writes magazine articles—when not getting her own breakfast.

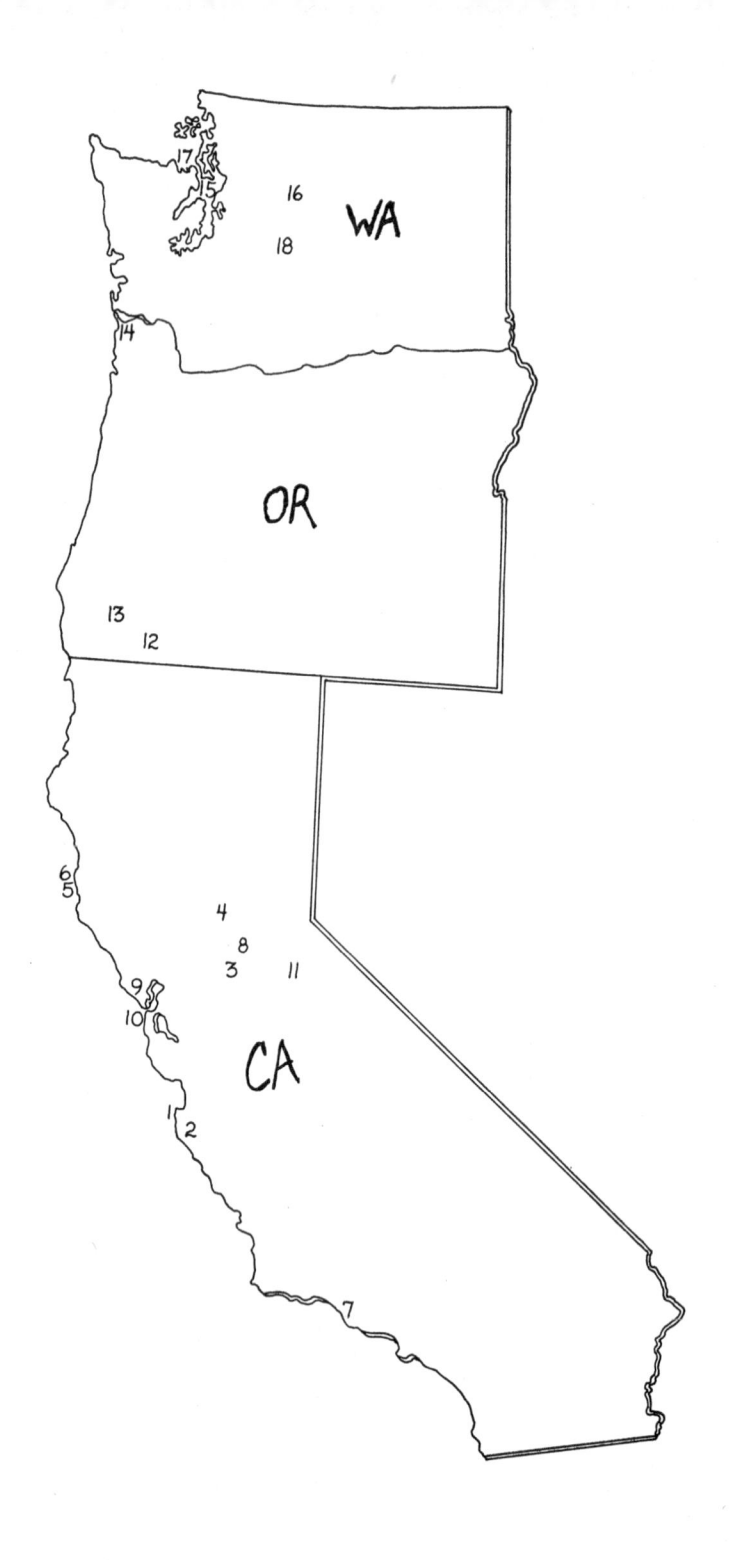

West Coast

Numbers on map refer to towns numbered below.

CALIFORNIA
1. Carmel-by-the-Sea, Mission Ranch 244
2. Carmel Valley, Stonepine 246
3. Columbia, City Hotel 248
4. Georgetown, The American River Inn 250
5. Little River, Little River Inn 252
6. Mendocino, MacCallum House 254
7. Montecito, San Ysidro Ranch 256
8. Placerville, Fleming Jones Homestead 258
9. Point Reyes Station, Holly Tree Inn 260
10. San Francisco, The Washington Square Inn 262
11. Twain Harte, Twain Harte's Bed and Breakfast 264

OREGON
12. Ashland, Chanticleer Bed and Breakfast Inn 266
13. Grants Pass, Paradise Ranch 268
14. Seaside, The Boarding House 270

WASHINGTON
15. Bainbridge Island, The Bombay House 272
16. Leavenworth, Haus Rohrbach Pension 274
17. Port Townsend, Arcadia Country Inn 276
18. South Cle Elum, The Moore House 278

Mission Ranch
Carmel-by-the-Sea, California
93923

Innkeeper: Joyce Kutchins
Address/Telephone: 26270 Dolores; (408) 624–6436
Rooms: 6 in The Farmhouse, plus cottages and motel units; all with private bath.
Rates: $68 to $80 for Farmhouse rooms; $85 to $115 for cottages; $45 to $70 for motel units; continental breakfast buffet.
Open: All year.
Facilities and activities: Lunch, dinner, piano bar, cocktail lounge. Nature trails; 8 tennis courts, tennis clinics offered. Party Barn available for parties, dancing. Play in lagoon formed by the Carmel River; short walk to beach, Carmel Mission. Short drive to Point Lobos, Big Sur.

A friend waxing nostalgic about his college days (more than thirty-five years ago) remembered when he and his friends would drive down to Carmel from San Francisco to dine and dance at the Mission Ranch. It's downright reassuring to see that places that gave us happy memories are still around and looking good.

The Mission Ranch is charming a new generation with its historic buildings, ☛ hundred-year-old cypresses, and its outlook on the rugged beauty of Point Lobos. The restaurant still serves hearty dinners, and the ☛ piano bar—how's *that* for nostalgia?—

still gives repressed saloon singers an atmosphere for crooning.

One change at the Ranch is that the family homestead is now a bed-and-breakfast inn. The Farmhouse, built a century ago, was home to the Martins, a family of Scottish immigrants who came to California in 1856 and bought large acreage encircling an old Spanish mission.

The two-story, white frame house, sitting under several enormous cypress trees, is now sound-proofed and newly decorated in a homey, not high-fashion style. The large rooms are furnished very simply with odd pieces from the 1920s and 1930s. Bathrooms are large too, with showers added, and complimentary toiletries. All six rooms in the Farmhouse share a spacious parlor with Victorian sofas flanking a wood-burning fireplace, a television, and a telephone.

The cottages are ideal for families. They vary in size, and the largest, the Bunkhouse, sleeps six people and has a kitchen.

The dining room is where a generous continental breakfast is set up buffet style in the morning: fruit, juices, breads, cold cereals, coffee, and teas.

This is an atmosphere different from the usual Carmel lodgings—an authentic ranch, not a manicured resort. And it's a mere few blocks from the chichi streets of art galleries and stylish shops. Twenty acres to roam and enjoy, with long vistas of fields and water. In a tourist town that caters mostly to adults, the Mission Ranch is an offbeat haven for families.

How to get there: At Carmel, exit State Highway 1 on Rio Road west, toward the ocean. Immediately past the mission, turn left on Lasuen Drive; follow around to the Ranch on your left.

※

J: *The mission just up the road is officially "San Carlos Borromeo de Carmelo," a romantic gem in the mission chain, with a Moorish tower and tranquil gardens. It's the resting place of Father Junipero Serra, who founded nine missions and died there in 1784. It is an interesting piece of history to show the children.*

Stonepine
Carmel Valley, California
93924

Innkeepers: Owners Gordon Hentschel and Noel Irwin-Hentschel; resident manager, Richard Buelow
Address/Telephone: 150 East Carmel Valley Road; (408) 659–2245
Rooms: 12 suites; all with private bath with Jacuzzi and cable television, most with wood-burning fireplace.
Rates: $150 to $500 double occupancy, continental breakfast. Exclusive use of the chateau (up to 16 people) $3,500 per night; Paddock House exclusive (up to 8 people) $1,000. Children welcome in Paddock suites.
Open: All year.
Facilities and activities: Dinner by reservation. 330 acres of meadows, gardens, and woodlands to explore over miles of riding and running trails or by horse-drawn Victorian carriages. Swimming pool, tennis court, croquet, archery range, soccer field. Health club, steam bath. Equestrian Center; instruction, moonlight hayrides. Minutes from Carmel, Monterey, Big Sur.

If F. Scott Fitzgerald had wanted Gatsby to make his splash in California's Carmel Valley instead of East Egg, the once-private estate of Stonepine would have been the perfect background. Fitzgerald missed it, but you need not. The splendid Mediterranean-style house is now a remarkable country inn.

Carmel Valley, California

When you press the button that opens an electric gate guarding a mile-long road to the main house, you enter a world of quiet luxury and 330 acres of natural beauty. After three years of restoration and redecoration, the Chateau Noel has eight magnificent suites, and four less formal suites in the Paddock House.

The common rooms include an elegant foyer, living room, dining room, and handsome library paneled with burnished nineteenth century French oak. Every detail is first-class, even to the library shelves stocked with hardback copies of current titles and classics. Across the back of the estate is the 🖙 loggia with stone arches supported by centuries-old columns from Rome. In daylight, you look out to gnarled olive trees and gardens that frame a rolling meadow. At night, it's a romantic place to watch the sunset or dine by a blazing fire.

In the early 1930s, the estate was the foremost thoroughbred horse–breeding farm in California. (The owner was the daughter of the Crocker banking family of San Francisco, and the social set motored over from Pebble Beach to play polo and ride.) Today, the 🖙 Equestrian Center is the primary attraction at Stonepine with the finest examples of classic breeds in residence. Debby and Tommy Harris run the center. They give English and western riding lessons and two-day equestrian clinics—beginners welcome. Tommy's drives around the estate and moonlight hayrides are popular with guests.

To dine here is to feast on superb food and drink served on Limoges, Waterford, and Baccarat with sterling silver at a prix fixe of $40 per person. If you want to entertain, a creative 🖙 staff will produce a unique party with music, food, and entertainment. A recent Civil War extravaganza even had hairdressers and costumes for the guests—everything but live bullets in the battle re-enactment that took place off the loggia.

How to get there: From Highway 1 proceed east on Carmel Valley Road past a 13.0 mile marker; Stonepine will be on your right. Pick up telephone at the gate for entry. Complimentary airport pickups available in a Phantom V Rolls Royce. Monterey airport 30 minutes from Stonepine.

~~

J: *If you're striving to acquaint your little darlings with the finer things in life—this is the right country inn.*

olive Metcalf

City Hotel
Columbia, California 95310

Innkeeper: Tom Bender
Address/Telephone: Box 1870; (209) 532–1479
Rooms: 9; all with private half-bath, share showers down the hall.
Rates: Balcony rooms, $75; parlor and hall rooms, $60 to $65; double occupancy, continental breakfast. Children 2 and under, free; over 2, $10. Ask about theater, lodging, and dinner packages. Ski packages in season.
Open: All year.
Facilities and activities: Lunch, dinner, Saturday and Sunday brunch. What Cheer Saloon. Stroll the town with its restored buildings, working weavers, blacksmith, harness, and saddle shops. Stagecoach rides. Productions at Fallon House Theatre year round. Special events: Fire Muster in May, old-fashioned Fourth of July Celebration, two-week Miners' Christmas Celebration.

Early one morning in Columbia, I walked alone down Main Street's boardwalk, passed a stagecoach and team standing by the Wells Fargo Office, saw a woman in pioneer costume opening her candy store, and listened to the barber outside his shop playing a tune on a harmonica. This is the heart of gold-rush country, and no town captures that spirit better than Columbia. Children will feel a truer sense of that era in these streets than in any theme park you might visit.

In its gold-fever days, Columbia had forty saloons, 150 gambling houses, and eight hotels. Today the entire town is a state park, with ☞ tree-shaded Main Street barred to cars during the day to enhance the 1850–1870 atmosphere. But this is no static museum ghost town. Columbia is alive and bustling, and the jewel of the town is the City Hotel.

The two-story red-brick building has an upstairs parlor opening onto a wrought-iron balcony. A continental breakfast is served here each morning. Bedrooms are furnished with ☞ unusually impressive antiques, massive Victorian bedsteads and marble-topped bureaus. Half-baths in each room are restoration additions, but showers down the hall are scarcely a hardship when you're provided with a wicker basket to tuck over your arm holding robe, slippers, and all the essentials.

The handsome, high-ceilinged dining room is an improbable surprise. Gold-rush-country explorers usually don't expect white linen, silver napkin rings, and haute cuisine. Although it served classic French-style cooking for many years, the hotel has recently shifted to a more contemporary California cuisine, emphasizing fresh, seasonal, local ingredients. Among the sophisticated starters are house-cured salmon with crème fraîche, and fresh oysters in a roasted tomato vinaigrette. Entrees include roasted range chicken with Andouille sausage, and Sierra Foothill rabbit with wild-mushroom ragout. At this writing, they are working on a menu especially for children. Meanwhile, they offer half orders of many choices, such as a grilled lamb chop or fresh fish.

With all its gold-rush attractions, Columbia is a colorful addition to a Yosemite trip and only two hours from the valley floor.

How to get there: From San Francisco, take Highway 580 to Tracy, then 205 to Manteca. Take Highway 120 east, past Knights Ferry, to Highway 108 intersection. Continue on 108 east to Sonora; then Highway 49 to Columbia.

olive Metcalf

The American River Inn
Georgetown, California
95634

Innkeepers: Will and Maria Collin, Neal and Carol La Morte
Address/Telephone: Orleans Street at Main (mailing address: Box 43); (916) 333–4499 or (800) 245–6566 in California
Rooms: 25, including 7 suites; 12 with private bath, 7 additional baths shared. Queen Anne House separate from main inn, with 5 bedrooms, 3 baths, living room. Facilities for the handicapped. Prefer children 8 and over, but innkeepers will negotiate.
Rates: $68 to $78; suites $85; double occupancy; EPB and early evening wine and refreshments.
Open: All year.
Facilities and activities: Pool, Jacuzzi, formal croquet field, badminton, horseshoes, table tennis, bicycles. Walk to fishing streams, hiking trails, Indian Village, gold mine. Ten minutes from Gold Discovery Park. Arrangements made for white-water rafting, kayaking, hot-air ballooning. Antique/gift shop.

This is upscale, beautiful lodging for the gold country. But that's only fitting for a town that in 1853 estimated it had mined two million dollars in gold since the discovery in 1848. Once-rich, booming Georgetown, which then enjoyed the more picturesque name of Growlersburg, is now the setting of an ☞ impressive inn.

Georgetown, California

There's no escaping the fact that a lot of money has been spent restoring the original American Hotel, but the four young innkeepers have also lavished love, hard work, and attention to detail on the effort.

Antiques, polished pine floors, and bright provincial fabrics invite you into the attractive common rooms. In the late afternoon, the innkeepers serve local wines and hors d'oeuvres in the tasteful parlor. They'll also tell you about restaurants you can stroll to for dinner, or others a short drive away. Tall, handsomely draped windows, and antique tables and chairs are in the light-filled dining room. Breakfast here is a full production: fresh fruit (from the inn's own garden), juice, quiche or other egg dishes, Canadian bacon, berry muffins, and freshly ground coffee.

The spacious bedrooms have each been individually decorated and have luxurious bathrooms with thoughtful touches like robes. Rooms that open onto porches are especially pleasant. On a midweek visit, when the town is quiet, these are delightful spots for reading in a comfortable wicker chair.

Besides the fresh mountain air and the clear rivers and lakes, history's footprints are everywhere in these foothills of the Sierra Nevada. ☞ Georgetown, itself, is well worth your time. It's a pleasure to see some of the stately homes built in the 1870s and 1880s, surrounded by well-tended gardens. Georgetown is one of those gold towns with charm but few tourists ... always a winning combination.

If your family is looking for adventure, the innkeepers will arrange hot-air ballooning, rafting, or kayak trips down the American River. They'll even provide the bicycles and pack you a luxury picnic basket to take along while you explore, and you keep the basket for future trips. But a look at the beautiful ☞ natural stone swimming pool or the Jacuzzi could easily persuade you that relaxing right here has a lot of merit.

How to get there: From Sacramento, take I–50 or I–80 to Highway 49 to Highway 193. Follow the signs to Georgetown. The inn is 2 short blocks from the junction of California 193 and Main Street. Fly-in: Georgetown Airport. Free airport pickup.

J: School-age children will enjoy this area's gold-rush attractions.

olive Metcalf

Little River Inn
Little River, California 95456

Innkeepers: Charles D. Hervilla and Susan Kimberly
Address/Telephone: Highway 1; (707) 937–5942 reservations; 937–5051 restaurant
Rooms: 54, including inn rooms, cottages, motel-type units; all with private bath.
Rates: Rooms, $68 to $80; cottages, $80 to $175; double occupancy, EP. Children under 12, free; 12 and over, $10. No credit cards. Cribs available.
Open: All year.
Facilities and activities: Breakfast, dinner, bar. Lighted tennis courts. Golf course (nine holes), pro shop, putting greens; hiking, bicycling Van Damme State Park; beachcombing, good tide-pool exploring. Minutes from Mendocino art galleries, antique shops, restaurants.

Anyone who has driven north on Highway 1 along the dramatic Mendocino coastline has seen this rambling white inn off on the right. It looks "New England" because it was built in 1853 by a pioneer from Maine, Silas Coombs.

Three generations later, the parlors are lobbies and dining rooms, and the conservatory is the bar. The long front porch used to be the place to watch for arriving schooners. Now it's where you

Little River, California

follow the movements of the salmon fleet and, during the winter months, a favorite place for watching the migration of gray whales.

The range of accommodations here means you can have exactly what tickles your family's fancy. Rooms in the inn are decorated in early California style with antiques. If you prefer more modern appointments, try the motel wing. These pleasant, single-story rooms have big decks looking out at the ocean. Quiet spots to read are interrupted occasionally by deer wandering in the meadow below.

The cottages are especially cozy when you want to snuggle in for a few days with your family. They have one or two bedrooms, and some have sitting areas and fireplaces. One of my favorites for many years and through several refurbishings is the ☞ Van Damme Property. It sits across the road from the inn with three other units directly above the rugged coastline. The downstairs of a farmhouse called Mallory House is an outstanding choice for a family; it is the only one with a kitchen and a TV. It also has a comfortable living room, fireplace, two bedrooms, and a yard where the children can let off steam.

A continuous refurbishing of the inn goes on, but longtime fans will notice a new flair in recently done rooms. Ms. Kimberly has an eye for comfortable furnishings and tasteful appointments.

Little River's dining room is known up and down the coast for fine cooking. ☞ Whatever is freshest from the sea will be on the menu, along with good steaks and other choices. Salmon, abalone, snapper, and ling cod are specialties, and they are prepared with the delicate touch fresh fish deserves. (It ought to be a crime for kitchens to *claim* that they specialize in seafood, when their only technique is to beat, batter, and deep-fry!)

There's a down-to-earth quality about food here that you get only when things are homemade. This kitchen makes soups from scratch and its own breads. For dessert, try a fresh berry cobbler with tender crust and softly whipped cream.

How to get there: Three hours north of San Francisco on Coast Highway 1. The inn is on the right just south of Mendocino. Fly-in: Mendocino County Airport, 2 miles from the inn.

MacCallum House
Mendocino, California 95460

Innkeeper: Patti Raines; owners, Joe and Melanie Redding
Address/Telephone: 45020 Albion Street (mailing address: Box 206); (707) 937-0289
Rooms: 21; 7 with private bath, some rooms with sink.
Rates: $45 and up, double occupancy, $200 for 4-person suite; continental breakfast. Children, $15. Special family and midweek rates. Prefer cash or checks.
Open: All year.
Facilities and activities: Dinner, bar. Walk to everything in Mendocino: restaurants, shops, galleries, theater. Whale watching, fishing, hikes.

Daisy MacCallum was the lucky bride who, in 1882, moved into this beguiling New England–style Victorian house, a gift from her father. Gingerbread trim, gables, and a white picket fence decorate the yellow house that sits on three acres.

This is an inn for lovers of flowers and flounces, quilts and old trunks. In the old house, the rooms have been cheerfully preserved, many still containing the ☞ original furnishings, Tiffany lamps, and Persian rugs. Facilities are down the hall, but most rooms have a sink. The third floor is a cozy haven with walls papered with rotogravures of the period, and it has a small parlor with splendid views of the town.

Other accommodations are in cottages around the garden. Among these, The Watertower and The Green House have private baths and wood-burning stoves. The Carriage House is convenient for families because it has two separate units, each with a Franklin fireplace and privacy. The most luxurious rooms are those in The Barn. The ☞ upstairs unit has a private deck with sweeping views and a sitting room with a massive stone fireplace.

The Gray Whale Bar and sun porch are additions so skillfully done you would think they were part of Daisy's house. Remember, a bar means music and laughter (naturally), so if you plan to rise early for bird watching, you might want one of the garden or barn suites, a little more removed from the action.

Rob Fertero oversees the restaurant. Dinners are served in the book-lined dining room at tables set with fresh flowers and oil lamps, before a huge cobblestone fireplace. Like all good chefs, he cooks what is freshest and in season. No cans in this kitchen. Poached salmon with Béarnaise sauce, bouillabaisse, beef Bordelaise, and veal and champignons are typical fare. On the porch off the bar, you can order light items rather than a full dinner. This gives children the option of a simpler meal, as there is a nice variety of pasta dishes and salads. I had tasty homemade linguine with red peppers and snow peas. A continental breakfast is served strictly for house guests.

How to get there: From Highway 1, enter Mendocino on Main Street. On Lansing, turn right and go 1 block to Albion; then turn left. The inn is on the right in the center of the village.

❇

J: A big, old-fashioned yard where children can run around and play will soothe their travel blahs.

olive Metcalf

San Ysidro Ranch
Montecito, California
93108

Innkeeper: Jan Martin Winn, manager
Address/Telephone: 900 San Ysidro Lane; (805) 969–5046
Rooms: 43; all with private bath, television, fireplace, porch, and stocked refrigerator.
Rates: $160 for cottage rooms to $350 for cottages with private Jacuzzi; double occupancy, EP. Children, $15. Two-night minimum on weekends.
Open: All year.
Facilities and activities: Breakfast, lunch, dinner, Sunday brunch. Horses, guided rides, swimming pool, tennis courts, golf.

Meanwhile, back at the ranch, things are changing. The San Ysidro has been around since 1893, always a premier hideaway and favorite of celebrities and writers. I admit being worried when I heard about its new corporate ownership, but the blue business suits have wisely not changed the unique feeling at this gorgeously situated inn. There are more elegant room appointments now—televisions, telephones, and fresh decor, but I was relieved to see the ranch has not gone California chic. Those infamous cheery signs announcing "I am a Catalpa Tree," or "late check-outs will be charged an arm and a leg" have disappeared, but the special low-key ambience, elegant but not slick, still prevails.

Montecito, California

Admittedly, the San Ysidro is not inexpensive, but I think you'd have the curiosity of a turnip if you didn't want to see the ☞ place where John and Jacqueline Kennedy honeymooned, Laurence Olivier and Vivien Leigh married, and where Winston Churchill and John Galsworthy relaxed and wrote.

Privacy, in a setting of great natural beauty, was and still is the story of the ranch's appeal. The soft foothills of the Santa Ynez Mountains offer miles of riding trails with ☞ breathtaking views. You can disappear into one of the cottages and not see another soul for days, though the innkeepers claim if a guest doesn't come out for twenty-four hours, they do force-feeding.

There is no typical room in the buildings scattered around the lush grounds. Some are parlor suites with patio or deck; some are individual cottages nestled here and there. They're not all equally spiffy, it must be admitted. There's the odd piece of antique plumbing or worn upholstery, but luxury appointments aren't what has attracted people here for so long.

A kind of "we're all country gentlemen here" atmosphere is also part of the charm. Take the stocked refrigerators in every room that serve as honor bars. Mix your own and keep tabs. Very upper class, don't you think? The refrigerators are a great help for families who want a place to keep snacks.

One other major lure is the outstanding food at the Plow and Angel restaurant. From al fresco breakfasts on the deck to candlelit continental dinners in the beautiful white-stuccoed dining room, the cuisine ranges from Western to sophisticated. Its reputation attracts even diners who aren't ranch guests. Children will enjoy the food too, but finicky eaters may request lighter fare or a hamburger.

How to get there: From Highway 101, take San Ysidro Road exit in Montecito, 4 miles south of Santa Barbara. Follow signs to San Ysidro Ranch, 2 miles toward the mountains.

Olive Metcalf

Fleming Jones Homestead
Placerville, California
95667

Innkeeper: Janice Condit
Address/Telephone: 3170 Newton Road; (916) 626–5840
Rooms: 6, including Bunkhouse; 4 with private bath, 2 share 1 bath. Wheelchair access. Smoking only on decks and balconies.
Rates: $80 to $100, double occupancy, EPB. Children, $15. 3 nights for price of 2 Sunday through Thursday. No credit cards.
Open: All year.
Facilities and activities: "Picnic supper in a basket" available by arrangement. Restaurants nearby. Children over 12 (or with parent attending) can help feed burros, ponies, range chickens, and ducks. Hiking. Nearby: fishing, skiing, gold panning, local historical museum, Gold Discovery Park, Gold Bug Mine, Apple Hill Orchards (in autumn watch pressing, cider making, pick your own). Spanish spoken.

When you have a yen to leave big city woes behind you and show your children the simple satisfactions of rural life, this 1883 farmhouse in the Sierra foothills is a satisfying place to try. It was under a cloudless, blue August sky that we drove up the lane to the back garden. An American flag flapped in the breeze from an upstairs porch; flowers, fruit trees, and vegetables were growing in an amiable hodge-podge; and a dozen or so exotic chickens roamed the yard. The aroma of honeysuckle, roses, and green grass was pure summer.

Innkeeper Janice Condit and Rocky, the "fetchin' dog," greeted us. She is a rural whirlwind, very much the capable 1980s woman, and proof that all female entrepreneurs aren't in offices wearing dress-for-success suits. Besides running her inn and an expanding catalog business for her farm's products, she grows vintage roses, organizes an annual tour of some of the Mother Lode's most beautiful gardens, nurtures her fancy-breed chickens, and plays cello for the Sierra Symphony. Just your average down-home farm girl.

You enter through the back door to the kitchen that looks and smells like a country boutique. Rows of county fair blue-ribbon preserves and jellies gleam on counters and cupboards in addition to potpourri (some packaged and some drying in bowls), herbal vinegars, and fresh farm eggs–all for sale; all Janice's enterprises.

As you pass through into the dining room and parlor, you'll notice that not all the animals are outside. Dozens of stuffed ones have seats of honor and hidden perches throughout the house. The parlor also has a 1917 Steinway grand that Janice invites guests to try. She is a trained concert pianist and especially likes to have guests bring instruments with them to play along with her.

The separate Bunkhouse is a good setup for families: two large rooms, each with a bath, and a deck overlooking an English-style garden and the meadow.

Breakfast was particularly relaxed around the oak dining-room table. Most guests had already been out to watch the animals have their morning nosh; ☛ children over 12 may even help with the feeding. I preferred the porch swing and the morning paper, but aromas from the kitchen were too good to dawdle when the call for breakfast came. You feel you're honestly back to basics, knowing ☛ the eggs, fresh fruit, and preserves for the homemade muffins all came from the farm where you slept.

How to get there: From Sacramento take Highway 50 east to Placerville. Continue through the town. Exit right at Newton Road. At the end of exit road jog right to a stop sign. Turn left onto Broadway. It becomes Newton Road. Continue 1.4 miles to the inn's driveway on the right.

Holly Tree Inn
Point Reyes Station, California 94956

Innkeepers: Tom and Diane Balogh
Address/Telephone: 3 Silverhills Road (mailing address: Box 642); (415) 663-1554
Rooms: 4, all with private bath; 1 cottage with private bath and fireplace.
Rates: $70 to $130, double occupancy, EPB. Children, $10.
Open: All year.
Facilities and activities: Swings. Creek and bridge on property. One mile from Point Reyes National Seashore. Area offers horseback riding, hiking, fishing, boating, bird watching, mushrooming, nature walks, unique shops, fine restaurants. Horses boarded.

There is something especially pleasing about fine houses built before World War II: They're modern enough for comfort, yet old enough to have a spacious elegance few of us enjoy at home. Holly Tree Inn has those qualities and sits on ☛ nineteen lush acres of lawns and gardens. It was built in 1939 by a Swede with a British wife, who probably accounts for the arbor of holly trees, the English laurels, lilacs, privet, and the herb garden.

The house is decorated in understated British taste that suits it perfectly: Laura Ashley prints, plump upholstered chairs and sofas, antiques, fresh flowers, and whimsy. A row of tiny wooden

Point Reyes Station, California

buildings ranges across both fireplace mantels in the dining and living rooms. A guest sipping a sherry in the big sofa might look at it for some time before realizing it is Point Reyes in miniature—made by innkeeper Tom Balogh.

Bedrooms are each different and delightfully English. The smallest, Mary's Garden Room, is done in a red-and-green-sprigged Ashley print and opens onto a patio and perennial flower garden. The larger rooms are equally tasteful and have beautiful views.

Diane's enthusiasm for decorating this great house extends even to a newly tiled bathroom sink. She pointed out the pretty gray-green color of the grouting. "Did you know grout comes in almost any color you want? It doesn't have to be white!"

A separate cottage is probably the best family setup with a king-size bed and two futons. And since breakfast is delivered to you here, you have the additional flexibility of setting your own morning schedule.

Christmas at Holly Tree Inn is special. Polished wood gleams in the glow of both blazing fireplaces, and there are decorations galore. Santa made an unexpected appearance once by way of a working electric dumbwaiter beside the fireplace, usually used for bringing up logs.

Mid-January is 🐳 whale-watch time on cool, misty Point Reyes Peninsula, an experience for older children but not for the little ones. The Baloghs arrange for a naturalist to speak about the phenomenon to guests, followed by a short drive out to the coast to watch the migration.

A fine breakfast is served in the dining room—juice, fresh fruit, bran muffins or croissants, homemade poppy-seed bread, several cheeses, and then something special, like individual asparagus soufflés. For other meals, there is a wide choice of good restaurants in the area.

How to get there: From San Francisco, exit Highway 101 north at Sir Francis Drake Boulevard. Stay on Drake 45 minutes to Olema and turn right onto Highway 1. Drive 1 block north, then turn left onto Bear Valley Road. At Holly Tree Inn sign, turn left onto Silverhills Road. Turn left at second driveway. Look for Holly Tree Inn sign.

The Washington Square Inn
San Francisco, California 94133

Innkeepers: Nan and Norman Rosenblatt
Address/Telephone: 1660 Stockton Street; (415) 981–4220
Rooms: 15; 10 with private bath, 4 with shared baths; 1 with half-bath.
Rates: $75 to $160, double occupancy, continental breakfast and afternoon tea and wine. Children under 6 months, free; 6 months and older, $10.
Open: All year.
Facilities and activities: Television available on request at no charge. Playground just across the street in Washington Square Park. Great walking area of San Francisco: restaurants, shops, markets. Close to cable car line; 1 block from Telegraph Hill; easy walk to Ghirardelli Square, the Cannery, financial district.

It would be a shame to bring the children to San Francisco and not introduce them to the city's diversity. Here is a stylish city lodging that puts you in a great location.

The inn faces Washington Square, in the heart of North Beach—to my eye the ☞ most colorful neighborhood in the city. Saints Peter and Paul Church dominates one side of the square; on the other sides are wonderful restaurants (the Washington Square Bar and Grill is a mecca for politicians and literary types), shops, and markets displaying fresh pasta, salamis, and produce. In the park a covey of shining black bangs clutching brown bags (a Chinese kindergarten class) settles down on the grass for a picnic lunch. Several old men practice *tai chi* exercises, oblivious to the bustle on all sides. Over all is the aroma of freshly ground coffee.

You can see much of this scene from the comfort of the inn's lobby/sitting room. There is a handsomely carved fireplace, comfortable provincial furniture on a blue rug, magazines, and books. A big basket of fresh fruit looks as if you're actually supposed to take a piece. Continental breakfast with freshly squeezed juice is served here or in your room. Since this is North Beach, with some of the best restaurants and bakeries anywhere, the croissants and pastries will be the best. Afternoon tea is served here, too, with tiny sandwiches and shortbread.

The inn is as ☛ convenient for a business traveler who wants a personal atmosphere as it is for a family of four who can settle comfortably into a bedroom/sitting room combination with a sofa bed. From arranging baby-sitting or tours, to packing a picnic lunch, to hiring you a stenographer, the staff is ready to help. High-anxiety types may find that the most considerate personal service is an innkeeper who will find at 10:00 P.M. that aspirin or Alka Seltzer you forgot to pack.

The rooms are pure pleasure. Nan Rosenblatt is a San Francisco designer and has decorated them with English and French antiques and a good eye for comfort. She has chosen bright French floral fabrics for quilted comforters and matching canopies. Some rooms look out on a small courtyard, and those in front overlook the square and a bit of city skyline.

The colors, aromas, and sights of North Beach are the very essence of San Francisco. And you can ☛ walk to most of the city's attractions from this location.

How to get there: From Van Ness, take Union Street east; turn left on Stockton. The inn is on your right.

Twain Harte's Bed and Breakfast
Twain Harte, California 95383

Innkeepers: El and Pat Pantaleoni
Address/Telephone: 18864 Manzanita Drive (mailing address: Box 1718); (209) 586–3311
Rooms: 6, including 1 suite with kitchen; 2 with private bath, 4 with sink in room share 2 baths.
Rates: $45 to $70, double occupancy, EPB. Children, $5. Ask about ski and theater packages.
Open: All year.
Facilities and activities: Recreation room with pool table, television. Walk to downtown Twain Harte and restaurants. Hike surrounding woods, fishing, hunting, boating, water-skiing. Nearby: Yosemite, Dodge Ridge Ski Resort (cross-country and downhill).

Mark Twain lived and wrote around this area, and Bret Harte lived here for a time. It's beautiful country just to walk in and enjoy quietly, but the variety of recreational activities in the area make Twain Harte an exceptional headquarters for family vacations.

This rambling inn welcomes children and makes it convenient

for parents to bring them. An unpretentious living room with a fireplace opens to a spacious recreation room complete with a pool table, games, and television. A family suite upstairs can sleep six. It has a large living room and kitchen with a microwave oven for fixing your own snacks.

A big sun porch upstairs is a sunny place to play. El says several people have had winter weddings up here. In summer, the outdoor decks are perfect places for a mountain wedding.

Newly expanded skiing facilities at Dodge Ridge make lodging at Twain Harte all the more interesting. Families who used to ski all day and then face a long drive home will enjoy coming back to Twain Harte for dinner at one of the good restaurants nearby, then a cozy evening at the inn. After a comfortable sleep and a hearty breakfast, you can be off to ski again.

A long glassed-in front porch is the breakfast room. The entire house is heated with wood, and a huge farmer's boiler in here serves as a unique and efficient stove. The morning menu is usually a fruit combination, eggs poached or scrambled, bacon or sausage, and muffins.

The gold-rush town of Columbia is only 15 miles away with many attractions, including a theater company. One of the inn's promotions is a package that includes dinner at Twain Harte's Villa D'Oro Restaurant, theater tickets to the Columbia Actors Repertory, and a night and breakfast at the Twain Harte, all for $95 for two people.

How to get there: From Sonora, take Highway 108 to Twain Harte. Just past the town center, look for Manzanita Drive; turn right. Inn is on the left, across from schoolyard. Guest parking behind.

Chanticleer Bed and Breakfast Inn
Ashland, Oregon
97520

Innkeepers: Jim and Nancy Beaver
Address/Telephone: 120 Gresham Street; (503) 482–1919
Rooms: 7, including a suite with kitchen; all with private bath. Best for children over 12; all ages if you book entire inn.
Rates: $75 to $140, double occupancy, EPB and afternoon refreshments.
Open: All year.
Facilities and activities: Walk to Ashland theaters, shops, and restaurants. Band concerts at Lithia Park. Convenient to Rogue River white-water rafting, Mt. Ashland skiing.

With the success of its Shakespearean festival, Ashland has become a mecca for bed-and-breakfast inns. In the past year I've collected a file of clippings about them, mostly letters written to travel editors from past visitors singing the praises of one particular inn—the Chanticleer. Now that I've been there too, I can appreciate the enthusiastic chorus. It's undoubtedly one of the most attractive, romantic inns in Ashland.

The name comes from Chaucer's tale of Chanticleer and the fox, a European barnyard fable. That's the feeling here—cozy and

Ashland, Oregon

European. The country living room has a warm appeal with its blue rug and rock fireplace and hearth. Comfortable, cushy furniture, books, and an ever-welcome tray of sherry complete the picture. I'm always favorably predisposed toward *any* room that includes these amenities. Younger guests will appreciate the mineral water, fresh fruit, and temptingly filled cookie jar that are always at hand.

Everything about you looks freshly painted and is immaculate. If you're not off to a matinee, it's a pleasure to spend your day at this inn. Some of the rooms overlook Bear Creek Valley and Cascade foothills; others open onto a ☞ brick patio and a perfectly lovely rock garden.

The seven cheerful bedrooms are engagingly decorated with crisp linens, cotton slipcovers on puffy goose-down comforters, wallpapers, and fresh flowers. Complimentary toiletries and thick towels appoint your private bath. Several of these rooms accommodate a family of four nicely.

Jim and Nancy think of many ways to be obliging. They're endlessly helpful in choosing where to have dinner and what to see in the area. But most thoughtful, I think, is having in your room ☞ copies of all the current plays running in Ashland's three theaters. Wonderful for resolving after-the-play discussions. With an advance request, Jim and Nancy will even engage a speaker to discuss the plays you'll be seeing.

Everyone who stays here raves about the breakfasts, and with good cause. Even the orange juice and fresh fruit seem tastier than when you prepare them at home. Maybe it's Jim and Nancy's solicitude for everyone's comfort, or perhaps it's the lively conversation with other guests that accounts for this. Of course, the baked pears with orange sauce, blintzes, quiche, or shirred eggs with cream, the hot breads and blueberry muffins, the superb coffee and teas have something to do with it, too.

How to get there: Driving north to Ashland on I-5, take exit 11; proceed along Siskiyou to Iowa Street, and turn left. At Gresham Street, turn right. Inn is on your right.

Paradise Ranch Inn
Grants Pass, Oregon
97526

Innkeepers: Oliver and Mattie Raymond
Address/Telephone: 7000 Monument Drive; (503) 479–4333
Rooms: 14, including a 2-bedroom Gardener's Cottage; all with private bath. Pets welcome. Cribs available.
Rates: Beginning at $49.50 (October through May 15) and $83 summer, double occupancy, continental breakfast. Children under 5, $10; 5 and over, $20. Ask about package rates including dinners; special honeymoon package.
Open: All year.
Facilities and activities: Sunday breakfast, dinners open to public. Winter dinners served only Thursday through Sunday. Full bar. Swimming pool, hot tub, golf, bicycles, tennis, volleyball, boats, fishing, jogging trails. Recreation center with billiards, television, table tennis. Baby-sitters available. Arrangements made for white-water Rogue River trips; one-day scenic fishing trips.

Once I saw the Paradise Ranch Inn I had two immediate thoughts: 1) its name is right on the button, and 2) how *could* I have missed it all these years? The mini-resort has been operating for almost twenty years, but major renovations have brought it to a very classy status for an inn that ☛ dares to welcome children and pets.

Grants Pass, Oregon

It's only 3 miles from Interstate 5 and an hour from Ashland, but this is a little world of its own that pushes every button for rural getaway fantasies. Everywhere you look over the 300-acre ranch, the natural beauty of Oregon is inspiring. But the ranch has gilded that lily even further. There are three ponds, a lake, miles of white fences, an elegant barn, jogging trails through the woods, a triangle golf course, tennis courts, and a swimming pool.

All the recreation facilities are included in your room rate, and you don't even have to bring equipment with you. Fishing gear, tennis rackets, bicycles, and golf clubs are all for loan with a deposit. This is a wonderful opportunity to borrow a rod and fish on a ☞ willow-lined pond stocked with rainbow trout.

A new ☞ triangle golf course is an experience you just might find even more fun than the real thing. Each hole has three tees, so it plays like a nine-hole course. You play at your own pace—use all your clubs—and lose your fear of water.

The atmosphere around the ranch seems to emphasize opportunities for enjoying the quiet pleasures, too, in this beautiful setting. Watch the black swans and Canada geese, or row out on the lake and gaze at the awesome Cascades.

The fourteen guest rooms are in a long, low white building, one side facing the pond and the other facing the barn and green grounds. They are unpretentious, completely comfortable rooms, simply decorated in Ethan Allen–style furniture.

You won't find any straw on the floor in this barn. It's an attractive, carpeted recreation area, a place to have a quiet glass of wine, watch television, or enjoy the fire. On the upper level are billiard tables, Ping-Pong, another television, and games.

Great food, the kind that brings the locals out for dinner and summer Sunday brunch, is a major ingredient in this blend of sophistication and dude ranch. Fresh Oregon coast seafood and local lamb are elegantly prepared along with beef and pork entrees, so the children will find a variety of choices they will enjoy.

How to get there: Driving south on I–5, take Hugo exit; turn right and follow Monument Drive 3.9 miles to the inn. Driving north on I–5, take the Merlin exit; continue left 1.9 miles. Fly-in: Josephine County Airport. Free shuttle to the inn.

olive Metcalf

The Boarding House
Seaside, Oregon
97138

Innkeepers: Dick and Barb Edwards
Address/Telephone: 208 North Holladay Drive; (503) 738–9055
Rooms: 6, plus a cottage; all with private bath, television.
Rates: $55 to $85 for cottage, double occupancy, EPB. Deduct $5 for single. Children under 3, free; 3 and over, $10.
Open: All year.
Facilities and activities: Beach walks, clam digging, swimming; fishing on Necanicum River. Stroll to downtown shops, restaurants. Ocean 4 blocks away.

"This old house serves comfort" is the motto posted at the door. The rustic, 1898 Victorian boarding house keeps that promise, and at a refreshingly modest price. Built entirely of fir tongue-and-groove lumber, with beamed ceilings and paneling throughout, the house has recently been completely restored. New comforts include private baths, color TVs, and a private side entrance. Brass and white iron beds, down quilts, antiques, and wicker add a country touch. Sleeping accommodations are flexible with queen-size beds and daybeds with trundles.

Behind the house is a 100-year-old cottage sitting right on the river. It has been renovated and is a wonderful family accommodation sleeping six. Children will love the sleeping loft. Parents will appreciate that it is self-contained with a microwave. The river is also great for entertainment, watching the ducks and heron, or taking out the paddleboat available for rent.

There is a delightful paneled parlor for relaxing with a piano, comfortable sofa and chairs, and a window seat. Breakfast is served in a sunny, paneled dining room with beamed ceilings, a built-in buffet, touches of stained glass, and another big window seat. Tables are covered to the floor with blue and white cloths. You can also take your breakfast outside to a wraparound porch.

The Edwards' menu is a full one with juices, lots of fresh fruit, and something like a fancy French toast with fresh berry sauce and whipped cream, or a special egg dish and rich coffee cake as typical entrees.

The town of Seaside is in the extreme northwest corner of Oregon in an area called the North Coast. It marks the ☞ end of the Lewis and Clark Trail and encompasses the oldest settlement in the West: Astoria.

One of the joys of being in a quaint seaside town is to forget the car and walk to all the attractions. From the Boarding House, you are 4 blocks from the ocean and 2 blocks from downtown. The nearly 2-mile beach promenade is lined with charming old houses. You can rent horses, or dig for clams, or surf fish. The resort-atmosphere town has small shops and a variety of restaurants. Teenagers will love the arcades of games.

How to get there: Exit Highway 101 at Seaside and follow signs to City Center; the street becomes Holladay Drive. Inn is on the right.

※

J: *In February, Seaside hosts the highly regarded Trail's End Marathon—one of the country's top road runs.*

The Bombay House
Bainbridge Island, Washington 98110

Innkeepers: Bunny Cameron and Robert Kanchuk
Address/Telephone: 8490 N.E. Beck Road; (206) 842-3926
Rooms: 5, including 1 suite; 3 with private bath and all with air conditioning. Smoking restricted.
Rates: $55 to $93, double occupancy, expanded continental breakfast. Children, $15. All ages welcome weekdays; age 4 and over on weekends. American Express or checks preferred.
Open: All year.
Facilities and activities: An island to bicycle. Fort Warden State Park, Eagle Harbor Waterfront Park, Indian battlegrounds. Nearby: Boating, beach walks, picnic areas, tennis courts, golf. Shopping, restaurants in Winslow. Ferry to Seattle.

At Bombay House, you can sit at the breakfast table enjoying muffins, homemade granola, and fresh fruits and ☛ watch the big white ferries gliding through Rich Passage. All the ships bound for the Bremerton Navy Yards go through, too. In the daytime, it is endlessly fascinating; at night, the lighted ferries look like ocean liners in the dark waters.

"Unlikely" is the way the big house strikes me. Part Victorian, part nautical, and part just the independent ideas of the master shipbuilder who built it in 1907. The house sits on a half acre of green lawn, a hilltop location with marine views and wonderful unstructured gardens. It's a delightful place for a country-style wedding—there is even a rustic, rough cedar gazebo. During my May visit, a big American flag was flapping in the breeze, the flowers were glorious, and twisted old apple trees looked romantic.

If you have visited the inn before, you will surely remember the unexpected sight of a full-size rabbit named James Brown snoozing on the brick open-hearth fireplace. It seems he began to add electrical cords to his diet, and now poor James no longer has the run of the house. He still thrives, but outdoors.

The bedrooms are all roomy, except for the cozy Crows Nest, which has one of the best views from the house—but you have to be in bed to see it. The Captain's Suite is the spacious master bedroom upstairs that is well suited to a family. You have good views from here, a sitting area with a wood stove, small refrigerator, game table, and sleeper couch. The bathroom facilities include a claw-footed tub and a shower. The first-floor King Room has a unique, blue-tin soaking tub in the room. The Red Room has a brass bed, a sitting area, and a tub and hand-shower across the hall.

This is an informal house with a casual kind of atmosphere that children enjoy. The morning meal is served in the kitchen, not a formal dining room, and the innkeepers have a young child. Bunny says that at Christmas they have custom decorations that are great.

How to get there: From Seattle, take Winslow Ferry to Bainbridge. Proceed left on Winslow Way, right on Madison, left on Wyatt. Turn right at the "Y" in the road. Past the elementary school on your left, veer to the right down the hill. Turn right on Beck. The inn is on the corner. Free ferry pick-up available.

J: *On a scale of one to ten, the thirty-minute ferry ride from Seattle Harbor to Bainbridge Island rates a ten: a glorious panorama of that city's skyline and the romantic fun of heading for an island!*

Haus Rohrbach Pension
Leavenworth, Washington
98826

Innkeepers: Kathryn and Bob Harrild
Address/Telephone: 12882 Ranger Road; (509) 548–7024
Rooms: 10; 6 with private bath, 4 share 2 baths, and all with air conditioning. Chalet for 6 with kitchen and bath. No smoking.
Rates: $55 for single to $98 for Chalet for two, EPB. Children 12 and under, $10; over 12, $15.
Open: All year except November until day after Thanksgiving.
Facilities and activities: Heated pool, hot tub, sledding, snowshoeing in front meadow. Two mountain bikes for rent. Explore Bavarian-style village of Leavenworth; spring Mai Fest, white-water rafting, winter skiing, tobogganing, year-round fishing, hiking.

Forget about the high price of getting to Europe and take your family to the country byways of central Washington's Eastern Cascade Mountains. In the Swiss-looking Tumwater Valley, you'll discover an entire town that has adopted the image of a ☛ Bavarian village. Believe it or not, it works.

Similar gimmicks imposed on a town by the local merchants can sometimes have grotesque results, but in this instance, the natural setting is so perfect that the effect is quite pleasing. There are several streets of Alpine-decorated shops and restaurants, with ☛ hanging baskets of brilliant flowers in every doorway.

Leavenworth, Washington

Haus Rohrbach is a country inn nestled among the foothills overlooking the entire valley and only minutes from the town. The ☛ three-story Chalet has wide balconies adjoining almost every room, overflowing flower boxes, and views of meadow and mountains, cows, geese, and gardens.

A comfortably furnished common room and an adjoining deck overlooking the valley are where guests gather. After a day of outdoor fun, it's inviting to relax around the fire for conversation.

The Harrilds are always improving their deservedly popular inn. A few years ago, they added the pool and hot tub; most recently, Bob has redone several of the bedrooms and baths. The feeling is rustic, or at least as rustic as you can feel with down comforters, good reading lights, and modern baths. These are appealing rooms with pine details and colorful cotton fabrics. Families will appreciate the several rooms with daybeds and trundles.

Kathryn serves breakfast on the balcony in good weather—sourdough pancakes, cinnamon rolls, and other delights she bakes while you watch. She'll pack your family a picnic, too, for a day of exploring the beautiful countryside.

The Terrace Bistor is *the* place to go in town for fine dining. The Harrilds agree the chef is world-class, but I advise you to come back to the pensione for your "afters." Get into something with a stretchy waistband and cast your eyes over the variety of desserts available every night: old-fashioned sundaes and shakes; apple, peach, blueberry, and (oh, joy!) peanut butter pies; rhubarb crisps; a white chocolate mousse cake, and Schwarzwalder Kirsch Torte. Courage. Your bed is just up the steps.

How to get there: Going east on Highway 2 after Stevens Pass, turn left on Ski Hill Drive at entrance to Leavenworth. Go 1 mile; turn left on Ranger Road. You'll see the inn on the hillside.

Olive Metcalf

Arcadia Country Inn
Port Townsend, Washington 98368

Innkeeper: Yvonne Rose; owners, The Flying Karamozov Brothers
Address/Telephone: 1891 South Jacob Miller Road; (206) 385–5245
Rooms: 5; all with private bath.
Rates: $49.50, midweek; $60 to $80, weekends; double occupancy, generous continental breakfast. Lower winter rates. Children 5 and older preferred, $10.
Open: All year except for some winter closings.
Facilities and activities: Hot tub, playground, walking trails through woods, pond. On ☞ route of Port Townsend Marathon and bicycle-racing teams; pasture is site of Jefferson County Air Show ultralight airplane races. Tour town's Victorian homes, antique shops, Fort Warden State Park. Nearby: clam digging, scuba diving, sailing on Straits of Juan De Fuca and Puget Sound. Many summer music festivals.

What a shame people don't survive a wild youth looking as good as the Arcadia Inn does. Nestled in a pastoral setting of seventy acres of thick forest and meadows, the 1908 red-brick house reveals nothing of its rowdy past. Quite the contrary. You have to smile at its wholesome appeal as you wind down the driveway and catch sight of the bright flower beds, the big swing on the front porch, and the flagpole waving Old Glory.

Port Townsend, Washington

During Prohibition, the city fathers, having vowed to rid the city of prostitution, decided that since Arcadia was already the local "speakeasy," why not make it the centralized location for vice. They made Arcadia an offer it couldn't refuse: In exchange for the public-service gesture of providing a home for the working girls, the city agreed to provide them a 2-mile-long private water line from the city water system. What could be neater? The town was made pure, and the inn had all the water it needed.

An occasional federal raid kept business from being completely peaceful, and "The Untouchables" eventually destroyed the still in the biggest law enforcement raid ever held on the Olympic Peninsula. So much for creative politics.

Since its renovation, the big house in its idyllic country setting is the essence of gentility and comfort. A 40-foot living room has a beamed ceiling, easy seating before a fireplace, and an 1890s upright piano. One bedroom is on the first floor, and a stairway leads upstairs to the others. A family will like one of the quiet rooms on the second floor. There are double beds, twins, and futons that can be moved around. They're spacious, antique-filled rooms with views from all of them—rolling meadows, forests, and the Olympic Mountains.

Guests breakfast together at a 10-foot-long table in the dining room where an all-you-can-eat continental breakfast is set out—many fresh fruits, homemade granola, a variety of muffins and breads, coffee, and teas.

The surrounding land is a country paradise. Besides all the meadow to run free in, there's an outfitted children's play yard. Trails through the woods lead to a stocked pond—no fishing or swimming, but it's pretty. Another kind of attraction are the May and September house tours of Port Townsend's Victorians. They are very popular, so you may want to ask the innkeeper to reserve your tickets ahead of time.

How to get there: From downtown Port Townsend, follow the main street (Highway 20) south out of town to South Jacob Miller Road, 100 feet north of Johnson's Rentals. Turn right; continue to inn on the right.

J: Nearby is a place to watch a dying skill—a school teaching some of the last wooden-boat building in the country. Visitors are welcome.

Olive Metcalf

The Moore House
South Cle Elum, Washington
98943

Innkeepers: Connie and Monty Moore

Address/Telephone: 526 Marie Avenue (mailing address: P.O. Box 2861); (509) 674-5939

Rooms: 10; 4 with private bath, 6 share 2 large compartmentalized baths. Separate, self-contained caboose sleeps 5.

Rates: $30 for bunk beds to $89, double occupancy, EPB. Ask about family rates.

Open: All year.

Facilities and activities: Additional meals by pre-arrangement. Hot tub, horse-drawn covered wagon rides, paddock facilities. Cross-country skiing from back door, sleigh rides. Trail rides, river rafting, floating, hiking, fishing, apple picking. Nearby old towns to explore. Special events as planned by innkeepers.

Connie and Monty Moore have salvaged a bit of 🚂 railroad history in quiet little South Cle Elum. They've turned a 1913, L-shaped building originally used as a crew house for the Chicago, Milwaukee, St. Paul and Pacific Railroad into a homespun country inn. It's an inn that will delight railroad buffs and give children a taste of once-thriving railroad days.

What were thirty-two bare-essential rooms for a group of rugged men have been turned into ten cheerful guest rooms, many

South Cle Elum, Washington

with brass beds, quilts, and antique wardrobes. Each one has a small brass plaque on the door bearing the name of one of the men who actually worked the Milwaukee and stayed at the crew house. Outside the two-story colonial-blue building are several working railroad breaker signals, and inside is a steadily growing collection of that era's memorabilia.

But the railroad theme goes beyond a mere decorating ploy. Both the Moores have researched that time period and their building. Connie has traced some of the men on the crews, some of whom became interested and involved in the restoration. Many have contributed ☞ wonderful photographs of their railroad days, now displayed on the inn's walls. The Moores also have letters, a conductor's uniform, even china from the dining car.

You'll find an unpretentious, relaxed atmosphere in the dining room and sitting area that opens through French doors to a deck and hot tub. It's a house furnished for casual comfort, conversation, and children. (The Moores have two young daughters.) There are an upright piano, games, books, and a large wooden train that younger children love to ride. While I visited, children played games on the big dining-room table, enjoyed the hot tub, and downed platters of Monty's blueberry pancakes.

The Moores are a brainstorming duo of innkeeping ideas that always keep them busy. They host parties, weddings, meetings, covered-wagon trail rides (make reservations ahead for this midweek entertainment), and have barbecues in the yard. Monty (I believe he could persuade Eskimos they need more snow) has instigated the nation's first Volksport-sanctioned, long-distance round walk, persuading twelve fellow innkeepers to participate by checking in participants and just incidentally, introducing walkers to some remote Washington inns. His mystery weekends sound like the funniest I've encountered, and now there are four more cabooses sitting in the backyard just waiting to be turned into private guest rooms. . . when he has some spare time.

How to get there: From Seattle on I–90, take first Cle Elum exit. Turn right at sign for South Cle Elum and follow the Moore House signs.

❈

J: *Try a "why don'tcha" idea on Monty and watch him go. These innkeepers are always ready to spend time with their guests and are always ready for fun.*

Alphabetical Index to Inns

American Club, The (WI) 148
American River Inn, The (CA) 250
Anderson House, The (MN) 140
Aquarena Springs Inn (TX) 198
Arcadia Country Inn (WA) 276
Asa Ransom House (NY) 54
Aspen Lodge at Estes Park, The (CO) 208
Asphodel Village (LA) 100
Averill's Flathead Lake Lodge and Dude Ranch (MT) . . 226
Bark Eater Lodge, The (NY) 56
Bay Shore Inn (WI) 156
Bear Mountain Guest Ranch (NM) 178
Beaverkill Valley Inn (NY) 58
Bethel Inn, The (ME) 8
Beverly Hills Inn (GA) 90
Boarding House, The (OR) 270
Bombay House, The (WA) 272
Bonnie Oaks Estate (WI) 154
Boone Tavern Hotel (KY) 96
Brookstown Inn (NC) 110
Bullis House Inn (TX) 196
Casa Europa (NM) 180
Cedar Grove Mansion-Inn (MS) 102
Chalfonte, The (NJ) 48
Chanticleer Bed and Breakfast Inn (OR) 266
Chinguague Compound (NM) 174
Christmas Farm Inn (NH) 20
City Hotel (CA) 248
Corner Cupboard Inn, The (DE) 44
Country Inn, The (TN) 118
Dan'l Webster Inn, The (MA) 14
Das Essenhaus Country Inn (IN) 128
Davidson's Country Inn (CO) 220
Dexters (NH) 26
Dillard House Farms (GA) 92
Dixie Dude Ranch (TX) 184
Elk Lake Lodge (NY) 60

281

Indexes

El Monte Lodge (NM)	182
Fleming Jones Homestead (CA)	258
Flying E Ranch (AZ)	170
Franconia Inn (NH)	18
Garnet Hill Lodge (NY)	62
Gateway Lodge (PA)	66
Grand Hotel (MI)	134
Haus Rohrbach Pension (WA)	274
Heartstone Inn and Cottages (AR)	84
Hedges, The (NY)	52
High Hampton Inn and Country Club (NC)	106
Highland Lodge (VT)	34
Historic Taylors Falls Jail (MN)	138
Hobson's Bluffdale (IL)	124
Holly Tree Inn (CA)	260
Home Ranch, The (CO)	206
Homestead, The (UT)	232
Idaho City Hotel (ID)	224
Indian Lodge (TX)	192
Inn at Starlight Lake, The (PA)	70
Inn on Lake Waramaug, The (CT)	4
Inn on the Common, The (VT)	32
Jordan Hollow Farm Inn (VA)	72
Kohl's Ranch Resort (AZ)	166
Lawnmeer Inn, The (ME)	12
Lazy L & B Ranch (WY)	238
Little Red Ski Haus (CO)	204
Little River Inn (CA)	252
Little St. Simons Island (GA)	94
Log Cabin Guest House (IL)	126
Long Point Inn (TX)	190
MacCallum House (CA)	254
Mayan Dude Ranch (TX)	186
Mission Ranch (CA)	244
Moore House, The (WA)	278
Mormon Lake Lodge (AZ)	164
Mountain Top Inn (VT)	30
Nantahala Village (NC)	104
Nevada City Hotel (MT)	228
Old Harbor Inn (MI)	136
Old Miners' Lodge, The (UT)	234
Old Pioneer Garden (NV)	230

Indexes

Osceola Mill Country Inn and Mangus House, The (VA) .	74
Outlook Lodge (CO)	212
Ozark Folk Center (AR)	86
Paradise Ranch Inn (OR)	268
Peaceful Valley Lodge and Guest Ranch (CO)	218
Philbrook Farm Inn (NH)	24
Pines, The (NC)	108
Portland Inn, The (CO)	222
Publick House & Country Motor Lodge (MA)	16
Queen Victoria, The (NJ)	50
Ram's Head Inn, The (NY)	64
Rancho Encantado (NM)	176
Randall's Ordinary (CT)	6
Redstone Inn, The (IA)	130
Rimrock Dude Ranch (WY)	236
River View Farm (TX)	194
Roscoe Village Inn (OH)	144
San Ysidro Ranch (CA)	256
Serendipity (SC)	114
1735 House, The (FL)	88
Shaker Village of Pleasant Hill (KY)	98
Shelter Harbor Inn (RI)	28
Siebken's (WI)	146
Silver Springs Inn and Resort (WI)	152
Smoke Hole Lodge (WV)	78
Sterling Inn, The (PA)	68
Stonepine (CA)	246
Sylvan Dale Ranch (CO)	216
Tanque Verde Ranch (AZ)	168
Tidewater Inn, The (MD)	46
Tip Top Inn (SC)	116
Tumbling River Ranch (CO)	210
Twain Harte's Bed and Breakfast (CA)	264
Twin Elm Guest Ranch (TX)	188
Vermont Inn, The (VT)	36
Village B & B (SC)	112
Village Inn, The (VT)	38
Washington Square Inn, The (CA)	262
Watervale Inn (MI)	132
Waunita Hot Springs Ranch (CO)	214
Westways Country Inn (ME)	10
Whitney's Village Inn (NH)	22

Indexes

Wickenburg Inn (AZ) 172
Wilderness Lodge (MO) 142
Williamsburg Inn and Colonial Houses (VA)   76
Wolf River Lodge (WI) 158
Woods Manor (WI) 150

Inns on or near a Lake

Aquarena Springs Inn (TX) 198
Aspen Lodge at Estes Park, The (CO) 208
Averill's Flathead Lake Lodge and Dude Ranch (MT) . . 226
Bay Shore Inn (WI) 156
Bethel Inn, The (ME)   8
Elk Lake Lodge (NY)   60
Garnet Hill Lodge (NY)   62
Hedges, The (NY)   52
High Hampton Inn and Country Club (NC) 106
Highland Lodge (VT)   34
Homestead, The (UT) 232
Inn at Starlight Lake, The (PA)   70
Inn on Lake Waramaug, The (CT)   4
Inn on the Common, The (VT)   32
Jordan Hollow Farm Inn (VA)   72
Kohl's Ranch Resort (AZ) 166
Mormon Lake Lodge (AZ) 164
Mountain Top Inn (VT)   30
Outlook Lodge (CO) 212
Paradise Ranch Inn (OR) 268
Pines, The (NC) 108
Siebken's (WI) 146
Twain Harte's Bed and Breakfast (CA) 264
Watervale Inn (MI) 132
Westways Country Inn (ME)   10

Inns at or near the Seashore

Boarding House, The (OR) 270
Bombay House, The (WA) 272
Chalfonte, The (NJ)   48

Corner Cupboard Inn, The (DE) 44
Dan'l Webster Inn, The (MA) 14
Holly Tree Inn (CA) 260
Lawnmeer Inn, The (ME) 12
Little River Inn (CA) 252
Little St. Simons Island (GA) 94
MacCallum House (CA) 254
Mission Ranch (CA) 244
Queen Victoria, The (NJ) 50
Ram's Head Inn (NY) 64
Randall's Ordinary (CT) 6
Serendipity (SC) 114
1735 House, The (FL) 88
Shelter Harbor Inn (RI) 28
Tip Top Inn (SC) 116
Village B & B (SC) 112

Riverside Inns

Anderson House, The (MN) 140
Boarding House, The (OR) 270
Bonnie Oaks Estate (WI) 154
Chinguague Compound (NM) 174
Mayan Dude Ranch (TX) 186
Nantahala Village (NC) 104
Old Harbor Inn (MI) 136
River View Farm (TX) 194
Silver Springs Inn and Resort (WI) 152
Smoke Hole Lodge (WV) 78
Twin Elm Guest Ranch (TX) 188
Wilderness Lodge (MO) 142
Wolf River Lodge (WI) 158

Island Inns

Bombay House, The (WA) 272
Grand Hotel (MI) 134
Lawnmeer Inn, The (ME) 12
Little St. Simons Island (GA) 94

Indexes

Ram's Head Inn (NY)	64
1735 House, The (FL)	88
Tip Top Inn (SC)	116
Woods Manor (WI)	150

Inns with Cabins

Aspen Lodge at Estes Park, The (CO)	208
Averill's Flathead Lake Lodge and Dude Ranch (MT)	226
Bark Eater Lodge, The (NY)	56
Bay Shore Inn (WI)	156
Boarding House, The (OR)	270
Bonnie Oaks Estate (WI)	154
Chinguague Compound (NM)	174
Chirstmas Farm Inn (NH)	20
Dexters (NH)	26
Dillard House Farms (GA)	92
Dixie Dude Ranch (TX)	184
Elk Lake Lodge (NY)	60
El Monte Lodge (NM)	182
Fleming Jones Homestead (CA)	258
Gateway Lodge (PA)	66
Heartstone Inn and Cottages (AR)	84
Hedges, The (NY)	52
High Hampton Inn and Country Club (NC)	106
Highland Lodge (VT)	34
Historic Taylors Falls Jail (MN)	138
Holly Tree Inn (CA)	260
Home Ranch, The (CO)	206
Homestead, The (UT)	232
Kohl's Ranch Resort (AZ)	166
Lazy L & B Ranch (WY)	238
Little River Inn (CA)	252
Log Cabin Guest House (IL)	126
MacCallum House (CA)	254
Mayan Dude Ranch (TX)	186
Mission Ranch (CA)	244
Moore House, The (WA)	278
Mormon Lake Lodge (AZ)	164
Mountain Top Inn (VT)	30
Nantahala Village (NC)	104

Indexes

Nevada City Hotel (MT) 228
Old Pioneer Garden (NV) 230
Osceola Mill Country Inn and Mangus House, The (VA) . 74
Paradise Ranch Inn (OR) 268
Philbrook Farm Inn (NH) 24
Pines, The (NC) 108
Rancho Encantado (NM) 176
Rimrock Dude Ranch (WY) 236
San Ysidro Ranch (CA) 256
1735 House, The (FL) 88
Siebken's (WI) 146
Silver Springs Inn and Resort (WI) 152
Sylvan Dale Ranch (CO) 216
Tumbling River Ranch (CO) 210
Watervale Inn (MI) 132
Westways Country Inn (ME) 10
Whitney's Village Inn (NH) 22
Wickenburg Inn (AZ) 172
Wilderness Lodge (MO) 142

Inns or Locations of Historical Interest

American Club (WI) 148
American River Inn, The (CA) 250
Anderson House, The (MN) 140
Aquarena Springs Inn (TX) 198
Arcadia Country Inn (WA) 276
Asa Ransom House (NY) 54
Asphodel Village (LA) 100
Bark Eater Lodge, The (NY) 56
Bethel Inn, The (ME) 8
Bonnie Oaks Estate (WI) 154
Brookstown Inn (NC) 110
Bullis House Inn (TX) 196
Cedar Grove Mansion-Inn (MS) 102
Chalfonte, The (NJ) 48
City Hotel (CA) 248
Dan'l Webster Inn, The (MA) 14
Das Essenhaus Country Inn (IN) 128
Dillard House Farms (GA) 92
Grand Hotel (MI) 134

Indexes

Hedges, The (NY)	52
Historic Taylors Falls Jail (MN)	138
Idaho City Hotel (ID)	224
Indian Lodge (TX)	192
Jordan Hollow Farm Inn (VA)	72
Lawnmeer Inn, The (ME)	12
Log Cabin Guest House (IL)	126
Moore House, The (WA)	278
Nevada City Hotel (MT)	288
Old Miners' Lodge, The (UT)	234
Osceola MIll Country Inn and Mangus House, The (VA)	74
Outlook Lodge (CO)	212
Philbrook Farm Inn (NH)	24
Portland Inn, The (CO)	222
Publick House & Country Motor Lodge (MA)	16
Queen Victoria, The (NJ)	50
Randall's Ordinary (CT)	6
Redstone Inn, The (IA)	130
Roscoe Village Inn (OH)	144
Shaker Village of Pleasant Hill (KY)	98
Tanque Verde Ranch (AZ)	168
Vermont Inn, The (VT)	36
Village Inn, The (VT)	38
Watervale Inn (MI)	132
Williamsburg Inn and Colonial Houses (VA)	76

Inns Offering Educational Experiences

Aquarena Springs Inn (TX)	198
Asphodel Village (LA)	100
Bear Mountain Guest Ranch (NM)	178
Boone Tavern Hotel (KY)	96
Bullis House Inn (TX)	196
Cedar Grove Mansion-Inn (MS)	102
Chinguague Compound (NM)	174
City Hotel (CA)	248
Das Essenhaus Country Inn (IN)	128
Little St. Simons Island (GA)	94
Ozark Folk Center (AR)	86
Roscoe Village Inn (OH)	144
Shaker Village of Pleasant Hill (KY)	98

Indexes

Tanque Verde Ranch (AZ) 168
Wickenburg Inn (AZ) 172
Williamsburg Inn and Colonial Houses, The (VA) . . . 76

Inns near Cross-Country Skiing
(*denotes on property)

Aspen Lodge at Estes Park, The (CO) 208
Bark Eater Lodge, The (NY) (*) 56
Beaverkill Valley Inn (NY) (*) 58
Bethel Inn, The (ME) 8
Christmas Farm Inn (NH) (*) 20
Davidson's Country Inn (CO) 220
Franconia Inn (NH) (*) 18
Garnet Hill Lodge (NY) (*) 62
Gateway Lodge (PA) (*) 66
Highland Lodge (VT) (*) 34
Home Ranch, The (CO) 206
Homestead, The (UT) 232
Inn at Starlight Lake, The (PA) (*) 70
Inn on the Common, The (VT) 32
Little Red Ski Haus (CO) 204
Log Cabin Guest House (IL) 126
Moore House, the (WA) (*) 278
Mormon Lake Lodge (AZ) (*) 164
Mountain Top Inn (VT) 30
Old Miners' Lodge, The (UT) (*) 234
Peaceful Valley Lodge and Guest Ranch (CO) 218
Philbrook Farm Inn (NH) (*) 24
Publick House & Country Motor Lodge (MA) 16
Randall's Ordinary (CT) (*) 6
Silver Springs Inn and Resort (WI) 152
Sterling Inn, The (PA) (*) 68
Twain Harte's Bed and Breakfast (CA) 264
Village Inn, The (VT) (*) 38
Waunita Hot Springs Ranch (CO) 214
Westways Country Inn (ME) 10
Wolf River Lodge (WI) (*) 158

Indexes

Inns near Downhill Skiing

Anderson House, The (MN) 140
Aspen Lodge at Estes Park, The (CO) 208
Bark Eater Lodge, The (NY) 56
Bethel Inn, The (ME) 8
Chanticleer Bed and Breakfast Inn (OR) 266
Christmas Farm Inn (NH) 20
Davidson's Country Inn (CO) 220
Franconia Inn (NH) 18
Garnet Hill Lodge (NY) 62
Haus Rohrback Pension (WA) 274
Home Ranch, The (CO) 206
Homestead, The (UT) 232
Inn at Starlight Lake, The (PA) 70
Inn on Lake Waramaug, The (CT) 4
Little Red Ski Haus (CO) 204
Mountain Top Inn (VT) 30
Old Harbor Inn (MI) 136
Old Miners' Lodge, The (UT) 234
Peaceful Valley Lodge and Guest Ranch (CO) 218
Philbrook Farm Inn (NH) 24
Redstone Inn (IA) 130
Silver Springs Inn and Resort (WI) 152
Twain Harte's Bed and Breakfast (CA) 264
Vermont Inn, The (VT) 36
Village Inn, The (VT) 38
Waunita Hot Springs Ranch (CO) 214
Westways Country Inn (ME) 10
Whitney's Village Inn (NH) 22

Guest Ranches or Inns with Horseback Riding

Aspen Lodge at Estes Park, The (CO) 208
Averill's Flathead Lake Lodge and Dude Ranch (MT) . . 226
Bark Eater Lodge, The (NY) 56
Dixie Dude Ranch (TX) 184
Flying E Ranch (AZ) 170
Franconia Inn (NY) 18

Indexes

Grand Hotel (MI) 134
Hobson's Bluffdale (IL) 124
Homestead, The (UT) 232
Jordan Hollow Farm Inn (VA) 72
Kohl's Ranch Resort (AZ) 166
Lazy L & B Ranch (WY) 238
Little St. Simons Island (GA) 94
Mayan Dude Ranch (TX) 186
Mormon Lake Lodge (AZ) 164
Mountain Top Inn (VT) 30
Nantahala Village (NC) 104
Peaceful Valley Lodge and Guest Ranch (CO) 218
Philbrook Farm Inn (NH) 24
Rancho Encantado (NM) 176
Rimrock Dude Ranch (WY) 236
San Ysidro Ranch (CA) 256
Stonepine (CA) 246
Sylvan Dale Ranch (CO) 216
Tanque Verde Ranch (AZ) 168
Tumbling River Ranch (CO) 210
Twin Elm Guest Ranch (TX) 188
Waunita Hot Springs Ranch (CO) 214
Wickenburg Inn (AZ) 172

Guests Farms or Inns with Farm Animals

Averill's Flathead Lake Lodge and Dude Ranch (MT) .. 226
Dexters (NH) 26
Dillard House Farms (GA) 92
Fleming Jones Homestead (CA) 258
Hobson's Bluffdale (IL) 124
Jordan Hollow Farm Inn (VA) 72
Long Point Inn (TX) 190
Old Pioneer Garden (NV) 230
Peaceful Valley Lodge and Guest Ranch (CO) 218
Publick House & Country Motor Lodge (MA) 16
River View Farm (TX) 194
Sylvan Dale Ranch (CO) 216
Tumbling River Ranch (CO) 210
Waunita Hot Springs Ranch (CO) 214

291

Indexes

Inns that Accept or Consider Pets

Anderson House (MN)	140
Bear Mountain Guest Ranch (NM)	178
Boone Tavern Hotel (KY)	96
Chinguague Compound (NM)	174
Corner Cupborad Inn, The (DE)	44
Davidson's Country Inn (CO)	220
Dexters (NH)	26
Dillard House Farms (GA)	92
El Monte Lodge (NM)	182
Gateway Lodge (PA)	66
High Hampton Inn and Country Club (NC)	106
Kohl's Ranch Resort (AZ)	166
Lazy L & B Ranch (WY)	238
Mormon Lake Lodge (AZ)	164
Philbrook Farm Inn (NH)	24
Rimrock Dude Ranch (WY)	236
River View Farm (TX)	194
Shaker Village of Pleasant Hill (KY)	98
Siebken's (WI)	146
Tidewater Inn, The (MD)	46
Woods Manor (WI)	150